189.4

BLACKWELL'S POLITICAL TEXTS

General Editors: C. H. WILSON and R. B. McCALLUM

AQUINAS
SELECTED POLITICAL WRITINGS

AQUINAS
SELECTED POLITICAL WRITINGS

Edited with an Introduction by
A. P. D'ENTRÈVES
Serena Professor of Italian Studies in the University of Oxford

Translated by
J. G. DAWSON

BASIL BLACKWELL

OXFORD

1948

Political Science

Printed in Great Britain for BASIL BLACKWELL & MOTT LTD.
by A. R. MOWBRAY & CO. LIMITED, London and Oxford.

CONTENTS

CONTENTS

PART II. FROM THE PHILOSOPHICAL WORKS

INTRODUCTION

1. The approach to politics

Biographical details have little or no bearing upon the interpretation of St. Thomas Aquinas's political thought. His scholarly and uneventful life was spent in the comparative seclusion of monastery and classroom. He was born at the Castle of Roccasecca near Naples, towards the end of 1224 or at the beginning of 1225, of a noble and powerful South-Italian family. He received his early education from the Benedictines of Monte Cassino, and pursued his studies in the University of Naples. Notwithstanding the bitter opposition of his family, he joined the order of St. Dominic at the age of twenty. A Dominican monk, he was sent to Paris and studied philosophy under Albert the Great, whom he followed to Cologne in 1248. He returned to Paris in 1252 to complete his study of theology, and was admitted to the *licentia docendi* in 1256—on the same day as his contemporary and fellow-countryman, John of Fidanza, better known to posterity under the name of St. Bonaventura. His teaching in Paris lasted only three years. It was followed by a long period in Italy, in the train of the Papal court. Back in Paris in 1269 he found himself in the turmoil of philosophic controversy. The great struggle between Augustinianism and Aristotelianism had come to a head, and it was St. Thomas who fought the decisive battle. These were the culminating years of his life and activity. He returned to Italy in 1272, a director of the Dominican *Studium* in Naples. He was not yet fifty when he died —on the 7th of March, 1274—in the monastery of Fossanuova, while he was on his way to the Council of Lyons.

We cannot expect a man of this kind to have much in common with the professional political theorist. Unlike many of his contemporaries, he kept aloof from the strife of a turbulent age. He was no counsellor of Princes or Popes like Giles of Rome, no passionate patriot and partisan like Dante. The story of his friendship with St. Louis of France has probably been embellished by hagiography. That he was poisoned by order of Charles of Anjou, King of Naples, as Dante believed, is certainly a legend. With the political conditions of his days he could not fail, however, to be well acquainted. Rome, Paris, Cologne and Naples were points of vantage from which to observe the world. An Italian by birth, he was, like most medieval

thinkers, thoroughly European in education and outlook. But his approach to politics was essentially theoretical. It did not arise from any practical issue. The impact of philosophy was the determining factor. His views on State and government were a deduction from metaphysical premisses.

It has been said that there are no 'politics' of St. Thomas Aquinas. This is certainly true in the sense that he has left us no complete work to which we can turn, as we do to the *Politics* of Aristotle or to the *Social Contract* of Rousseau, for a systematic treatment of politics. The treatise *De Regimine Principum* is of little avail for the purpose. Only the first book and a small part of the second can be attributed with certainty to St. Thomas's authorship. They cover a limited ground and cannot be considered exhaustive. The treatise was compiled for the education of a prince and followed the pattern of many similar handbooks which were popular in the Middle Ages. The Commentaries on the *Ethics* and the *Politics* of Aristotle are a valuable source of information. But apart from the doubts as to the authenticity of some of their parts, the Scholastic form of expounding the Aristotelian texts makes it difficult to distinguish St. Thomas's own views from those which he attributed to his author. By far the most important material is to be found in the philosophical works, from the Commentary on the *Sentences* of Peter Lombard to the great *Summae*. But it is scattered and fragmentary, and the greatest care must be taken in severing such fragments from the general frame in which they fit and from which they derive their significance.

There is, however, another and deeper sense in which it can be said that there are no politics in St. Thomas Aquinas. The contrast with the modern approach is complete and far-reaching. It is a contrast of method, of the deductive method as opposed to the empirical. It is also a contrast of importance. We have become so entangled in particulars, in the practical side of politics, that it is only with an effort that we can be brought to realize the existence of the more general issues which lie behind our immediate predicament. The medieval thinkers had them in mind all the time. They started from the beginning, not, as we do, from the end. And 'in the beginning was the Word': the supreme values, the standard of good and evil. Politics were to St. Thomas a branch of Ethics.

This does not mean that he was entirely indifferent to the technicalities and to the concrete problems of political experience. In a system which purported to be complete, each particular question had

to find its place, and actually found it. It is fairly easy to gather together the scattered material and to shape it into a coherent body of doctrine. We may call this, if you like, the 'politics' of St. Thomas Aquinas. But the results are disappointing. Some questions which St. Thomas discusses sound strangely obsolete to modern ears: whether honour or glory are sufficient incentives for a Monarch to govern wisely; whether the power of a King may be compared to that of the soul over the body and of God over the Universe; whether unjust laws are binding in conscience, and so forth. Yet even this side of his teaching bears the mark of his genius. St. Thomas's handling of practical difficulties shows a spirit of realism, an adherence to evidence which compares most favourably with the day-dreams of some of his contemporaries or immediate successors. We have only to glance at Dante's Utopia to convince ourselves of the qualities of St. Thomas's political thought. They are qualities which we would hardly expect from a medieval theologian casting his eyes on what we would call nowadays the field of sociology rather than of politics proper. But they are qualities which we can only explain and fully appreciate if we bear in mind that general attitude which I have mentioned above. And this attitude in turn is directly connected with an interpretation of Christianity which has remained down to the present day associated with the name of St. Thomas.

This is not the place for a full appreciation of the value and meaning of Thomism in the history of Christian, and indeed of European thought. But the full implications of St. Thomas's attitude to politics can only be grasped in the light of the great issues which it lays bare, the issues which confronted medieval Christianity. St. Thomas stood at a crossing in the development of European thought. His age was an age of transition and crisis, and nowhere, perhaps, was that crisis more apparent than in the field of political theory. Let us try to form a clear notion of what was at stake.

We like to think of the Middle Ages as a great age of faith. The notion is true, but slightly misleading. As far as its spiritual life was concerned, the West—down to the thirteenth century—had lived, so to say, on its capital. The great Christian tradition handed down in the works of the Fathers had provided an endless storehouse of subjects for meditation and discussion. Above all, the teaching of St. Augustine had offered an interpretation of life which admirably fitted the other-worldliness of the medieval mind. With his eyes fixed in rapture on the splendours of the Heavenly City, the Christian could only

conceive of the world as a world of corruption. History, indeed, was nothing else than a tale of two cities: the tale of the failure of man and of the triumph of faith, of sin and redemption. The earthly city must be recast as a godly theocracy. It was a pessimistic conception of politics, which well corresponds to our conventional notion of the 'Dark Ages.'

But in the age of St. Thomas that pessimism was being challenged on all sides. Men were beginning to take pride in the work of their hands, to doubt whether all that they did was utterly sinful. A richer blood was beginning to circulate inside Western Europe. The impact of new ideas and modes of thought was shaping the intellectual life which had found its focus in the Universities. The study of Roman Law, which had spread from Bologna, had disclosed new perspectives to government and administration. A number of Aristotle's writings, which had long been ignored, were brought within reach of the student. A strange and insidious philosophy was percolating through the iron curtain separating the Arab from the Christian world.

The philosophical controversies which form the background of St. Thomas's thought are directly reflected in his approach to the problem of politics. It was not only a question of deciding whether Aristotle's conceptions could be squared with the Christian interpretation of life. It was also a question of interpreting Aristotle correctly. The doctrines which Averroism purported to derive from Aristotle were striking at the roots of Christian belief and Christian philosophy. And from the very pages of Aristotle was revealed a new conception of the State as the highest achievement of man which could well set the stage for the transfiguration of the earthly into the heavenly city. Never had a peril so great threatened Western Christianity. Some thought that it could be met by simply restoring the basis of the godly theocracy, by denying the State any right of existence. The uncompromising dilemma of St. Augustine could provide a refuge against doctrines so subversive and alien. In later days, when, after the Renaissance, a large part of Europe was on the verge of becoming altogether pagan, Protestantism was to find in it once again a powerful inspiration for action and reform. Luther restored the fundamental values of Christianity within the sanctuary of the heart. But he also abandoned entirely the realm of politics to the rule of the sword. This was not the answer of medieval Catholicism. It was not the answer of St. Thomas Aquinas.

The victory which St. Thomas achieved over the Averroist interpre-

tation of Aristotle has been compared to the victory of Charles Martel over the Arabs five centuries earlier. It was celebrated as a capital event even by medieval painters. But the picture has another side which must not be overlooked. It was also a victory over the rigid Augustinianism of many of St. Thomas's predecessors and contemporaries. It was a victory of common sense and of progress. St. Thomas was the best interpreter of the spirit of his time and of its deepest aspirations. Some comforting signs of a more lenient attitude to politics were not entirely lacking in medieval thought, nor even indeed in St. Augustine. Was not the State, by the very fact of being entrusted with the task of securing the *pax terrena*, endowed with some positive value? Was it not an expression of God's providence and good will? The Augustinian notion of the *Civitas Dei* had gradually been transformed into the ambitious programme of a society thoroughly imbued with the Christian ideal. And now the heathen conception of the State, as expressed by Aristotle, could be called upon to implement that programme and to provide a justification of it. Surely that conception might contain some permanent elements of truth. It might make it possible to retrace the foundations of the State in nature rather than in sin. It might allow a good Christian to be a good citizen as well.

The political theory of St. Thomas Aquinas is thus but one aspect of his great enterprise of reconciling Aristotelianism and Christianity, of grafting on to the teaching of the Church the old and yet newly discovered wisdom of Greece. It is our task to examine the conditions which made that enterprise possible and which ensured its success. Some of these conditions are strictly relevant to the problem of politics, others apply to the whole philosophical system of St. Thomas. But all reflect the characters which are prominent in Thomist thought, a truly humanistic sense of proportion, a sustained effort to maintain the balance between opposite extremes.

First with regard to the importance of politics and to the part which must be attributed to it in the range of human activity and thought. How could the teaching of the *Ethics* and the *Politics* be reconciled with the Christian interpretation of life? St. Thomas's first answer is to distinguish carefully between the different spheres of knowledge and action. The distinction between speculative and practical sciences, which is emphasized in the Introduction to the Commentary on the *Politics*, must always be borne in mind if we are to

understand in what sense the medieval philosopher is ready to accept the Aristotelian notion of the paramount importance of politics.[1] But so must the distinction between contemplative and active life, which is one of the cornerstones of the *Summa Theologica*.[2] Politics, however important, are not the last word in human wisdom and in human behaviour. The ultimate end of man, the *perfecta beatitudo*, is only to be attained in a future life, and will consist entirely in contemplation. In this life also the practice of virtue and the enjoyment of human fellowship are but the handmaids to the pursuit of truth. This closes the door to any interpretation of politics in the modern sense, as distinct and separate from the rest of a moral Christian life.

Then as to the nature of politics, the full implications of their pursuit. Here again the Commentary on the *Politics* is revealing. The art of politics is anything but a mere technique. It cannot and must not be measured solely by its achievements, by standards of efficiency and success. And the reason for this is that politics always imply a moral responsibility, a deliberation, a willing, a choice. They are not a purely pragmatic science. They are a part of morals. The door is shut to the modern glorification of political leadership, though not to a proper appreciation of leadership as such. Indeed, prudence is a virtue—the virtue of good council and right decision—and nowhere does that virtue shine more brightly than in the leadership of men.[3] This means that a large field of action is left to the skilled politician, but it does not mean that all his actions are justified because of his skill. St. Thomas's 'political prudence' has little to do with the *raison d'état* of the Machiavellian. It deals with the choice of means, but the means are dependent on the end, and the end is a moral one. This end is the common good, an end which is higher in value than that of the individual and that of the family, and which constitutes the proper object of politics.

We are thus led back again to a problem of ends and of values, and the question now is, how are we to attain the knowledge of them, how are we to determine their nature, how, above all, are we to distinguish them and to assess their proper place within the rich complexity of a life fully determined by the Christian ideal? It is not surprising that St. Thomas's teaching should link up at this point with those meta-

---

[1] See below, pp. 198–199.
[2] *S. Theol.*, 1a2ae, III, 5; LXVI, 3; 2a2ae, CLXXIX, 1 and 2; also 2a2ae, XLVII, 2.
[3] *S. Theol.*, 2a2ae, XLVII and L, *passim*; and below, pp. 162–3.

physical premisses upon which his whole philosophy ultimately rests. For unless the distinction is firmly established between what man is able to discover and to do by himself, and that which he is unable to achieve without supernatural help, it is clear that there will be little room left for his nature to expand and to assert itself. All the wisdom of the Ancients will be of little avail. The city of man will be absorbed once again into the city of God. Now according to St. Thomas the revealed truths of Christianity are not in contradiction to the testimony of reason. The practice of Christian life does not exact from man a renunciation of what is essential to him as man. Reason and faith, human nature and supernatural values are fundamentally in harmony. *Gratia non tollit naturam sed perficit*: this is the key-motif of St. Thomas's speculations, this, if any, his stroke of genius and the reason of his success. The well-known formula expresses an entirely different attitude to life from the diffidence and hostility of earlier Christian thought. It indicates a frame of mind which has remained closely linked with Western Christianity. It is indeed a Catholic interpretation of life in its endeavour to embrace and comprehend the whole range of human activity and thought, to make room for every aspect of life but at the same time to distribute them in an ordered hierarchy. St. Thomas's assertion that Grace does not abolish Nature but perfects it, implies that human values and truths are not necessarily obliterated by the revelation of higher ones; however modest and low, they deserve to be considered as possible tools for the great task of building up a Christian civilization. It also implies the recognition of the existence and dignity of a purely 'natural' sphere of rational and ethical values. This essentially human standard of justice is not vitiated by sin nor absorbed in the glare of absolute and divine justice. It is rather the first and necessary step in the long ascent towards the fulfilment of the Christian ideal. This standard of justice is embodied in the law of nature.

The doctrine of natural law is the pivot of St. Thomas's treatment of politics. But it is an entirely different doctrine from that which has played so prominent a part in days nearer to us in shaping the modern world. It has nothing to do with the doctrine of the natural rights of the individual. It is not from the individual that we are asked to make our start, but from the Cosmos, from the notion of a world well ordered and graded of which law is the highest expression. Natural law is like a bridge, thrown as it were across the gulf which divides man from his divine Creator. It expresses the dignity and power of

man, who alone of created beings is called upon to participate intellectually and actively in the rational order of the universe. There is a rationalist bent in all this, but nothing of the proud spirit of modern rationalism. There is also (as Hooker discovered) a most interesting notion of law, conceived as the expression not so much of will as of reason. Natural law is the pattern of all positive legislation: what is stressed is the duty of the State rather than the right of the individual. Natural law is the basis of political allegiance, the ground upon which social and political relations can be secured and comprehended.

Thus was the Aristotelian conception of the State received and embedded within the framework of the Scholastic conception of the law of nature; a combination less paradoxical than would seem at first sight, for was not human nature the problem at issue? Aristotle had provided a rational explanation of the State. He had attributed a positive value to social and political institutions, as being grounded on the very nature of man. As a great historian of political thought has pointed out, it is significant that St. Thomas did not in all respects directly and categorically contradict the older explanation of those institutions as the result of and the divine remedy for sin. The idea of sin and of its consequences remained for him, and could not but remain, a fundamental dogma of the Christian faith. But sin itself has not invalidated *ipsa principia naturae*. Its consequences therefore only concern the possibility of man's fulfilling the dictates of the *naturalis ratio*, not his capacity of attaining to their knowledge; in other words they do not shatter the existence of a sphere of purely natural ethical values, and it is in this sphere that the State finds its *raison d'être*. It can indeed be said that the different manner of conceiving the necessity and foundation of the State, before and after St. Thomas, derived from a different conception of human nature. Instead of considering the State as an institution which may well be necessary and divinely appointed, but only in view of the actual conditions of corrupted mankind, Thomas Aquinas followed Aristotle in deriving the idea of the State from the very nature of man. But here again the idea of natural law, and the conception of a harmonious correspondence between the natural and the divine order which it expressed, provided a solid ground for further developments. For the Aristotelian conception, with its insistence on the 'natural' character of the State and the exaltation of the State itself as the fulfilment and end of human nature, contained at bottom a challenge to the Christian idea of the existence of higher and ultimate values, and of the inadequacy of

merely human means for their attainment. The natural order, which comprises and sufficiently justifies political experience, is for St. Thomas only a condition and a means for the recognition of a higher order, as natural law is but a part of the eternal law of God. If *Gratia non tollit naturam*, certainly also *Natura non tollit gratiam*. Nature requires to be perfected by Grace. The action of the State, as part of the natural order, must be considered in the general frame of the divine direction of the world, and is entirely subservient to that direction. This clear-cut delimitation made it possible for St. Thomas to attempt the reconciliation of the classical and the Christian idea of the State. Within these well-drawn limits, and subject to these cautions, the influence of Aristotelian ideas caused a deep and thorough-going reconstruction of medieval political thought.

2. POLITICAL OBLIGATION

If political institutions are an aspect of 'natural' morality, this means that the justification of the State and the ground of political obligation must be sought in the very nature of man. This is precisely the leading idea which St. Thomas derives from Aristotle. Few expressions are repeated so often, every time St. Thomas approaches the problem of politics, as that *homo naturaliter est animal politicum et sociale* (*ut Philosophus dicit, ut probatur in I° Politicae*, etc.). The words are significant. William of Moerbecke, whose Latin translation of the *Politics* was the source of St. Thomas's knowledge of Aristotle's work, had translated the Aristotelian expression πολιτικόν ζῷον with the words *animal civile*. St. Thomas maintained this expression in his Commentary on the *Politics*, but he constantly used *animal politicum et sociale* in all his other works. It is not so much a question as to whether they are a more correct rendering of Aristotle's thought. What is interesting is the emphasis which is laid upon the social character of politics. Man is a political animal because he is a social being. This means that the State must have its roots in social experience, that it cannot be, or cannot be solely, the creation of human will. The State is not a work of art, but a historical product. It is the highest expression of human fellowship. All that pertains to that fellowship is natural to man. All that renders it possible is open to rational enquiry and susceptible of rational justification.

St. Thomas never tires of emphasizing the importance of the political nature of man. In one place[1] he describes man as subject to a

[1] Below, pp. 108–9.

xvi   INTRODUCTION

triplex ordo, divine law, reason, and political authority. If man had been by nature a solitary animal, the order of reason and that of revealed law would have been sufficient. But man is a political being. It is necessary, if he is to attain his proper end and the highest forms of life and of virtue, that he should share in political life, that he practise the *virtutes politicae*.[1]

The doctrine of the political nature of man has an immediate bearing upon the treatment of political obligation. It implies that the historical origins of the State must not be confused with the problem of its rational justification. Whatever the earliest conditions of mankind, political relationship is its 'natural' condition. It is therefore quite pointless to argue about the causes of some supposed change in human conditions, and to seek in them an explanation and justification of the State and political institutions. There is no place in such doctrine for a contrast between 'nature' and 'convention'. There is no need for a social contract. St. Thomas makes full use of Aristotle's notion of man as a political animal. He does not hesitate in breaking away, when necessary, from the tenets of earlier Christian writers. His difficulties are clearly apparent in his careful discussion of the state of nature and of the natural equality of men.[2] Stoic and Christian philosophy had been strangely consonant on this point. The teaching of the Fathers left no doubt as to the conditions in which mankind had originally been placed by God. St. Augustine, in a famous passage which St. Thomas did not fail to remember, had stated that God had made the rational man to be the master of animals, not of his fellow-men, thus showing by visible signs what is the proper order of nature and what are the consequences of sin.[3] The same conception was repeated by Gregory the Great, and by St. Isidore of Seville, a Christian writer of the beginning of the seventh century, whose great work of compilation was constantly referred to by medieval writers. The older doctrine of the law of nature, laid down by some of the Roman lawyers and transmitted in Justinian's *Corpus Juris*, had also emphatically asserted the natural freedom and equality of all men, contrasting the institutions which can be referred to the *ius naturale* with those which are grounded upon the *ius gentium* and on human conventions.

Here again St. Thomas did not directly and categorically contradict these conceptions. His answer to the difficulty raised by two contrasting modes of thought shows his effort of adaptation and is a typical

---

[1] *S. Theol.*, 1a2ae, LXI, 5.   [2] Below, pp. 98–107.   [3] *De Civitate Dei*, XIX, 15.

instance of scholastic subtlety. But the distinction which makes the answer possible is important and has important results. Yes, God has made man to his image and likeness. Had men remained in the state of innocence the more jarring inequalities between them, such as the distinction between masters and slaves, would not have existed. But even in the state of innocence the fundamental difference between man and man would have been apparent; for, as Aristotle points out, men are not equal, but unequal. Everything is clear if we distinguish between two different sorts of subjection. Slavery—the *subiectio servilis* in which man is degraded to a tool—is undoubtedly contrary to nature, and can therefore only be explained as a consequence of sin. But political relationship—the *subiectio civilis* of man to man which is necessary for the attainment of the common good—is not a consequence of sin, for it is founded upon the very nature of man. Authority and obedience would still have been required even if the state of innocence had been preserved. The reason for this is again that, according to Aristotle, man is a social and political animal. Society would not be possible without authority, and without those who are more wise and righteous having command over the rest. The idea of sin, without being rejected, is confined to narrow limits, merely to explain certain inevitable hardships of social and political experience, such as slavery, the penal character of laws, or the existence of unjust rulers. It has no part in the rational justification of the State, because political obligation is inherent in man's nature. Man is unthinkable without the State, because it is only in the State and through the State that he can achieve perfection.

But at this point another difficulty was bound to arise, perhaps even more serious. Surely a doctrine such as the one which we have analysed ran counter to some very old and deep *motifs* of Christian experience. If man can only achieve perfection in the fellowship of other men, what about hermits and saints? There is an interesting passage in the Commentary on the *Politics* about this. St. Thomas is commenting here on the Aristotelian doctrine of the 'monstrous' condition of man deprived of society and isolated from political life. He finds it necessary to make an express reservation with regard to asceticism, in favour of the idea of a higher degree of perfection to be attained by retiring from the world rather than by participating in it. But he is at pains to emphasize the exceptional character of a life of this kind, and the necessity, for the attainment of such an ideal, of more than human capacities. 'If any man should be such that he is not a

b

political being by nature, he is either wicked—as when this happens through the corruption of human nature—or he is better than man—in that he has a nature more perfect than that of other men in general, so that he is able to be sufficient to himself without the society of men, as were John the Baptist and St. Anthony the hermit.'[1] The Aristotelian doctrine has opened up new perspectives. The idea of the social and political nature of man leads to an emphatic assertion of the full and harmonious integration of individual life in the life of the community. 'All men being a part of the city, they cannot be truly good unless they adapt themselves to the common good.'[2]

It is upon the ultimate meaning of this 'integration' that we must focus our attention. What are the real implications of so much emphasis laid on the common good as being greater, and indeed more divine (maius et divinius)[3] than that of the single individual? Does it not imply in some way a belittlement of human personality? Can it not lead to a complete absorption of individual life in that of the State? We are clearly here faced with that 'organic' conception of the State which Gierke stressed as one of the essential features of medieval political theory: and an organic conception can only mean that the State, as the whole, is prior to its parts, that the end of the individual is subordinate to that of the community, that, in fact, the individual has no independent meaning nor value apart from the whole of which it is a part. Such views seem hardly compatible with the Christian conception of the absolute value of human personality. They tend to make the State a sort of Leviathan, which devours its components. They conjure up the notion of the 'mortal God' in a Hegelian sense, still more than in Hobbes's familiar wording. It is interesting to find that they are by no means a modern invention. Historians have coined the expression 'political Averroism' to indicate the direction in which medieval Aristotelianism was moving. The impact of Averroist ideas has been clearly traced back in Marsilius of Padua, and even in Dante. It is therefore of the greatest importance that we should interpret St. Thomas correctly on this momentous issue. But this is far from being an easy task. For there is no doubt that he conceives of the State as an organism,[4] of the individual as subordinate to the community,

[1] Comm. on the Politics, lib. I, lectio 1.
[2] Below, pp. 118–19.
[3] De Regimine Principum, I, ix.; also in S. Theol., 2a2ae, XXXI, 3, and Summa contra Gent., III, 17.
[4] S. Theol., 1a2ae, LXXXI, 1: ('secundum quod in civi[li]bus omnes homines qui sunt unius communitatis, reputantur quasi unum corpus, et tota communitas unus homo').

and of the common good as the supreme value to which all others are instrumental.[1] He repeats and endorses the Aristotelian statement, that the family and all other groups differ from the city not only in size, but 'specifically', and derives from it the conclusion that 'the common welfare is different in nature from that of the individual, just as the nature of the part is different from that of the whole'.[2]

We have, however, only to look a little more deeply into the matter in order to realize to how many cautions the 'organic' conception of the State is subject in St. Thomas's interpretation. To begin with, the unity which is achieved through any form of human association is a unity of a very peculiar kind. 'It must be noted'—we read in the first chapter of the Commentary on the *Ethics*[3]—'that this unity which is the political community or the unity of the family, is only a unity of order and not an unconditional unity. Consequently the parts which form it can have a sphere of action which is distinct from that of the whole; just as in an army a soldier can perform actions which are not proper to the whole army. At the same time the whole has a sphere of action which is not proper to any of its parts: as for example the general action in battle of the entire army; or again, like the movement of a ship which results from the combined action of the rowers.' This seems to exclude that the grouping together of men should be creative of a new and separate being, different in substance from the parts that compose it. The rôle of the individual is neither minimized nor denied; it is simply enhanced and brought as it were upon a higher plane. The integration of the individual in the whole must be conceived as an enlargement and an enrichment of his personality, not as a degradation to the mere function of a part without a value of its own. Above all, the difference between the end of the individual and that of the whole does not imply a difference in the standards by which both can and must be judged. Ultimately these ends are one and the same.[4]

Thus could the interplay of man and society be assessed and the value of individual personality secured with all due concession to the new conceptions which were revealed from the reading of Aristotle. A solid safeguard was provided by natural law. Though the emphasis is never on 'natural rights' in the modern sense, the action of the State is delimited by objective rules of justice which ensure the respect of the fundamental demands of the Christian conception of human

---

[1] *S. Theol.*, 1ª2ªe, XC, 3 (below, pp. 112–3); cp. also *Summa contra Gent.*, III, 17.
[2] *S. Theol.*, 2ª2ªe, LVII, 7 (below, pp. 164–5). [3] Below, pp. 190–3.
[4] *De Regimine Principum*, I, xiv.

*b**

personality. It is further delimited by the fact that the laws of the State cannot aim at making men perfectly virtuous. They are confined to pass judgement only upon external actions.[1] The spirit of Christian individualism remains unabated. The individual can never be entirely absorbed by the State. Something in him is reserved for a higher end. The value of the single soul is sealed by the price of Redemption.[2] No human authority can be absolutely binding in conscience. And a higher authority is given to man, which rises high above the authority of the State and of all other earthly power. It is the authority of the Church, which has its source directly from God and finds its justification not only in Scripture, but in that very progression of ends which inspires St. Thomas's whole treatment of Ethics.

Thus in the end does St. Thomas's theory of politics lead us back to medieval theocracy. The State is no longer denied any right of existence. But it must fit into the scheme of a hierarchical and graded society, and accept its subordinate part. We can now measure all the distance which separates St. Thomas's from the modern conception of politics. It is unfortunate that he should not have left us a systematic treatment of the problem of State and Church. But a clear account of his doctrine is to be found in the fourteenth chapter of the *De Regimine Principum*. It is the doctrine of the necessity of a dual direction of human affairs, of the insufficiency of the *humanum regimen* and of its completion through the *divinum regimen*. This duality is reflected in the distinction between the *regnum* and the *sacerdotium*. It is the traditional doctrine, which had found its solemn expression in the famous letter of Pope Gelasius I to the Emperor Anasthasius at the end of the fifth century, and had been enshrined in the great collection of Gratian towards the middle of the twelfth century. What is new and startling is its development on the basis of the Aristotelian theory of ends. It is with a view to the full attainment of human ends, culminating in the *fruitio divina*, that the necessity of the two powers is shown. The duality converges into unity in Christ, who is both *rex* and *sacerdos*. In this world the two powers are committed separately, the one to earthly kings, the other to priests, and principally to the Roman Pontiff, 'so that temporal affairs may remain distinct from those spiritual.' But the different value of the ends necessarily implies a subordination of the one power to the other, of the *regnum* to the *sacerdotium*. Hence it follows that to the *Summus Sacerdos*, the successor

---

[1] *S. Theol.*, 1ª2ᵃᵉ, 96, 2 and 3; C, 9 (below, pp. 132–5, and 146–7).
[2] *S. Theol.*, 1ª2ᵃᵉ, XXI, 4 (below, pp. 108–9), and ibid., CXIII, 9, ad 2um.

of Peter and Vicar of Christ, 'all Kings in Christendom should be subject, as to the Lord Jesus Christ Himself.'

However clear and definite in its outlines, this doctrine is far from being free of all ambiguities. Let us remark for one thing that St. Thomas does not conceive of a relation between two different societies, between State and Church in any modern sense, but of a distinction of functions (*gubernationes, regimina, ministeria, potestates*). We are entirely on the lines of what historians have called the Gelasian doctrine, the doctrine of the distinction and interrelation of two great spheres of human life within one single society—the Christian society, the *respublica christiana*. But it is the relationship itself that leaves the field open to uncertainty. What does the necessary 'subjection' of all temporal rulers to the authority of the Pope really amount to? If we relate the doctrine laid down in the *De Regimine Principum* with other passages from St. Thomas's other works[1], and especially if we compare it with the extreme claims of what we may call the 'theocratic' doctrine proper, such as set forth by Boniface VIII and his supporters, we are inclined to appreciate its moderation. There is no mention of the *plenitudo potestatis*, of a direct sovereignty of the Pope in temporal matters. The subordination or *subiectio* of the civil to the spiritual power of which St. Thomas speaks, is such only with regard to the end. It comes much nearer to the *potestas indirecta*, the typical doctrine of the post-Tridentine Church, although this doctrine represents an adaptation to social and political conditions greatly different from those of the Middle Ages, and implies the definite abandonment of the medieval idea of the unity of the two societies, the Church and the State. But it is this unity that matters. The spiritual and the temporal spheres are not independent. 'The temporal power is subject to the spiritual as the body to the soul'[2], as philosophy is to theology, as the natural is to the supernatural. It is all right to speak of an indirect power, inasmuch as 'the spiritual Prelate should interest himself in temporal affairs with respect to those things in which the temporal power is subject to him or in matters which have been left to him by the secular power.'[3] But when we come to examine the actual working of this indirect power, we do not only find that, as could later be said of the Jesuits, what is granted with one hand is immediately withdrawn with the other. We also find that the matters which the

---

[1] *Comm. on the Sentences*, book II, dist. xliv, q. 3, a. 4 (below, pp. 186–7); and *S. Theol.*, 2a2ae, CXLVII, 3.

[2] *S. Theol.*, 2a2ae, LX, 6 (below, p. 166–7). [3] Below, p. 167.

State is supposed to leave to the Church are precisely those which the modern man has struggled for centuries to secure against the interference of Church and of State alike: such as the pursuit of truth and the worship of God according to his conscience. There is no room for religious freedom in a system which is based on orthodoxy.

The theory of St. Thomas is the theory of the orthodox State. We are apt to forget it. We have grown so accustomed to the threat which comes from the State, that we are only too ready to hail the Church as the champion of freedom. Medieval intolerance had at least one great advantage over modern totalitarianism. It subtracted entirely the definition of orthodoxy from the hands of the politician. It put a bar on Erastianism. It would never have allowed that 'the General Will is always right.' It was an intolerance of a different and more noble brand. But it was intolerance all right, and a thorough, totalitarian intolerance. I am not drawing a fanciful picture. I would like to refer the reader to pp. 153–9 of this book, as well as to the little treatise *De Regimine Judaeorum* which is included in this selection. Here is a picture of a society thoroughly Christian, led by the two authorities to the attainment of the ultimate goal. The fact that this society is a society of the faithful does not exclude that there may be infidels among them. But, as such, they are not members of the society proper. They are *qui foris sunt*, without the community altogether. However, 'we must bear ourselves honestly, even to those that are outcasts.' They must be tolerated. They must even be respected. The great spirit of Christianity speaks in the words: 'Gentiles and Jews ... should in no way be constrained to embrace the faith and profess belief. For belief depends upon the will.' But the Jews are and remain outcasts in the Christian community. Their rites, which after all bear testimony to our faith, may be allowed, in the same way as prostitution is allowed to avoid greater evils. But they must be obliged to bear some special sign to distinguish them from the Christians. They should be compelled to work for their living rather than be allowed to live in idleness and grow rich by usury.

The unhappy lot of the Jews is a paradise compared with that of the heretic or the apostate. They had at one time accepted the faith and professed it. They must be 'constrained, even physically, to fulfil what they have promised and to observe what once they accepted for ever.' Their sin is one which can hope for no pardon. 'If it be just that forgers and other malefactors are put to death without mercy by the secular authority, with how much greater reason may heretics

not only be excommunicated, but also put to death, when once they
are convicted of heresy.' But the Church is merciful. She will not
condemn heretics unless they remain pertinacious. She will even go
so far as to tolerate their rites when they are in very great numbers
or in the case that their suppression should be a cause of discord or of
scandal. Yet the principle of intolerance is unflinchingly maintained.
It casts a sinister light upon this part of St. Thomas's teaching. There
can be no doubt as to the ultimate meaning of the indirect power and
the separation of spiritual and temporal matters. In theory the power of
the Church is purely spiritual. Her weapons are not temporal weapons.
But they carry a temporal weight because of the subservience of the
State to the higher direction of the Church in all temporal matters.
By the sentence of excommunication the heretic is not only separated
from the Church. He is passed on 'to the secular judgement to be
exterminated from the world by death.'

Very little seems to be left at this point of all the effort to secure an
independent and proper platform to the State and to politics. And yet
here is the final paradox: indeed, not a paradox at all, but a strictly
logical consequence of the accepted premises. Political authority
has a value of its own, independent of religion. It has such value as
the expression of a natural and rational order. This implies that even a
non-Christian State is endowed with a positive value, over and against
St. Augustine's conception of the pagan State as the embodiment of
the *civitas terrena* and a work of sin. But though based on the very
nature of man, political obligation cannot avoid being subordinate to
religious obligation. It is a question of interpreting correctly the
fundamental principle that Grace does not abolish Nature, but perfects
it. Let us quote St. Thomas again, for his words are better than any
commentary. 'We must note that government and dominion depend
from human law, but the distinction between the faithful and infidels
is from divine law. The divine law, however, which is a law of
grace, does not abolish human law which is founded on natural reason.
So the distinction between the faithful and the infidel, considered in
itself, does not invalidate the government and dominion of infidels
over the faithful. Such right to dominion or government may, however, with justice be abrogated by order of the Church in virtue of her
divine authority; for the infidel, on account of their unbelief, deserve
to lose their power over the faithful, who are become the sons of God.
But the Church sometimes does and sometimes does not take such
steps.' It is a momentous step and such as to make the holder of the

spiritual power hesitate before taking it. But its very possibility makes in certain cases the final decision inevitable. It is in the power of the Church to release those bonds of allegiance to the State which are founded in Nature. These bonds can and must be released whenever a danger threatens religion. Christian rulers must know the price of having embraced the faith, of being a part of the Christian republic. Political obligation ultimately rests upon religious obligation. 'It is not the province of the Church to punish infidelity in those who have never embraced the faith, according to what the Apostle says, 'What have I to do to judge them that are without?' But the infidelity of those who have once embraced the faith, she may punish by judicial sentence; and it is just that they be punished by loss of the right to rule believers. For this could lead to widespread corruption of the faith: as it is said, 'the apostate breeds evil in his heart, and sows discord,' seeking to detach men from their faith. And therefore, as soon as a ruler falls under sentence of excommunication for apostasy from the faith, his subjects are *ipso facto* absolved from his rule, and from the oath of fealty which bound them to him.' St. Thomas lays down with uncompromising clearness the principles which underlie the medieval conception of the State. The student of history will have little difficulty in providing the necessary illustrations of its practice.

3. PRACTICAL POLITICS

Practical politics, in a system such as the one which we are examining, can obviously be nothing else than an application of general principles to particular cases. But practical applications require practical sense. Enough has been said of the balance of St. Thomas's mind. Now is the time to assess his realism. He has been spoken of as 'the first whig.' This must not necessarily be taken to mean that he was a champion of democracy. But that he was remarkably progressive is shown by his treatment of the more burning questions of his age. We must now turn to examine that treatment.

Many references have been made so far to 'the State.' Would it not have been more correct always to use the words 'temporal authority'? Did the medieval writers have a notion of the State which may be said to correspond even approximately to the modern? The question is a much disputed one. I have no doubts that the answer, as far as St. Thomas is concerned, should be in the affirmative. Here again he stands at a crossing. On one side was the old idea of the fundamental

unity of mankind, expressed in a universal Empire and in a universal Church. On the other, the new and modern experience of a number of independent communities, gradually becoming aware of their independence. St. Thomas set himself to interpret that experience in the light of Aristotelian ideas as well as of the most recent developments of the legal theory of his days. Gierke has vividly depicted the impact of the Aristotelian definition of the State upon the political thought of the Middle Ages. It is evident, he notes, that as soon as men took that definition in earnest, only some among the various subordinate and superordinated communities could be regarded as being States. The revival of the classical conception of the State thus helped to destroy the medieval ideal of a universal community or *Imperium Mundi*. It prepared the way for the modern notion of the particular and sovereign State.

St. Thomas's teaching affords a striking confirmation of Gierke's remark. The State, as the *communitas perfecta*, he conceives to be of an intrinsically different nature from all other communities. The difference consists in the State's capacity for making laws endowed with a *potestas coactiva*, and its possession of a *sufficientia ad omnia necessaria vitae*. These are the two Aristotelian attributes of autonomy and autarky. They are fulfilled by two main types of organizations, the *civitas* and the *regnum*, which thus deserve the name of *communitates perfectae*, and are properly States. The Aristotelian notion of the πόλις undergoes a noteworthy extension. It is made to square with the particular types of political organization which St. Thomas had more directly under his eyes in Italy and in France. But in its essence the Aristotelian notion of the particular State bears full sway. There is no open mention, in the whole of St. Thomas's work, of the idea of a universal empire. No doubt the idea of the fundamental unity of mankind is preserved in the general outlines of St. Thomas's conception of politics. It survives in the very notion of a natural law, common to all men, from which the several systems of positive laws derive their substance and value. It survives in the conception of the *unus populus Christianus*, which embraces all countries and nations, and which finds its highest expression in the *Corpus mysticum Ecclesiae*.[1] But in the sphere of practical politics it is the particular State which carries the day. *Rex in regno suo est Imperator, Civitas sibi Princeps*: St. Thomas never commits himself to the sweeping formulae which were already set forth in his days. He even admits

---

[1] *Summa contra Gent.*, IV, 76; *S. Theol.*, 3ª, VIII, 1–4.

that in certain cases the single communities may depend on some superior authority. But his silence on an issue so important as the powers of the Emperor is significant. His notion of a 'free community,' which can make its own laws and does not depend on any further control[1] clearly reflects the trend of contemporary thought. It is from France and from South Italy that the idea of the modern sovereign State sets out on its revolutionary course over Europe.

I have mentioned democracy. It is a misleading word. But how tempting it is to retrace the origins of democratic thought in medieval political theory! Dr. Carlyle has shown conclusively that the idea that the foundation of political power lies in the community is a common idea in the Middle Ages. It is one to which, as again he pointed out, both the older idea of the supremacy of customary law and the revival of Roman conceptions equally contributed. However different in their premisses as well as in their practical applications, both could be interpreted, and were in fact interpreted, as containing the idea that the people is the ultimate source of law and authority. This doctrine can be clearly retraced in several passages of St. Thomas's works.[2] But this does in no way authorize us to read into his teaching, as some interpreters have done, an assertion of popular sovereignty. Although clearly admitting that the proper foundation of positive law and political authority is the will, or at least the consent of the community, St. Thomas never committed himself to anything which may be said to approach even remotely the notion of an 'original' or 'natural' right of the people. The acknowledgement of the human source of authority is qualified by the fundamental Christian idea that all power is from God, and that authority has therefore always a divine and sacred character. If *dominium et praelatio introducta sunt ex iure humano*, it is also true that *non est potestas nisi a Deo*. These two aspects of authority are reconciled in one place[3], in typically scholastic manner, in the distinction between the 'form' and the 'substance' of authority. The ultimate divine source of all authority (its *causa formalis*) does not exclude, but on the contrary requires (as its *causa materialis*), an intervention on the side of man in the setting up of a particular form of government. Finally, along with these two traditional views, the influence of a third notion can be clearly traced in St. Thomas's theory of

[1] *De Regimine Principum*, I, vi and S. *Theol.*, 1a2ae, XCVII, 3 (below, pp. 30–1 and 144–5).

[2] S. *Theol.*, 1a2ae, XC, 3; 2a2ae, LVII, 2 (below, pp. 110–3 and 162–3).

[3] *Comm. on the Sent.*, II, xliv, 2, 2 (below, pp. 182–3).

the foundation of power. It is the Aristotelian doctrine that, since political relationship is natural to man, the real foundation of the *ordo inter homines* must be sought in the different capacities of men, in their 'natural' inequality. Political authority is based on that inequality. 'Lack of order arises from the fact that somebody is in control, not because of his superior intelligence, but because he has seized power by physical violence or has been set up to rule through ties of sensible affection.' The best *ordinatio* of the *humanum regimen* is that which corresponds more closely to that inequality, and respects that *praeeminentia intellectus* which is the real justification of power. This lends to St. Thomas's teaching a bias in favour of aristocracy rather than of democracy.[1]

The same undemocratic leaning is further apparent in what we may call not improperly St. Thomas's theory of government. But this time it is not so much the Aristotelian as the medieval conception of kingship which leaves its mark upon Thomistic thought. The best form of government, it is said in the second chapter of the *De Regimine Principum*, must be determined in accordance with the highest and more abstract metaphysical premisses. The lesson of experience can only provide a confirmation of what is revealed by the very order of the universe. Monarchy is the best form of government because it best corresponds to the government of God.[2] The arguments in favour of monarchy are mainly of a deductive kind. First and foremost is that *principium unitatis* which, as Gierke pointed out, assumed in medieval eyes the value of a constitutional principle of the universe, and which Dante was soon to use as his main argument in favour of the *Monarchia*. All this seems very abstract and remote. We get back to realities with the discussion of the relation between the prince and the law. This is a fundamental issue with medieval political theory, one which clearly reveals the contrast between the old and the new. 'Medieval doctrine'—wrote Gierke—'while it was truly medieval, never surrendered the thought that law is by its origin of equal rank with the State and does not depend upon the State for its existence.' *Lex facit Regem*: Bracton's famous dictum provides the best illustration of the way in which the relationship between the prince and the law was conceived by the medieval lawyer. But the revival of Roman law had brought about a deep transformation. It had worked havoc with the archaic concep-

---

[1] *S. Theol.*, 1a, XCII, 1; XCVI, 4; and esp. *Summa contra Gent.*, III, 81 (below, pp. 98–107).

[2] Cp. also *S. Theol.*, 1a CIII, 3 (below, p. 106–7) and *S. contra Gent.*, IV, 76.

tion of custom, which was the starting-point of the medieval theory of law. It had substituted a notion of the law as the product of a deliberate act of lawgiving, of a will paramount and supreme. It was thus providing the basis for that legal conception of sovereignty which has often been decried as the *damnosa hereditas* of Roman Law. If law proceeds from the will of the lawgiver, then surely that will is above the law. And if—as was stated in a famous passage of the *Digest*—the lawgiving power has been transmitted from the people, its original holder, to the prince, then the prince is the holder of an absolute power. The sovereignty of the prince within the State is the counterpart of the sovereignty of the State in international relations.

Now it is most interesting to find that St. Thomas discusses at some length the two Roman principles *quod principi placuit legis habet vigorem* and *princeps legibus solutus*.[1] The discussion is of capital importance for a correct understanding not only of St. Thomas's thought, but of the impact of Roman legal ideas upon medieval political theory. It is a useful reminder of the dangers of oversimplification in history, as well as an important qualification to the current association of the legal notion of sovereignty with the spread of 'absolutist' ideas. St. Thomas shows a clear understanding of the Roman doctrine. The prince (or whoever has the function of making the law: the lawgiving power may also belong to the whole community) is superior to the law from the point of view of legal experience itself—that is to say with regard to positive law. For it is from the authority of the prince, or, generally speaking, from the *potestas publica* or the sovereign, that law derives its *vis coactiva*, its positive legal quality. Hence with regard to the coercive power of the law, the *potestas publica* is really *legibus soluta*. This acknowledgement of a principle which, with the necessary qualifications, comes remarkably close to the modern Austinian notion of sovereignty, ought to induce reflection in the many who still repeat the old slogan that 'there was no conception of sovereignty in the Middle Ages.' But in St. Thomas the principle is at once qualified by the important proviso that, *quantum ad vim directivam*, the prince is no doubt subject to the law. The *voluntas principis* has *vigorem legis* only inasmuch as it is *ratione regulata*. The *vis directiva*, the *regula rationis* are nothing else than the expression of that natural order of justice which limits the sovereignty of the particular State.

Thus albeit sovereignty is an attribute—and indeed the essential attribute—of political power, its exercise can and must be subject to

[1] *S. Theol.*, 1 2^{ae}, XC, 1; XCVI, 5 (below, pp. 110–11, 138–41).

careful delimitations. The limits of sovereignty are clearly laid down by St. Thomas both with regard to internal and to international relations. The most interesting illustration of the duties of the State in the international order is to be found in the theory of war.[1] There is no doubt that from the Christian viewpoint war is an evil. St. Thomas found his path clearly traced by St. Augustine. War is an evil, but a necessary evil. The Christian doctrine of non-violence must not be interpreted to mean that injustice should not be resisted and that the *licentia iniquitatis* should not be taken away from the evil-doer. *Esto bellando pacificus*: the common good and the preservation of peace may make the recourse to force inevitable. But war can be justified only within the strictest limits. It must be a 'just war', and for a war to be just special conditions are required: a legitimate authority, a just cause, a rightful intention. War is the ultimate resort in the absence of a superior authority. It is connected with the very existence of the particular State, a consequence of its sovereignty and at the same time the proof that such sovereignty is not absolute nor unlimited.

The limits of sovereignty in the internal sphere are equally apparent. St. Thomas's preferences are all for precise constitutional limitations of political authority. Much has been written about the theory of a 'mixed constitution' which is referred to in two passages of the *Summa Theologica*.[2] They provide a convenient illustration of the idea of a limited monarchy which is only mentioned incidentally in the first book of the *De Regimine Principum* (chap. vi). It would seem that the essential feature of the best form of government is for St. Thomas some sort of constitutional system in which the principles of monarchy, aristocracy and democracy are combined, and the prince is dependent on the rule of law as the expression of the will of the community. The real meaning and importance of St. Thomas's teaching on this point can clearly only be assessed by referring it to the actual constitutional practice of his times. It is significant that it was precisely to his authority that, two centuries later, one of the first theorists of the English constitution, Sir John Fortescue, repeatedly referred, when he defended limited monarchy not only as the traditional system inherited of old, but as the best of all possible forms of government.[3]

---

[1] *S. Theol.*, 2a2ae, XL (below, pp. 158–61).
[2] *S. Theol.*, 1a2ae, XCV, 4; CV, 1 (below, pp. 130–33, 148–51).
[3] *De Natura Legis Naturae*, c. XVI, XXVI; *De Laudibus Legum Angliae*, c. IX; *The Governance of England*, ch. 1.

The limitations of sovereignty have an immediate bearing upon the problems of obedience and resistance.[1] It is clear that in a system such as the one which has been described, allegiance cannot and must not be unconditional. It is circumscribed with remarkable precision by the very nature of political authority, as a means to achieve the common good, and by the fundamental constitutional laws which determine the position and the powers of the ruler within the body politic. The emphasis is on law and on the legal basis of authority. A purely *de facto* ruler is not a ruler at all. Authority must be legitimate, or subsequently legitimized. The first condition of obedience is therefore that there should be no 'defects' in the acquisition of power: such defects would exclude allegiance altogether. As for legitimate authority, it is by definition an authority based on the law. The commands of the ruler must not exceed the powers vested in him, nor impose useless or uneven burdens on the subjects. In all such cases obedience is conditioned by the rightful exercise of authority. Unjust commands are not binding. Evil rulers must be resisted. St. Thomas's attitude on this point bears witness to a deep transformation of the Christian notion of obedience, as laid down in the text of *Romans* xiii, 1–4: 'Let every soul be subject unto the higher powers. For there is no power but of God.' The roots of that transformation go far back in history. From the basic text of St. Paul very different inferences were drawn. The Christian notion of obedience was developed in turn into a doctrine of passive obedience and into a theory of the possibility and, indeed, of the duty of resistance. The fighting spirit of medieval Christianity shines in the teaching of Thomas Aquinas. Political authority is not only subject to the limits which are enacted in the fundamental constitutional laws which lay down and circumscribe its powers. It is subject to the fundamental requirements of justice, embodied in the law of nature. Natural law is the insurmountable barrier against which the will of the State is powerless. We are led back once again to the defence of certain supreme ethical values which is the gist of St. Thomas's theory of politics. It is essential that we should try and understand the real meaning of that defence before we close this brief survey and refer the reader to the actual words of St. Thomas.

Politics are subordinate to Ethics. Natural law is the guarantee of

---

[1] The more important texts on this question will be found below, pp. 134–9, 160–1, 174–9, 180–5. Chapter vi of the 1st book of *De Regimine Principum* should also be kept in mind.

that subordination. But, as has already been pointed out, this does not mean that St. Thomas's theory of politics is based on the recognition of the natural rights of man. There is an essential difference between the modern, 'subjective' idea of natural law, and the medieval conception of an objective rule of justice expressed in the law of nature. There is an essential difference between the vindication of abstract, inviolable rights, and the assertion of general principles susceptible of adaptation according to time and to circumstances. There is, above all, an essential difference in the very notion of individual personality and of its value and place in the structure of organized life. 'We hold'— wrote Jefferson—'these truths to be self-evident, that all men are created equal, that they are endowed by their Creator with certain inalienable rights, that among them are life, liberty, and the pursuit of happiness.' St. Thomas would never have written these lines. His emphasis is not on rights, but on duties, not on the single individual, but on the common good. Men are not equal in the State, although they all partake of a common humanity: indeed the best form of political organization is that which takes into account their unequal capacities. Men are not free in the State, although their souls are undoubtedly free: true freedom they can only attain by accepting an order of which they are not directly the makers. Men have no inalienable rights, neither of thought, nor of association, nor of property. St. Thomas's treatment of property is interesting from this angle. We have included in this selection some passages which deal with this subject, although they do not properly pertain to St. Thomas's political writings.[1] The student of social theory will find in them some valuable food for thought. What is important here to note is that private property can only be justified on grounds of expediency. All that natural law can tell us, is that God has made material goods for the use and the benefit of men. 'The right to private property is not opposed to natural law, but is an addition to it, devised by the human reason.' Private property, though permissible and even necessary under the circumstances, can and must not detract from the general welfare. Hence the poor man who out of necessity takes from another's superabundance of goods does not commit robbery. Hence also the accumulation of wealth for the mere sake of profit is to be condemned. Only a moderate profit should be allowed in the trade of goods. The return of interest on money is downright usury, and

---

[1] Below, pp. 166–75. The treatise *De Regimine Judaeorum* is also of interest for the question.

sinful. There is nothing here to make private property or the pursuit of riches a 'natural right'. In fact, all the conditions are laid down for a sweeping intervention of the State in the control and regulation of economic life.

Thus the common characters of St. Thomas's approach to social and political problems are confirmed once again. It looks as if, instead of providing us with a complete and elaborate system, he had been concerned with setting forth the principles from which such a system can be constructed. What matters is that the principles should not be betrayed. All the rest is a task for the 'prudent' legislator. I have stressed from the beginning the aloofness of the Angelic Doctor from the strain and the strife of his days. In the end, it is this aloofness which proves to be all-important. In it lies the true historical significance of St. Thomas Aquinas as a political thinker. In it also lies the explanation of the fact that the Roman Church could find for so many centuries, and still finds in his teaching, an answer not only to philosophical, but also to social and political questions. At the time of the Counter Reformation the Thomist conception of the *potestas indirecta* of the Church could be developed to meet the new situation created by the rise of the modern sovereign State. In later days the doctrine of the sacred character of authority had to be reasserted against the secularization of politics which was the outcome of rationalism and enlightenment. Later still St. Thomas's teaching could be invoked for an assertion of the duty of social and economic co-operation in the age of extreme individualism and *laissez-faire*. And now in our days the Church and Catholic apologists have brought that teaching even nearer to us in the battle against totalitarianism. We have learnt to appraise a doctrine which is founded upon the vindication of human personality and on the unflinching assertion of the primacy of spiritual values. We have become better aware of the debt we owe to our medieval and Christian inheritance.

But the apparent coincidence of Thomist political thought in many of its aspects with the demands of our times must not deceive us as to the fundamental differences. The Thomist ideal is a timeless ideal. Its adaptation to change is no concession to the *Zeitgeist*. Many evils can and must be tolerated *propter vitandum scandalum vel periculum*, which would never be allowed in a truly Christian State. An answer to new and pressing questions can always be found when the immutable principles of Christian ethics are kept clearly and firmly in mind, and are resorted to in a spirit of optimism.

It is this combination of a rigid intransigence with a spirit of compromise and adaptation which makes the reading of Thomas Aquinas so perplexing to the modern reader. It may well be that we cannot share his optimism any longer, that we are nearer to Augustine than to Thomas. But it is also that, however much we may have learnt to value the principles which he defends, we shrink from accepting their full implications. The 'primacy of the Spiritual' was perhaps the most important factor of Western civilization. But that ideal has lived on through centuries of suffering and hope, and it has come to mean for us something quite different from what it meant for the Middle Ages. And it is hardly possible for the modern man to accept the system which St. Thomas coherently founded upon it without renouncing that notion of civil and religious liberty which we have some right to consider the most precious conquest of the West.

A. P. D'ENTRÈVES.

I wish to express my warmest thanks and appreciation to Mr. J. G. Dawson for his excellent translation of the passages included in this selection, as well as for his help and co-operation in matters of detail. I owe to our discussions, and I daresay even to our disagreements, a better understanding of many problems relating to St. Thomas, which has led me to broaden and partly to revise the interpretation which I had set forth in my *Medieval Contribution to Political Thought* and in my Italian edition of the *Scritti Politici di San Tommaso d'Aquino* (Bologna, 1946).—A.P.D'E.

TRANSLATOR'S NOTE

THE editions from which the Latin text is taken are the Leonine (Rome, 1889–1918 ss.) for the passages from the *Summa Theologica*: the Parmense (Parma, Fiaccadori, 1852 ss.) for the passages from the *Summa Contra Gentiles*, the *Commentary* on the *Sentences*, and the *Commentaries* on the *Ethics* and *Politics* of *Aristotle*: the Mathis (Marietti, Turin, 1924) for the *De Regimine Principum* and the *De Regimine Judaeorum*. The unsatisfactory nature of the Mathis text is, of course, well known, and it was with regret that we were not able to make use of the very generous offer of a critical text, prepared but not yet published, by Professor A. O'Rahilly of University College, Cork. We understand, however, that a critical version of the *De Regimine Principum* is shortly to appear in the Mandonnet series of texts.

In making the translation I have consulted Professor d'Entrèves' Italian version of the same passages; the relevant French translations in the 'Revue des Jeunes' edition of the *Summa Theologica* (*La Loi*. Ia IIae, qq. 90–97. P. Laversin, 1935; *La Justice*. IIa IIae, qq. 57–62. P. Gillet, 1932) and, of course, the English Dominican translation of the two *Summae*. Unfortunately I was unable to consult Fr. G. B. Phelan's translation of the *De Regimine Principum*.

St. Thomas himself has some excellent advice to offer to the would-be translator. 'The good translator,' he says, 'should not only be concerned with the sense of the truths he translates, he should also adapt his style to the genius of the language in which he is expressing himself.' In trying, however unsuccessfully, to follow this advice I have found it necessary to adopt at times a certain freedom in translation which inevitably raises questions of interpretation. The solution of such questions, however, obviously lies outside the scope of the present volume.

J. G. D.

BIBLIOGRAPHICAL INDICATIONS

THE following bibliography is confined to English works of a general character, and even so is by no means exhaustive. Some of the works quoted contain fuller bibliographies, but for completeness reference should be made to the *Bibliographie Thomiste*, Mandonnet et Destrez (Revue des Sciences philosophiques et théologiques), and to the various numbers of the *Bulletin Thomiste*.

ENGLISH VERSIONS:

The Summa Theologica and *The Summa Contra Gentiles*. Translated by members of the Dominican Order. 25 vols. London, 1920.

The Summa Contra Gentiles. Translated by J. Rickaby. 1 vol. London, 1905.

The Basic Writings of St. Thomas. Anton C. Pegis. 2 vols. Toronto, 1946.

The De Regimine Principum. Translated by G. B. Phelan. Toronto, 1932.

WORKS OF GENERAL REFERENCE:

A Companion to the Summa Theologica. Farrell. 4 vols. London, 1946.

St. Thomas Aquinas. Cambridge Summer School Papers. Ed. C. Lattey. London, 1925.

M. C. D'Arcy, *Thomas Aquinas*. London, 1930.

E. Gilson, *The Philosophy of St. Thomas Aquinas*. Cambridge, 1924.

M. Grabmann, *Thomas Aquinas*. London, 1928.

J. Maritain, *St. Thomas Aquinas*. London, 1931.

POLITICAL THOUGHT:

R. W. and A. J. Carlyle, *A History of Medieval Political Theory in the West*. Vol. V. London, 1928.

A. P. d'Entrèves, *The Medieval Contribution to Political Thought*. Oxford, 1939.

O. von Gierke. Tr. Maitland. *Political Theories of the Middle Ages*. Cambridge, 1900 (reprinted 1913, 1922).

Bede Jarrett, *Social Theories of the Middle Ages*. London, 1926.

C. H. McIlwain, *The Growth of Political Thought in the West from the Greeks to the end of the Middle Ages*. London, 1932.

E. Troeltsch, *The Social Teaching of the Christian Churches*. 2 Vols. (tr. O. Wyon). New York, 1931.

F. Kern, *Kingship and Law in the Middle Ages* (tr. Chrimes). Oxford, 1939.

F. M. Powicke, *The Christian Life in the Middle Ages*. Oxford, 1935.

PART I

POLITICAL TREATISES

DE REGIMINE PRINCIPUM

AD REGEM CYPRI

LIBER PRIMUS

Caput I.—QUOD NECESSE EST HOMINES SIMUL VIVENTES AB ALIQUO DILIGENTER REGI.

Principium autem intentionis nostrae hinc sumere oportet, ut quid nomine regis intelligendum sit, exponatur. In omnibus autem quae ad finem aliquem ordinantur, in quibus contingit sic et aliter procedere, opus est aliquo dirigente, per quod directe debitum perveniatur ad finem. Non enim navis, quam secundum diversorum ventorum impulsum in diversa moveri contingit, ad destinatum finem perveniret, nisi per gubernatoris industriam dirigeretur ad portum; hominis autem est aliquis finis, ad quem tota vita eius et actio ordinatur, cum sit agens per intellectum, cuius est manifeste propter finem operari. Contingit autem diversimode homines ad finem intentum procedere, quod ipsa diversitas humanorum studiorum et actionum declarat. Indiget igitur homo aliquo dirigente ad finem. Est autem unicuique hominum naturaliter insitum rationis lumen, quo in suis actibus dirigatur ad finem. Et si quidem homini conveniret singulariter vivere, sicut multis animalium, nullo alio dirigente indigeret ad finem, sed ipse sibi unusquisque esset rex sub Deo summo rege, inquantum per lumen rationis divinitus datum sibi, in suis actibus se ipsum dirigeret. Naturale autem est homini ut sit animal sociale et politicum, in multitudine vivens, magis etiam quam omnia alia animalia, quod quidem naturalis necessitas declarat. Aliis enim animalibus natura praeparavit cibum, tegumenta pilorum, defensionem, ut dentes, cornua, ungues vel saltem velocitatem ad fugam. Homo autem institutus est nullo horum sibi a natura praeparato, sed loco omnium data est ei ratio, per quam sibi haec omnia officio manuum posset praeparare, ad quae omnia praeparanda unus homo non sufficit. Nam unus homo per se sufficienter vitam transigere non posset. Est igitur homini naturale, quod in societate multorum vivat.

2

ON PRINCELY GOVERNMENT

TO THE KING OF CYPRUS

BOOK ONE

Chapter I.—THE NECESSITY FOR A POLITICAL REGIME.

Our first task must be to explain how the term king is to be understood. Now whenever a certain end has been decided upon, but the means for arriving thereat are still open to choice, some one must provide direction if that end is to be expeditiously attained. A ship, for instance, will sail first on one course and then on another, according to the winds it encounters, and it would never reach its destination but for the skill of the helmsman who steers it to port. In the same way man, who acts by intelligence, has a destiny to which all his life and activities are directed; for it is clearly the nature of intelligent beings to act with some end in view. Yet the diversity of human interests and pursuits makes it equally clear that there are many courses open to men when seeking the end they desire. Man, then, needs guidance for attaining his ends. Now, every man is endowed with reason, and it is by the light of reason that his actions are directed to their end. So if it befitted man to live a solitary life, after the fashion of many other animals, he would need no other guide, but each would be a king unto himself, under God, the King of kings, and would have the full ordering of his own actions by the light of God-given reason. When we consider all that is necessary to human life, however, it becomes clear that man is naturally a social and political animal, destined more than all other animals to live in community. Other animals have their food provided for them by nature, and a natural coat of hair. They are also given the means of defence, be it teeth, horns, claws, or at least speed in flight. Man, on the other hand, is not so provided, but having instead the power to reason must fashion such things for himself. Even so, one man alone would not be able to furnish himself with all that is necessary, for no one man's resources are adequate to the fullness of human life. For this reason the companionship of his fellows is naturally necessary to man.

3

Amplius: aliis animalibus insita est naturalis industria ad omnia ea quae sunt eis utilia vel nociva, sicut ovis naturaliter aestimat lupum inimicum. Quaedam etiam animalia ex naturali industria cognoscunt aliquas herbas medicinales et alia eorum vitae necessaria. Homo autem horum, quae sunt suae vitae necessaria, naturalem cognitionem habet solum in communi, quasi eo per rationem valente ex universalibus principiis ad cognitionem singulorum, quae necessaria sunt humanae vitae, pervenire. Non est autem possibile, quod unus homo ad omnia huiusmodi per suam rationem pertingat. Est igitur necessarium homini, quod in multitudine vivat, ut unus ab alio adiuvetur, et diversi diversis inveniendis per rationem occuparentur, puta, unus in medicina, alius in hoc, alius in alio. Hoc etiam evidentissime declaratur per hoc, quod est proprium hominis locutione uti, per quam unus homo aliis suum conceptum totaliter potest exprimere. Alia quidem animalia exprimunt mutuo passiones suas in communi, ut canis in latratu iram, et alia animalia passiones suas diversis modis. Magis igitur homo est communicativus alteri quam quodcumque aliud animal, quod gregale videtur, ut grus, formica et apis. Hoc ergo considerans Salomon in *Ecclesiaste* IV, 9, ait: « *Melius est esse duos quam unum. Habent enim emolumentum mutuae societatis* ». Si ergo naturale est homini quod in societate multorum vivat, necesse est in hominibus esse per quod multitudo regatur. Multis enim existentibus hominibus et unoquoque id, quod est sibi congruum, providente, multitudo in diversa dispergeretur, nisi etiam esset aliquis de eo, quod ad bonum multitudinis pertinet, curam habens; sicut et corpus hominis et cuiuslibet animalis deflueret, nisi esset aliqua vis regitiva communis in corpore, quae ad bonum commune omnium membrorum intenderet. Quod considerans Salomon dicit (*Prov.* XI, 14): « *Ubi non est gubernator dissipabitur populus* ». Hoc autem rationabiliter accidit: non enim idem est quod proprium et quod commune. Secundum propria quidem differunt, secundum autem commune uniuntur. Diversorum autem diversae sunt causae. Oportet igitur, praeter id quod movet ad proprium bonum uniuscuiusque, esse aliquid, quod movet ad bonum commune multorum. Propter quod et in omnibus, quae in unum ordinantur, aliquid invenitur alterius regitivum. In universitate enim corporum per primum corpus, scilicet coeleste, alia corpora ordine

Furthermore: other animals have a natural instinct for what is useful or hurtful to them; the sheep, for instance, instinctively senses an enemy in the wolf. Some animals even appear to have an instinctive knowledge of the medicinal properties of certain herbs and of other things necessary to their existence. Man, on the other hand has a natural knowledge of life's necessities only in a general way. Being gifted with reason, he must use it to pass from such universal principles to the knowledge of what in particular concerns his well-being. Reasoning thus, however, no one man could attain all necessary knowledge. Instead, nature has destined him to live in society, so that dividing the labour with his fellows each may devote himself to some branch of the sciences, one following medicine, another some other science, and so forth. This is further evident from the fact that men alone have the power of speech which enables them to convey the full content of their thoughts to one another. Other animals show their feelings it is true, but only in a general way, as when a dog betrays its anger by barking and other animals in different ways. Man, then, is more able to communicate with his kind than any other animal, even those which appear to be the most gregarious, such as cranes, ants or bees. Solomon had this in mind when he said (*Ecclesiastes*, IV, 9): 'It is better for two to live together than solitary, for they gain by mutual companionship.' The fellowship of society being thus natural and necessary to man, it follows with equal necessity that there must be some principle of government within the society. For if a great number of people were to live, each intent only upon his own interests, such a community would surely disintegrate unless there were one of its number to have a care for the common good: just as the body of a man or of any other animal would disintegrate were there not in the body itself a single controlling force, sustaining the general vitality of all the members. As Solomon tells us (*Prov*. XI, 14): 'Where there is no ruler the people shall be scattered.' This conclusion is quite reasonable; for the particular interest and the common good are not identical. We differ in our particular interests and it is the common good that unites the community. But matters which differ thus are the products of different causes. So, in addition to the motives of interest proper to each individual there must be some principle productive of the good of the many. For this reason, whenever there is an ordered unity arising out of a diversity of elements there is to be found some such controlling influence. In the material universe, for example, there is a certain order of divine providence under which all bodies are

quodam divinae providentiae reguntur, omniaque corpora per creaturam rationalem. In uno etiam homine anima regit corpus, atque inter animae partes irascibilis et concupiscibilis ratione reguntur. Itemque inter membra corporis unum est principale, quod omnia movet, ut cor, aut caput. Oportet igitur esse in omni multitudine aliquod regitivum.

Contingit autem in quibusdam, quae ordinantur ad finem, et recte, et non recte procedere. Quare et in regimine multitudinis et rectum et non rectum invenitur. Recte autem dirigitur unumquodque, quando ad finem convenientem deducitur, non recte autem, quando ad finem non convenientem. Alius autem est finis conveniens multitudini liberorum, et servorum. Nam liber est, qui sui causa est; servus autem est, qui id quod est, alterius est. Si igitur liberorum multitudo a regente ad bonum commune multitudinis ordinetur, erit regimen rectum et iustum, quale convenit liberis. Si vero non ad bonum commune multitudinis, sed ad bonum privatum regentis regimen ordinetur, erit regimen iniustum atque perversum, unde et Dominus talibus rectoribus comminatur per *Ezech.* XXXIV, 2, dicens: « *Vae pastoribus qui pascebant semetipsos* (quasi sua propria commoda quaerentes): *nonne greges a pastoribus pascuntur?* » Bonum siquidem gregis pastores quaerere debent, et rectores quilibet bonum multitudinis sibi subiectae. Si igitur regimen iniustum per unum tantum fiat, qui sua commoda ex regimine quaerat, non autem bonum multitudinis sibi subiectae, talis rector tyrannus vocatur, nomine a fortitudine derivato, quia scilicet per potentiam opprimit, non per iustitiam regit: unde et apud antiquos potentes quique tyranni vocabantur. Si vero iniustum regimen non per unum fiat, sed per plures, siquidem per paucos, *oligarchia* vocatur, id est principatus paucorum, quando scilicet pauci propter divitias opprimunt plebem, sola pluralitate a tyranno differentes. Si vero iniquum regimen exerceatur per multos, *democratia* nuncupatur, id est potentatus populi, quando scilicet populus plebeiorum per potentiam multitudinis opprimit divites. Sic enim populus totus erit quasi unus tyrannus. Similiter autem et iustum regimen

controlled by the first or heavenly body. Similarly all material bodies are controlled by rational creatures. In each man it is the soul which controls the body, and within the soul itself reason controls the faculties of passion and desire. Lastly, among the members of the body itself one is the principal, moving all the others: some say it is the heart, but others the head. So in all multiplicity there must be some controlling principle.

When matters are thus ordered to some end it can sometimes happen that such direction takes place either aright or wrongly. So political rule is sometimes just and sometimes unjust. Now anything is directed aright when it is brought to an end which befits it, but wrongly when it is brought to an end which is not so fitting. The object of a community of free men differs, for instance, from that of a community of slaves. For a free man is one who is master of his own actions, but a slave owes all that he is to another. If, then, a community of free men is administered by the ruler for the common good, such government will be just and fitting to free men. If, on the other hand, the community is directed in the particular interest of the ruler and not for the common good, this is a perversion of government and no longer just. Such rulers were warned by God, speaking through *Ezechiel* (XXXIV, 2), when he said: 'Woe to those shepherds who fatten themselves (because they seek only their own comfort): is it not the duty of the shepherd to pasture his sheep?' Shepherds must care for the good of the flock, and all who are in authority for the good of those entrusted to them.

When government is unjustly exercised by one man who seeks personal profit from his position instead of the good of the community subject to him, such a ruler is called a tyrant. This word is derived from the idea of force, since a tyrant forcibly oppresses the people instead of ruling justly. The ancients were in the habit of calling all powerful chieftains tyrants. If, on the other hand, unjust government is exercised, not by one man alone, but by several banded together in a clique, such a state of affairs is called an oligarchy or rule by the few. This can happen when a few rich men take advantage of their wealth to oppress the rest of the people; and such government differs from tyranny only in the fact that the oppressors are many. Finally, unjust government can be exercised by a great number, and it is then called a democracy: such is mob rule when the common folk take advantage of their numbers to oppress the rich. In such a case the entire community becomes a sort of tyrant.

distingui oportet. Si enim administretur per aliquam multitudinem, communi nomine *politia* vocatur, utpote cum multitudo bellatorum in civitate vel provincia dominatur. Si vero administretur per paucos, virtuosos autem, huiusmodi regimen *aristocratia* vocatur, id est potentatus optimus, vel optimorum, qui propterea optimates dicuntur. Si vero iustum regimen ad unum tantum pertineat, ille proprie rex vocatur: unde Dominus per *Ezech*. (cap. XXXVII, 24) dicit: « *Servus meus David rex super omnes erit, et pastor unus erit omnium eorum* ». Ex quo manifeste ostenditur, quod de ratione regis est quod sit unus, qui praesit, et quod sit pastor commune multitudinis bonum, et non suum commodum quaerens. Cum autem homini competat in multitudine vivere, quia sibi non sufficit ad necessaria vitae, si solitarius maneat, oportet quod tanto sit perfectior multitudinis societas, quanto magis per se sufficiens erit ad necessaria vitae. Habetur siquidem aliqua vitae sufficentia in una familia domus unius, quantum scilicet ad naturales actus nutritionis, et prolis generandae, et aliorum huiusmodi; in uno autem vico, quantum ad ea quae ad unum artificium pertinent; in civitate vero, quae est perfecta communitas, quantum ad omnia necessaria vitae; sed adhuc magis in provincia una propter necessitatem compugnationis et mutui auxilii contra hostes. Unde qui perfectam communitatem regit, id est civitatem vel provinciam, antonomastice rex vocatur; qui autem domum regit, non rex, sed paterfamilias dicitur. Habet tamen aliquam similitudinem regis, propter quam aliquando reges populorum patres vocantur.

Ex dictis igitur patet, quod rex est qui unius multitudinem civitatis vel provinciae, et propter bonum commune, regit; unde Salomon in *Eccle.*, V, 8, dicit: « *Universae terrae rex imperat servienti* ».

Similarly we must distinguish the various types of just rule. If the administration is carried out by some large section of the community, it is commonly called a polity: as for instance when an army rules in a province or a city. If, however, the administration falls to a few but virtuous men, it is called an aristocracy: that is rule by the best; and on account of this they are called aristocrats. Finally, if just government is exercised by one man alone, such a person is rightly called a king. So the Lord, speaking through *Ezechiel* (XXXVII, 24), said: 'My servant David shall be king over all; he shall be the sole shepherd of them all.' So it is quite clear that it is of the nature of kingship that there should be one to rule and that he should do so with a view to the common good without seeking private gain.

We have already seen that a communal life is proper to man because he would not be able to provide all that is necessary to life out of his own resources if he were to live like a hermit. So it follows that a communal society is the more perfect to the extent that it is sufficient in providing for life's necessities. There is indeed a certain sufficiency in the family of one household, so far as the elementary necessities of nutrition and procreation and such like are concerned. Similarly in one locality you may find all that is necessary for a particular trade or calling. In a city, however, there is a perfect community, providing all that is necessary for the fulness of life; and in a province we have an even better example, because in this case there is added the mutual assistance of allies against hostile attack. Whoever, then, rules a perfect community, be it a city or a province, is rightly called a king. The head of a household, on the other hand, is not called king but father. Even so there is a certain similarity about the two cases, and kings are sometimes called the fathers of their people.

From what we have said, then, it is clear that a king is one who rules the people of a city or a province for their common good. So Solomon declared (*Ecclesiastes*, V, 8), 'The king commands over all the lands which are subject to him.'

Caput II.—QUOD UTILIUS EST MULTITUDINEM HOMINUM SIMUL VIVEN-
TIUM REGI PER UNUM QUAM PER PLURES.

His autem praemissis requirere oportet, quid provinciae vel civitati
magis expedit: utrum a pluribus regi, vel uno. Hoc autem considerari
potest ex ipso fine regiminis.

Ad hoc enim cuiuslibet regentis ferri debet intentio, ut eius quod
regendum suscepit, salutem procuret. Gubernatoris enim est navem
contra maris pericula servando, illaesam perducere ad portum salutis.
Bonum autem et salus consociatae multitudinis est, ut eius unitas
conservetur, quae dicitur pax, qua remota, socialis vitae perit utilitas,
quinimmo multitudo dissentiens sibi ipsi sit onerosa. Hoc igitur est
ad quod maxime rector multitudinis intendere debet, ut pacis unitatem
procuret. Nec recte consiliatur, an pacem faciat in multitudine sibi
subiecta, sicut medicus, an sanet infirmum sibi commissum. Nullus
enim consiliari debet de fine quem intendere debet, sed de his quae
sunt ad finem. Propterea Apostolus commendata fidelis populi unitate:
« *Solliciti*, inquit (*Ephes*. IV, 3), *sitis servare unitatem spiritus in vinculo
pacis* ». Quanto igitur regimen efficacius fuerit ad unitatem pacis
servandam, tanto erit utilius. Hoc enim utilius dicimus, quod magis
perducit ad finem. Manifestum est autem quod unitatem magis
efficere potest quod est per se unum, quam plures. Sicut efficacissima
causa est calefactionis quod est per se calidum. Utilius igitur est regimen unius, quam plurium.

Amplius, manifestum est, quod plures multitudinem nullo modo
conservant, si omnino dissentirent. Requiritur enim in pluribus
quaedam unio ad hoc, quod quoquo modo regere possint: quia nec
multi navem in unam partem traherent, nisi aliquo modo coniuncti.
Uniri autem dicuntur plura per appropinquationem ad unum. Melius
igitur regit unus, quam plures ex eo quod appropinquant ad unum.

Adhuc: ea, quae sunt ad naturam, optime se habent: in singulis
enim operatur natura, quod optimum est; omne autem naturale regimen ab uno est. In membrorum enim multitudine unum est quod

Chapter II.—MONARCHY THE BEST FORM OF GOVERNMENT.

Having introduced our question it is now our further task to enquire whether it is better for a realm or a city to be ruled by one person or by many: and this question is best approached by considering the object of government.

The aim of any ruler should be to secure the well-being of the realm whose government he undertakes; just as it is the task of the helmsman to steer the ship through perilous seas to a safe harbourage. But the welfare and prosperity of a community lies in the preservation of its unity; or, more simply, in peace. For without peace a communal life loses all advantage; and, because of discord, becomes instead a burden. So the most important task for the ruler of any community is the establishment of peaceful unity. Nor has he the right to question whether or no he will so promote the peace of the community, any more than a doctor has the right to question whether he will cure the sick or not. For no one ought to deliberate about the ends for which he must act, but only about the means to those ends. Thus the Apostle, when stressing the unity of the faithful, adds (*Ephesians*, IV, 3) 'Be ye solicitous for the unity of the Spirit in the bond of peace.' So, therefore, government is the more useful to the extent that it more effectively attains peaceful unity. For that is more fruitful which better attains its object. Now it is clear that that which is itself a unity can more easily produce unity than that which is a plurality: just as that which is itself hot is best adapted to heating things. So government by one person is more likely to be successful than government by many.

Furthermore. It is clear that many persons will never succeed in producing unity in the community if they differ among themselves. So a plurality of individuals will already require some bond of unity before they can even begin to rule in any way whatsoever. Just as the whole crew of a ship would never succeed in sailing it on any course unless they were in agreement among themselves. But many may be said to be united in so far as they approach a unity. So it is better for one to rule rather than many who must first reach agreement.

Again. That is best which most nearly approaches a natural process, since nature always works in the best way. But in nature, government is always by one. Among members of the body there is one which

omnia movet, scilicet cor; et in partibus animae una vis principaliter praesidet, scilicet ratio. Est etiam apibus unus rex, et in toto universo unus Deus factor omnium et rector. Et hoc rationabiliter. Omnis enim multitudo derivatur ab uno. Quare si ea, quae sunt secundum artem, imitantur ea, quae sunt secundum naturam, et tanto magis opus artis est melius, quanto magis assequitur similitudinem eius quod est in natura, necesse est quod in humana multitudine optimum sit, quod per unum regatur.

Hoc etiam experimentis apparet. Nam provinciae vel civitates, quae non reguntur ab uno, dissensionibus laborant, et absque pace fluctuant, ut videatur adimpleri quod Dominus per Prophetam conqueritur, dicens (*Jerem.* XII, 10): « *Pastores multi demoliti sunt vineam meam* ». E contrario vero provinciae et civitates, quae sub uno rege reguntur pace gaudent, iustitia florent, et affluentia rerum laetantur. Unde Dominus pro magno munere per Prophetas populo suo promittit, quod poneret sibi caput unum, et quod princeps unus erit in medio eorum.

moves all the rest, namely, the heart: in the soul there is one faculty which is pre-eminent, namely reason. The bees have one king, and in the whole universe there is one God, Creator and Lord of all. And this is quite according to reason: for all plurality derives from unity. So, since the product of art is but an imitation of the work of nature, and since a work of art is the better for being a faithful representation of its natural pattern, it follows of necessity that the best form of government in human society is that which is exercised by one person.

This conclusion is also born out by experience. For cities or provinces which are not ruled by one person are torn by dissentions, and strive without peace: so that the Lord's words seem to be fulfilled when He said, 'Many shepherds have destroyed my vineyard' (*Jeremias* XII, 10). On the other hand, cities and provinces which are governed by one king enjoy peace, flourish in justice and are made glad by an abundance of riches. So the Lord promised His people by the Prophets that, as a great favour, He would place them under one head, and that there would be one prince over them all.

Caput III.—QUOD, SICUT DOMINIUM UNIUS OPTIMUM EST, QUANDO
EST IUSTUM, ITA OPPOSITUM EIUS EST PESSIMUM, PROBATURQUE MULTIS
RATIONIBUS ET ARGUMENTIS.

Sicut autem regimen regis est optimum, ita regimen tyranni est
pessimum. Opponitur autem politiae quidem democratia, utrumque
enim, sicut ex dictis apparet, est regimen quod per plures exercetur;
aristocratiae vero oligarchia, utrumque enim exercetur per paucos;
regnum autem tyrannidi, utrumque enim per unum exercetur. Quod
autem regnum sit optimum regimen, ostensum est prius. Si igitur
optimo opponitur pessimum, necesse est quod tyrannis sit pessimum.

Adhuc: virtus unita magis est efficax ad effectum inducendum, quam
dispersa vel divisa. Multi enim congregati simul trahunt, quod divisim
per partes singulariter a singulis trahi non posset. Sicut igitur utilius
est virtutem operantem ad bonum esse magis unam, ut sit virtuosior
ad operandum bonum; ita magis est nocivum si virtus operans malum
sit una, quam divisa. Virtus autem iniuste praesidentis operatur ad
malum multitudinis, dum commune bonum multitudinis in sui ipsius
bonum tantum retorquet. Sicut igitur in regimine iusto, quanto regens
est magis unum, tanto est utilius regimen, ut regnum melius est quam
aristocratia, aristocratia vero quam politia; ita e converso erit et in
iniusto regimine, ut videlicet quanto regens est magis unum, tanto
magis sit nocivum. Magis igitur est nociva tyrannis quam oligarchia:
oligarchia autem quam democratia.

Amplius: per hoc regimen fit iniustum, quod spreto bono communi
multitudinis, quaeritur bonum privatum regentis. Quanto igitur magis
receditur a bono communi, tanto est regimen magis iniustum; plus
autem receditur a bono communi in oligarchia, in qua quaeritur bonum
paucorum, quam in democratia, in qua quaeritur bonum multorum;
et adhuc plus receditur a bono communi in tyrannide, in qua quaeritur
bonum tantum unius: omni enim universitati propinquius est multum
quam paucum, et paucum quam unum solum. Regimen igitur tyranni
est iniustissimum. Similiter autem manifestum fit considerantibus
divinae providentiae ordinem, quae optime universa disponit. Nam

Chapter III.—Tyranny, the corruption of monarchy, is the
worst form of government.

As government by a king is the best, so also government by a
tyrant is the worst form of rule. A polity is to be contrasted with a
democracy, each as we have already shown, being a form of government by the multitude. Similarly, an aristocracy contrasts with an
oligarchy, each being a form of government by the few. Lastly,
tyranny is contrasted with government by a king; each being exercised by one person alone. We have already shown that monarchy is
the best form of government; so, as the best is to be contrasted with
the worst, it follows that tyranny is the worst form of government.

Furthermore. A power which is united is more efficient than one
which is divided. Many united in one body can pull what divided, and
by single endeavour, they could not move. So, just as it is better for a
power which is productive of good to be more united, it is more
harmful for a power which is productive of evil to be united rather
than divided. Now the power of an unjust ruler is exercised to the
detriment of the community, because it substitutes his private interest
for the common welfare of the citizens. So, just government is the more
beneficial in so far as it proceeds from greater unity; and monarchy
is better than aristocracy, which, in turn, is better than a polity; in
unjust government the reverse is the case, since it will be the more
damaging to the extent that it proceeds from greater unity. So tyranny
is more harmful than an oligarchy, and an oligarchy is more damaging
than a democracy.

Again. That which makes government unjust is the fact that the
personal aims of the ruler are sought to the detriment of the common
welfare. So the greater the damage to the common well-being, the
greater will be the injustice of the government. Now there is a greater
disregard of the common welfare in an oligarchy, where the private
gain of a few citizens is considered, than in a democracy, in which the
ends of many are served. Even greater is the harm to the common
welfare in the case of a tyranny, where the satisfaction of one man
alone is considered. For a great number comes nearer to generality
than a few, while a few is nearer than one. Tyranny, then, is the most
unjust form of government.

The same conclusions are apparent from a study of the order of
divine providence, which disposes of all things in the most admirable

bonum provenit in rebus ex una causa perfecta, quasi omnibus adunatis quae ad bonum iuvare possunt, malum autem singillatim ex singularibus defectibus. Non enim est pulchritudo in corpore, nisi omnia membra fuerint decenter disposita; turpitudo autem contingit, quodcumque membrum indecenter se habeat. Et sic turpitudo ex pluribus causis diversimode provenit, pulchritudo autem uno modo ex una causa perfecta: et sic est in omnibus bonis et malis, tamquam hoc Deo providente, ut bonum ex una causa sit fortius, malum autem ex pluribus causis sit debilius. Expedit igitur ut regimen iustum sit unius tantum, ad hoc ut sit fortius. Quod si in iniustitiam declinat regimen, expedit magis ut sit multorum, ut sit debilius, et se invicem impediant. Inter iniusta igitur regimina tolerabilius est democratia, pessimum vero tyrannis.

Idem etiam maxime apparet, si quis consideret mala quae ex tyrannis proveniunt, quia cum tyrannus, contempto communi bono, quaerit privatum, consequens est ut in subditos diversimode gravet, secundum quod diversis passionibus subiacet ad bona aliqua affectanda. Qui enim passione cupiditatis detinetur, bona subditorum rapit: unde Salomon (*Prov.* XXIX, 4): « *Rex iustus erigit terram, vir avarus destruet eam* ». Si vero iracundiae passioni subiaceat, pro nihilo sanguinem fundit, unde per *Ezech.* XXII, 27, dicitur: « *Principes eius in medio eius quasi lupi rapientes praedam ad effundendum sanguinem* ». Hoc igitur regimen fugiendum esse, sapiens monet, dicens (*Eccle.* IX, 18): « *Longe esto ab homine potestatem habente occidendi* », quia scilicet non pro iustitia, sed per potestatem occidit pro libidine voluntatis. Sic igitur nulla erit securitas, sed omnia sunt incerta, cum a iure disceditur, nec firmari quidquam potest, quod positum est in alterius voluntate, ne dicam libidine. Nec solum in corporalibus subditos gravat, sed etiam spiritualia eorum bona impedit, quia qui plus praeesse appetunt quam prodesse, omnem profectum subditorum impediunt, suspicantes omnem subditorum excellentiam suae iniquae dominationi preiudicium esse. Tyrannis enim magis boni quam mali suspecti sunt, semperque his aliena virtus formidolosa est. Conantur igitur praedicti tyranni, ne ipsorum subditi virtuosi effecti magnanimitatis concipiant

manner. For goodness arises in things out of one perfect cause, everything being so arranged as to assist the production of goodness; but evil arises out of singularity and individual defect. There is no beauty in a body unless all its members are harmoniously disposed one to another: but there is ugliness as soon as one member is ill-fitting. So ugliness may occur in many ways and for a diversity of reasons; but of beauty there is only one and perfect cause. This happens in every case where good and bad are contrasted; as though it were the providence of God that good, proceeding from a single cause should be the stronger; while evil, proceeding from a diversity of reasons should be the weaker. It is best, therefore, that just government should be exercised by one man alone, and should be, thereby, the stronger. But if such government should fall into injustice it is better that it be exercised by many, and so be weakened by internal friction. So, of all forms of unjust government, democracy is the most tolerable and tyranny the worst.

The same conclusion will also be reached if one considers the evils which are consequent upon tyranny. For the tyrant, being heedless of the common welfare, seeks his personal satisfaction. In consequence, he oppresses his subjects in various ways, according to the nature of the passions by which he is swayed in the pursuit of self-indulgence. If he is a slave to avarice, he steals from his subjects; so Solomon says (*Proverbs*, XXIX, 4): 'A just king makes rich the earth, but the miser destroys it.' If, on the other hand, he is prone to anger, he will shed blood heedlessly: so it is said in Ezechiel (XXII, 27): 'The princes in their midst are like wolves ravening their prey, to the shedding of blood.' And the wise man advises us to avoid such government, saying (*Eccles*. IX, 18): 'Keep at a distance from him who has power to slay thee.' Under such a government death comes, not in satisfaction of justice, but violently and because of unbridled passion. In such circumstances there is no security, and all is uncertain: for there is no law; and no reliance can be placed upon that which depends upon the will, or rather the caprice, of another. Such oppression does not bear only upon the material welfare of the subjects; their spiritual welfare also is threatened. For those whose object is power rather than the service of the community put obstacles in the way of any progress by their subjects, being suspicious that such progress might threaten their wicked rule. Tyrants always suspect the good rather than the wicked, and are ever afraid of virtue. They seek always to hinder their subjects from becoming virtuous, and from

B

spiritum, et eorum iniquam dominationem non ferant, ne inter subditos amicitiae foedus firmetur, et pacis emolumento ad invicem gaudeant, ut sic dum unus de altero non confidit, contra eorum dominium aliquid moliri non possint. Propter quod inter ipsos discordias seminant, exortas nutriunt, et ea quae ad foederationem hominum pertinent, ut connubia et convivia, prohibent, et caetera huiusmodi, per quae inter homines solet familiaritas et fiducia generari. Conantur etiam ne potentes aut divites fiant, quia de subditis secundum suae malitiae conscientiam suspicantes, sicut ipsi potentia et divitiis ad nocendum utuntur, ita timens ne potentia subditorum et divitiae eis nocivae reddantur. Unde et *Job* (XV, 21) de tyranno dicitur: « *Sonitus terroris semper in auribus eius, et cum pax sit,* (nullo scilicet malum ei intentante) *ille semper insidias suspicatur* ». Ex hoc autem contingit, ut, dum praesidentes, qui subditos ad virtutes inducere deberent, virtuti subditorum nequiter invident, et eam pro posse impediunt, sub tyrannis pauci virtuosi inveniantur. Nam iuxta sententiam Philosophi apud illos inveniuntur fortes viri, apud quos fortissimi quique honorantur, et ut Tullius dicit: « *Iacent semper et parum vigent, quae apud quosque improbantur* ». Naturale etiam est, ut homines, sub timore nutriti, in servilem degenerent animum, et pusillanimes fiant ad omne virile opus et strenuum: quod experimento patet in provinciis, quae diu sub tyrannis fuerunt. Unde Apostolus, *Col.* III, 21, dicit: « *Patres, nolite ad indignationem provocare filios vestros, ne pusillo animo fiant* ». Haec igitur nocumenta tyrannidis rex Salomon (*Prov.* XXVIII, 12) considerans, dicit: « *Regnantibus impiis, ruinae hominum* », quia scilicet per nequitiam tyrannorum subiecti a virtutum perfectione deficiunt; et iterum dicit (*ibid.* XXIX, 2): « *Cum impii sumpserint principatum, gemet populus quasi sub servitute deductus* »; et iterum (XXVIII, 28): « *Cum surrexerint impii, abscondentur homines* », ut tyrannorum crudelitatem evadant. Nec est mirum, quia homo absque ratione secundum animae suae libidinem praesidens nihil differt a bestia, unde Salomon (*ibid.* XXVIII, 15): « *Leo rugiens et ursus esuriens princeps impius super populum pauperem* »; et ideo a tyrannis se abscondunt homines sicut a crudelibus bestiis, idemque videtur tyranno subiici, et bestiae saevienti substerni.

growing in magnanimity of soul, lest they become restless under un-just government: they prevent them from establishing ties of friend-ship and from enjoying the benefit of fraternal peace; so that being always suspicious one of the other they can never combine against the tyrant's power. So tyrants sow discord between their subjects, and encourage strife wherever it exists; while at the same time they prohibit all that makes for harmony among men, such as wedding feasts and banquets, and all such activities which normally produce familiarity and confidence among men. They also take steps to prevent anyone from becoming powerful or rich: for they judge their subjects by their own evil consciences, and themselves using power and riches to evil purpose, they go in fear lest the power or wealth of their subjects be harmful to them. So Job, speaking of a tyrant, said (XV, 21): 'The sound of terror is ever in his ears, and even when there is peace (that is when no evil is intended towards him), he is ever suspicious of plots.' For this reason, when rulers who should encourage their subjects in the pursuit of virtue, look instead with envy and malice upon all virtue, and obstruct it by all means in their power, there will be found few men of virtue living under a tyrannical government. As the Philosopher says, strong men will be found among those who hold strength in honour: and Cicero says: 'Whatever is universally des-pised decays and ceases to flourish.' It is natural that men who are nurtured in an atmosphere of fear should be weak and degenerate in spirit, and afraid of facing a difficult or strenuous task. This is also proved by the experience of those countries which have remained long under tyranny. So the Apostle says (Col. III, 21): 'Fathers, provoke not your children to indignation; lest they be discouraged.' It was the consideration of these evil consequences of tyranny which led Solomon to say (Prov. XXVIII, 12): 'When the wicked reign, men are ruined,' because by reason of the malice of tyrants men are led away from the perfection of virtue. And again he says (ibid., XXIX, 2), 'When the wicked shall bear rule, the people shall mourn'; and again, (ibid., XXVIII, 28) 'When the wicked rise up, men shall hide them-selves,'—to avoid the cruelty of tyrants. Nor is this to be wondered at. For a man who exercises authority, not according to reason, but according to the desires of passion, in no way differs from a beast. So Solomon says (ibid., XXVIII, 15): 'As a roaring lion and a hungry bear, so is a wicked prince over the poor people.' So men flee from tyrants as they would from a cruel beast; nor is it any different to be subject to a tyrant or to a savage beast.

Caput IV.—QUOMODO VARIATUM EST DOMINIUM APUD ROMANOS, ET
QUOD INTERDUM APUD EOS MAGIS AUCTA EST RESPUBLICA EX DOMINIO
PLURIUM.

Quia igitur optimum et pessimum consistunt in monarchia, id est
principatu unius, multis quidem propter tyrannorum malitiam red-
ditur regia dignitas odiosa. Quidam vero dum regimen regis desiderant,
incidunt in saevitiam tyrannorum, rectoresque quamplures tyrannidem
exercent sub praetexto regiae dignitatis. Horum quidem exemplum
evidenter apparet in romana republica. Regibus enim a populo
romano expulsis, dum regium vel potius tyrannicum fastum ferre non
possent, instituerant sibi consules et alios magistratus, per quos regi
coeperunt et dirigi, regnum in aristocratiam commutare volentes, et,
sicut refert Sallustius: « *Incredibile est memoratu, quantum, adepta libertate,
in brevi romana civitas creverit* ». Plerumque namque contingit, ut
homines sub rege viventes, segnius ad bonum commune nitantur,
utpote aestimantes id quod ad commune bonum impendunt, non sibi
ipsis conferre, sed alteri, sub cuius potestate vident esse bona communia. Cum vero bonum commune non vident esse in potestate
unius, non attendunt ad bonum commune quasi ad id quod est alterius,
sed quilibet attendit ad illud quasi suum: unde experimento videtur
quod una civitas per annuos rectores administrata, plus potest interdum
quam rex aliquis, si haberet tres vel quatuor civitates: parvaque servitia
exacta a regibus gravius ferunt quam magna onera, si a communitate
civium imponantur: quod in promotione romanae reipublicae serva-
tum fuerit. Nam plebs ad militiam scribebatur, et pro militantibus
stipendia exsolvebant, et cum stipendiis exsolvendis non sufficeret
commune aerarium, in usus publicos opes venere privatae, adeo ut
praeter singulos annulos aureos, singulasque bullas, quae erant dignitatis insignia, nihil sibi auri ipse etiam senatus reliquerit. Sed cum
dissensionibus fatigarentur continuis, quae usque ad bella civilia excre-
verunt, quibus bellis civilibus eis libertas, ad quam multum studuerant,
de manibus erepta est, sub potestate imperatorum esse coeperunt, qui
se reges a principio appellari noluerunt, quia Romanis fuerat nomen
regium odiosum. Horum autem quidam more regio bonum commune

Chapter IV.—THE TYPES OF GOVERNMENT AMONG THE ROMANS, AND
THE ADVANTAGES SOMETIMES PRESENT IN GOVERNMENT BY MANY.

Because both the best and the worst is to be found in monarchy,
or government by one man, many people, knowing the evils of
tyranny, regard the very name of king with hate. For it sometimes
happens that those who expect to be ruled by a king, fall instead under
a savage tyranny: and too many rulers mask the injustice of their rule
with the cloak of regal dignity. There are many examples of this
to be found in the history of the Roman Republic. Their first kings
were driven out by the Romans when they would no longer support
the burden of their rule—or rather, of their tyranny. Then they
set up for themselves consuls and other magistrates to rule and guide
them: wishing thus to change from a monarchy to an aristocracy.
Sallust refers to this, saying: 'It is almost incredible if we call to mind
how speedily the Roman State grew, when once it had achieved its
liberty.' For it often happens that men who are ruled by a monarch
are slow to interest themselves in the common welfare; since they
are of opinion that whatever they do for the common good will in no
way benefit themselves, but only serve to enrich whoever appears to
control the public interest. But if there is no one person with power
over the common interest, they go about the corporate task as though
it were their own business and not merely profitable to another. So
experience has shown that a single city, with an administration which
is changed annually, can sometimes accomplish more than three or
four cities under a monarchy; and small services exacted by a king
bear more heavily than much greater burdens imposed by the community of citizens. The Roman Republic provides a very good
example of this point. For under it the people were conscripted to
military service, and payment was made for such service. But when
the public funds were insufficient to meet this debt, private wealth
was taxed to such an extent that not even the senators retained any
gold, except for a ring and a seal which were the sign of office. But
later, being weakened by continual dissensions which developed into
civil wars, they lost that liberty for which they had striven so hard,
and fell under the government of the emperors; who would not at
first accept the title of king, since the very name of king was still odious
to the Romans. Certain of these emperors, after the fashion of good

fideliter procuraverunt, per quorum studium romana respublica et aucta et conservata est. Plurimi vero eorum in subditos quidem tyranni, ad hostes vero effecti desides et imbecilles, romanam rempublicam ad nihilum redegerunt. Similis etiam processus fuit in populo Hebraeorum. Primo quidem dum sub iudicibus regebantur, undique diripiebantur ab hostibus. Nam unusquisque quod bonum erat in oculis suis, hoc faciebat. Regibus vero eis divinitus datis ad eorum instantiam, propter regum malitiam, a cultu unius Dei recesserunt et finaliter ducti sunt in captivitatem. Utrinque igitur pericula imminent: sive dum timetur tyrannus, evitetur regis optimum dominium, sive dum hoc consideratur, potestas regia in malitiam tyrannicam convertatur.

kings, faithfully served the common interest; and by their efforts the Roman state grew in strength and power. The majority of them, however, were tyrants to their subjects and weak and impotent before their enemies; so that under them the Roman State fell away to nought. The same story can also be seen in the case of the Jews. When at first they were ruled by judges they were devastated by their enemies. For each man was in the habit of attending only to his own business. Then, in answer to their prayers, God gave them kings: but in consequence of the sinfulness of their kings they fell away from the worship of the true God and were finally reduced to captivity. From one side and from another, therefore, there is danger: whether from fear of tyranny the best benefits of monarchy are lost, or whether in the hope of achieving true kingship the government degenerates into evil tyranny.

Caput V.—Quod in dominio plurium magis saepe contingit
dominium tyrannicum quam ex dominio unius; et ideo regimen
unius melius est.

Cum autem inter duo, ex quorum utroque periculum imminet,
eligere oportet, illud potissime eligendum est, ex quo sequitur minus
malum. Ex monarchia autem, si in tyrannidem convertatur, minus
malum sequitur quam ex regimine plurium optimatum, quando
corrumpitur. Dissensio enim, quae plurimum sequitur ex regimine
plurium, contrariatur bono pacis, quod est praecipuum in multitudine
sociali: quod quidem bonum per tyrannidem non tollitur, sed aliqua
particularium hominum bona impediuntur, nisi fuerit excessus tyrannidis, quod in totam communitatem desaeviat. Magis igitur praeop-
tandum est unius regimen quam multorum, quamvis ex utroque
sequantur pericula. Adhuc: illud magis fugiendum videtur, ex quo
pluries sequi possunt magna pericula; frequentius autem sequuntur
maxima pericula multitudinis ex multorum regimine, quam ex regimine unius. Plerumque enim contingit ut ex pluribus aliquis ab
intentione communis boni deficiat, quam quod unus tantum.
Quicumque autem, ex pluribus praesidentibus, divertat ab intentione
communis boni, dissensionis periculum in subditorum multitudine
imminet, quia dissentientibus principibus, consequens est ut in
multitudine sequatur dissensio. Si vero unus praesit, plerumque
quidem ad bonum commune respicit; aut si a bono communi intentionem avertat, non statim sequitur ut ad subditorum depressionem
intendat, quod est excessus tyrannidis et in malitia regiminis maximum
gradum tenens, ut supra ostensum est. Magis igitur sunt fugienda
pericula quae proveniunt ex gubernatione multorum, quam ex gubernatione unius. Amplius, non minus contingit in tyrannidem verti
regimen multorum quam unius, sed forte frequentius. Exorta namque
dissensione per regimen plurium, contingit saepe unum super alios
superare et sibi soli multitudinis dominium usurpare, quod quidem
ex his, quae pro tempore fuerunt, manifeste inspici potest. Nam fere
omnium multorum regimen est in tyrannidem terminatum, ut in

Chapter V.—MONARCHY THE BEST DEFENCE AGAINST TYRANNY.

When a choice has to be made between two courses of action, both of which are fraught with danger, one should choose that which will lead to the lesser evil. Monarchy, however, if it degenerates into tyranny is accompanied by less evil consequences than when the government of many becomes corrupt. For the dissensions which commonly follow government by many are destructive of the benefits of peace, which is the most important thing for any social life. But this benefit is not altogether destroyed by a tyranny, since under tyranny it is individual satisfaction which is most affected: unless of course the tyranny be so unbounded as to enslave the entire community. So government by one is to be preferred to government by many, though each has its own dangers.

Furthermore: that course of action should rather be avoided from which danger can more frequently arise. But the greatest dangers to a community more often arise under a pluralistic government than under government by one person. For a man may more often be deflected from the common interest if he be one of many than if he be alone in government. And whenever one out of a number who form the government fails in his duty to the common welfare, he puts the whole community in danger of strife; for disagreement among rulers is followed by general dissension. If, on the other hand, there is one person alone at the head of the government, he will more often attend to the common interest; and even if he fails in such high intention, it does not necessarily follow that he will oppress the whole community and become straightway an absolute tyrant, which, as we have seen, is the worst form of bad government. So the dangers which arise out of government by many are more to be avoided than those consequent upon monarchy.

Again. The degeneration of government into tyranny is no less frequent under a pluralistic than under a monarchical form of government: in fact it is probably more frequent. For when dissension breaks out under a pluralistic form of government, one man will often take the lead among the others, and usurp to himself power over the whole community; as is clearly seen from what has happened in history. Nearly every pluralistic regime has ended in tyranny, as the history of

romana republica manifeste apparet. Quae cum diu per plures magistratus administrata fuisset, exortis simultatibus, dissensionibus et bellis civilibus, in crudelissimos tyrannos incidit; et universaliter si quis praeterita facta et quae nunc fiunt diligenter consideret, plures inveniet exercuisse tyrannidem in terris, quae per multos reguntur, quam in illis, quae gubernantur per unum. Si igitur regium, quod est optimum regimen, maxime vitandum videatur propter tyrannidem; tyrannis autem non minus, sed magis, contingere solet in regimine plurium, quam unius, relinquitur simpliciter magis esse expediens sub rege uno vivere, quam sub regimine plurium.

the Roman State abundantly shows. For when it had long been administered by magistrates, there began plots and dissensions and even civil wars; and the republic fell into the hands of the most cruel tyrants. As a general rule, in fact, when one considers the events both of history and of our own times, it is clear that tyranny has more frequently flourished in those lands which had a pluralistic government than in those which were governed by monarchs.

Thus, if monarchy, which is the best form of government, is to be avoided mainly because of the danger of tyranny; and if tyranny comes about, not less, but rather more frequently under a pluralistic regime, we are left with the simple conclusion that it is more expedient to live under a monarchy than under a pluralistic government.

Caput VI.—CONCLUSIO, QUOD REGIMEN UNIUS SIMPLICITER SIT OPTI-
MUM. OSTENDIT QUALITER MULTITUDO SE DEBET HABERE CIRCA IPSUM,
QUIA AUFERENDA EST EI OCCASIO NE TYRANNIZET, ET QUOD ETIAM IN
HOC EST TOLERANDUS PROPTER MAIUS MALUM VITANDUM.

Quia ergo unius regimen praeligendum est, quod est optimum, et
contingit ipsum in tyrannidem converti, quod est pessimum, ut ex
dictis patet, laborandum est diligenti studio ut sic multitudini provi-
deatur de rege, ut non incidant in tyrannum. Primum autem est
necessarium ut talis conditionis homo ab illis, ad quos hoc spectat
officium, promoveatur in regem, quod non sit probabile in tyrannidem
declinare.   Unde Samuel, Dei providentiam erga institutionem
regis commendans, ait I *Reg.* cap. XIII, 14: « *Quaesivit sibi Dominus
virum secundum cor suum* ». Deinde sic disponenda est regni gubernatio,
ut regi iam instituto tyrannidis substrahatur occasio. Simul etiam sic
eius temperetur potestas, ut in tyrannidem de facili declinare non
possit. Quae quidem ut fiant, in sequentibus considerandum erit.
Demum vero curandum est, si rex in tyrannidem diveret, qualiter
posset occurri.

Et quidem si non fuerit excessus tyrannidis, utilius est remissam
tyrannidem tolerare ad tempus, quam contra tyrannum agendo multis
implicari periculis, quae sunt graviora ipsa tyrannide. Potest enim
contingere, ut qui contra tyrannum agunt praevalere non possint, et
sic provocatus tyrannus magis desaeviat. Quod si praevalere quis
possit adversus tyrannum, ex hoc ipso proveniunt multotiens gravis-
simae dissensiones in populo: sive dum in tyrannum insurgitur, sive
post deiectionem tyranni erga ordinationem regiminis multitudo
separatur in partes. Contingit etiam ut interdum, dum alicuius auxilio
multitudo expellit tyrannum, ille, potestate accepta, tyrannidem
arripiat, et timens pati ab alio quod ipse in alium fecit, graviori servitute
subditos opprimat. Sic enim in tyrannide solet contingere, ut pos-
terior gravior fiat quam praecedens, dum praecedentia gravamina
non deserit, et ipse, ex sui cordis malitia, nova excogitat; unde Syracusis
quondam Dionysii mortem omnibus desiderantibus, anus quaedam,
ut incolumis et sibi superstes esset, continue orabat; quod ut tyrannus
cognovit, cur hoc faceret interrogavit. Tum illa: « Puella, inquit,
existens, cum gravem tyrannum haberemus mortem ejus cupiebam,

Chapter VI.—THE EXCELLENCE OF MONARCHY AND THE SAFEGUARDS NECESSARY TO PREVENT ITS DEGENERATING INTO TYRANNY.

Since government by one person, being the best, is to be preferred; and since, as we have shown, there is always a danger that it will develop into tyranny, which is the worst government, every precaution must be taken to provide the community with a ruler who will not become a tyrant. In the first place it is necessary that whoever of the possible candidates is proclaimed king shall be of such character that it is unlikely that he will become a tyrant. So Samuel, praising God's Providence in instituting kingship, says (1 *Kings* XIII, 14) 'The Lord hath sought out for Himself a man after His own heart.' Next, a monarchy should be so constituted that there is no opportunity for the king, once he is reigning, to become a tyrant. And, at the same time the kingly power should be so restricted that he could not easily turn to tyranny. The steps to be taken to this end will be considered later. Finally, we must consider the action to be taken should a king become tyrannical.

If the tyranny be not excessive it is certainly wiser to tolerate it in limited measure, at least for a time, rather than to run the risk of even greater perils by opposing it. For those who take action against a tyrant may fail in their object, and only succeed in rousing the tyrant to greater savagery. Even when action against a tyrant meets with success, this very fact breeds strife and grave discord among the populace, either in the moment of rebellion or after his overthrow when opinion in the community is factiously divided as to the new form of government. Again, a community sometimes succeeds in deposing a tyrant with the help of some other ruler, who in turn seizes absolute power. But fear of sharing the fate of his predecessor drives him to even greater severity against his new subjects. Thus it is often the case with tyranny that a new tyrant is worse than the old; for the newcomer abandons none of his predecessor's cruelties, but plans even greater oppression in the evil of his heart. So at a time when the Syracusans all desired the death of Dionysius, there was an old woman who continually prayed that he would survive her. The tyrant, coming to know of this, asked why she acted thus; and she replied, 'When I was yet a girl we were oppressed by a tyrant, and I desired his death;

quo interfecto, aliquantum durior successit; eius quoque dominationem finiri magnum existimabam: tertium te importuniorem habere
coepimus rectorem. Itaque si tu fueris absumptus, deterior in locum
tuum succedet ».

Et si sit intolerabilis excessus tyrannidis, quibusdam visum fuit
ut ad fortium virorum virtutem pertineat tyrannum interimere, seque
pro liberatione multitudinis exponere periculis mortis: cuius rei
exemplum etiam in veteri testamento habetur. Nam Aioth quidam
Eglon, regem Moab, qui gravi servitute populum Dei premebat, sica
infixa in eius femore, interemit, et factus est populi iudex. Sed hoc
apostolicae doctrinae non congruit. Docet enim nos Petrus non bonis
tantum et modestis, verum etiam dyscolis dominis reverenter subditos
esse (I *Petr.*, II): « *Haec est enim gratia, si, propter conscientiam Dei, susti-
neat quis tristitias patiens iniuste* »; unde cum multi romani imperatores
fidem Christi persequerentur tyrannice, magnaque multitudo tam
nobilium quam populi esset ad fidem conversa, non resistendo, sed
mortem patienter et animati sustinentes pro Christo laudantur, ut in
sacra Thebaeorum legione manifeste apparet; magisque Aioth iudican-
dus est hostem interemisse, quam populi rectorem, licet tyrannum:
unde et in veteri testamento leguntur occisi fuisse hi, qui occiderunt
Joas, regem Juda, quamvis a cultu Dei recedentem, eorumque filii
reservati secundum legis praeceptum. Esset autem hoc multitudini
periculosum et eius rectoribus, si privata praesumptione aliqui atten-
tarent praesidentium necem, etiam tyrannorum. Plerumque enim
huiusmodi periculis magis exponunt se mali quam boni. Malis autem
solet esse grave dominium non minus regum quam tyrannorum, quia
secundum sententiam Salomonis, *Prov.* XX, 26: « *Dissipat impios rex
sapiens* ». Magis igitur ex huiusmodi praesumptione immineret
periculum multitudini de amissione regis, quam remedium de sub-
tractione tyranni.

Videtur autem magis contra tyrannorum saevitiam non privata
praesumptione aliquorum, sed auctoritate publica procedendum.
Primo quidem, si ad ius multitudinis alicuius pertineat sibi providere
de rege, non iniuste ab eadem rex institutus potest destrui[1] vel refre-
nari eius potestas, si potestate regia tyrannice abutatur. Nec putanda

---

[1] In some editions 'destitui.'

he was slain, but was succeeded by another who oppressed us even more harshly; and again I was greatly pleased to see the end of his reign. But he was succeeded by you, who are an even harsher ruler. So I fear that if you are taken from our midst you will be succeeded by one who is even more terrible.'

If, however, tyranny becomes so excessive as to be intolerable, it has been argued that it would be an act of virtue for the more powerful citizens to kill the tyrant, even exposing themselves to the peril of death for the liberation of the community. There is an example of such a situation in the Old Testament. A certain Aioth slew Eglon, King of the Moabites, with a dagger thrust in the side, because he oppressed the people of God with dire bondage: and for this he was made a judge of the people. But this does not agree with Apostolic teaching. For Peter teaches us to obey not only good and temperate rulers, but also to bear reverence to those who are ill-disposed (I *Peter*, II, 20). 'It is the patience of the innocent sufferer that wins credit in God's sight.' Thus during the persecutions of many Roman emperors against the faith of Christ a great part of the people, both nobles and commoners, were converted to the faith and made no resistance, but suffered death for Christ with great courage and resignation; as is clear from the example of the holy legion of Thebes. As to the case of Aioth, it would appear that he slew an enemy rather than a legitimate, though tyrannical, ruler of the people. So, again in the Old Testament, we read that those who slew Joas, King of Juda, were put to death, even though he was an apostate; and that their children were spared according to the precept of the law. It would indeed be dangerous, both for the community and for its rulers, if individuals were, upon private initiative, to attempt the death of those who govern, albeit tyrannically. It is in fact more common for evildoers than for just men, to expose themselves to such dangers; because the rule of a just king is no less burdensome to the evil than that of a tyrant; for as Solomon says (*Prov.* XX, 26), 'The wise king scatters the impious.' The consequence of such presumption is more likely to be the loss of a good king to the community than any benefit from the suppression of tyranny.

It seems then, that the remedy against the evils of tyranny lies rather in the hands of public authority than in the private judgement of individuals. In particular, where a community has the right to elect a ruler for itself, it would not be contrary to justice for that community to depose the king whom it has elected, nor to curb his power should he abuse it to play the tyrant. Nor should the community be

est talis multitudo infideliter agere tyrannum destituens, etiam si eidem in perpetuo se ante subiecerat; quia hoc ipse meruit, in multitudinis regimine se non fideliter gerens ut exigit regis officium, quod ei pactum a subditis non reservetur. Sic Romani Tarquinium superbum, quem in regem susceperant, propter eius et filiorum tyrannidem a regno eiecerunt, substituta minori, scilicet consulari, potestate. Sic etiam Domitianus, qui modestissimis imperatoribus, Vespasiano patri et Tito fratri eius, successerat, dum tyrannidem exercet, a senatu Romano interemptus est, omnibus quae perverse Romanis fecerat per senatus-consultum iuste et salubriter in irritum revocatis. Quo factum est, ut Beatus Joannes Evangelista, dilectus Dei discipulus, qui per ipsum Domitianum in Pathmos insulam fuerat exilio relegatus, ad Ephesum per senatus-consultum remitteretur.

Si vero ad ius alicuius superioris pertineat multitudini providere de rege, expectandum est ab eo remedium contra tyranni nequitiam. Sic Archelai, qui in Judaea pro Herode patre suo regnare iam coeperat, paternam malitiam imitantis, Judaeis contra eum querimoniam ad Caesarem Augustum deferentibus, primo quidem potestas diminuitur ablato sibi regio nomine, et medietate regni sui inter duos fratres suos divisa: deinde, cum nec sic a tyrannide compesceretur, a Tiberio Caesare relegatus est in exilium apud Lugdunum, Galliae civitatem. Quod si omnino contra tyrannum auxilium humanum haberi non potest, recurrendum est ad regem omnium Deum, qui est adiutor in opportunitatibus in tribulatione. Eius enim potentiae subest, ut cor tyranni crudele convertat in mansuetudinem secundum Salomonis sententiam, *Prov.* XXI, 1: « *Cor regis in manu Dei, quocumque voluerit inclinabit illud* ». Ipse enim regis Assueri crudelitatem, qui Judaeis mortem parabat, in mansuetudinem vertit. Ipse est qui ita Nabuchodonosor crudelem regem convertit, quod factus est divinae potentiae praedicator. « *Nunc igitur*, inquit, *ego Nabuchodonosor laudo, et magnifico, et glorifico regem coeli, quia opera eius vera et viae eius iudicia, et gradientes in superbia potest humiliare* » (*Dan.* IV, vers. 34). Tyrannos vero, quos reputat conversione indignos, potest auferre de medio, vel ad infimum statum reducere, secundum illud Sapientis (*Eccle.* X, 17): « *Sedes ducum superborum destruxit Deus, et sedere fecit mites pro eis* ». Ipse est qui videns

accused of disloyalty for thus deposing a tyrant, even after a previous promise of constant fealty; for the tyrant lays himself open to such treatment by his failure to discharge the duties of his office as governor of the community, and in consequence his subjects are no longer bound by their oath to him. So the Romans deposed Tarquinius the proud, whom they had previously accepted as king, because of his and his children's tyranny, and substituted the lesser or consular power instead. So also Domitian, succeeding to those mildest of emperors, Vespasian, his father, and Titus his brother, was slain by the Roman Senate because of his tyranny: and all the injustices which he had brought upon the Romans were legally and wisely revoked and made void by decree of the Senate. It was thus that Saint John, the beloved disciple of God, who was banished into exile on the island of Patmos by Domitian, was by decree of the Senate brought back to Ephesus.

If on the other hand the right to appoint a king over a certain community belongs to some superior, then the remedy against tyrannical excess must be sought from him. Thus the Jews made complaint to Caesar Augustus against Archelaus, when the latter began to rule in the place of his father, Herod, in Judea and had begun to imitate his father's evil ways. At first, therefore, his power was curtailed; the title of king being taken from him and the half of his kingdom being divided between his two brothers. Then, when this proved insufficient to restrain his tyranny, he was exiled by Tiberius Caesar to Lyons, a city of France.

Finally, when there is no hope of human aid against tyranny, recourse must be made to God the King of all, and the helper of all who call upon Him in the time of tribulation. For it is in His power to turn the cruel heart of a tyrant to gentleness; and Solomon declares (*Prov.* XXI, 1): 'The heart of the king is in the hand of the Lord; whithersoever He will He shall turn it.' He turned the cruelty of the king of Assyria to pity when he meditated death to the Jews. It was He who so converted the cruel king Nabuchodonosor that he openly confessed the divine power: 'Now indeed, he said, I Nabuchodonosor do praise and magnify and glorify the King of heaven because all his works are true and his ways judgements, and them that walk in pride he is able to abase' (*Dan.* IV, 34). As for those tyrants whom He considers unworthy of conversion, He can take them from among us or reduce them to impotency, as we are told by the Wise Man (*Ecclesiastes,* X, 17) 'God hath overturned the thrones of proud princes and hath set up the meek in their stead.' Again it is He who seeing the

C

afflictionem populi sui in Aegypto, et audiens eorum clamorem, Pharaonem tyrannum deiecit cum exercitu suo in mare. Ipse est qui memoratum Nabuchodonosor prius superbientem non solum eiectum de regni solio, sed etiam de hominum consortio in similitudinem bestiae commutavit. Nec etiam abbreviata manus eius est, ut populum suum a tyrannis liberare non possit. Promittit enim populo suo per Isaiam requiem se daturum a labore et confusione, ac servitute dura, qua antea servierat. Et per *Ezech.* cap. XXXIV, 10, dicit: « *Liberabo meum gregem de ore eorum* », scilicet pastorum, qui pascunt se ipsos. Sed ut hoc beneficium populus a Deo consequi mereatur, debet a peccatis cessare, quia in ultionem peccati divina permissione impii accipiunt principatum, dicente Domino per *Oseam*, XIII, 11: « *Dabo tibi regem in furore meo* »; et in *Job.* XXXIV, vers. 30, dicitur quod « *regnare facit hominem hypocritam propter peccata populi* ». Tollenda est igitur culpa, ut cesset a tyrannorum plaga.

affliction of His people in Egypt, and hearing their cries, cast down the tyrant Pharaoh with his whole army into the sea. Not only did He depose the proud Nabuchodonosor, already mentioned, but cast him out like a beast from the company of men. Nor is His arm now any less strong to liberate His people from the oppression of tyrants. He promised His people by Isaias to give them peace from their labours and from the confusion and dire servitude under which they once suffered. And by Ezechiel He said (Chap. XXXIV, 10): 'I will deliver my flock from their mouth.' That is from those shepherds who feed only themselves. But for men to merit such benefit of God they must abstain from sinning, because it is as a punishment for sin that, by divine permission, the impious are allowed to rule, as the Lord Himself warns us by Hosea (XIII, 11): 'I will give thee a king in my wrath.' And again, in Job (XXXIV, 30) it is said, 'He maketh a man who is a hypocrite to rule because of the sins of the people.' So guilt must first be expiated before the affliction of tyranny can cease.

Caput VII.—Hic quaerit sanctus Doctor, quid praecipue movere debeat regem ad regendum, utrum honor, vel gloria; et ponit opiniones circa hoc, quid sit tenendum.

Quoniam autem, secundum praedicta, regis est bonum multitudinis quaerere, nimis videtur onerosum regis officium, nisi ei aliquod proprium bonum ex hoc proveniret. Oportet igitur considerare, in qua re sit boni regis conveniens praemium.

Quibusdam igitur visum est non esse aliud, nisi honorem et gloriam, unde et Tullius (*De repub.*) definit « *principem civitatis esse alendum gloria* », cuius rationem Aristoteles in lib. *Ethic.* assignare videtur, « *quia princeps, cui non sufficit honor et gloria, consequenter tyrannus efficitur* ». Inest enim animis omnium, ut proprium bonum quaerant. Si ergo contentus non fuerit princeps gloria et honore, quaeret voluptates et divitias, et sic ad rapinas et subditorum iniurias convertetur.

Sed si hanc sententiam receperimus, plurima sequuntur inconvenientia. Primo namque hoc regibus dispendiosum esset, si tot labores et sollicitudines paterentur pro mercede tam fragili. Nihil enim videtur in rebus humanis fragilius gloria et honore favoris hominum, cum dependeat ex opinionibus hominum, quibus nihil mutabilius in vita hominum, et inde est quod Isaias propheta, XX, huiusmodi gloriam nominat florem foeni. Deinde humanae gloriae cupido animi magnitudinem aufert. Qui enim favorem hominum quaerit, necesse est ut in omni eo, quod dicit aut facit, eorum voluntati deserviat, et sic dum placere hominibus studet, fit servus singulorum. Propter quod et idem Tullius in lib. *De officiis*, cavendam dicit gloriae cupidinem. Eripit enim animi libertatem, pro qua magnanimis viris omnis debet esse contentio. Nihil autem principem, qui ad bona peragenda instituitur, magis decet quam animi magnitudo. Est igitur incompetens regis officio humanae gloriae praemium.

Simul etiam est multitudini nocivum, si tale praemium statuatur principibus: pertinet enim ad boni viri officium, ut contemnat gloriam, sicut alia temporalia bona. Virtuosi enim et fortis animi est pro

Chapter VII.—WHETHER HONOUR OR GLORY ARE SUFFICIENT INCEN-
TIVES FOR A MONARCH TO GOVERN WISELY.

Since, as we have already shown, it is the duty of a king to provide
for the good of the community, and since such a task would appear
to be too heavy unless it were accompanied by some commensurate
reward, we must now consider what is the particular reward for a good
monarch.

Some have been of the opinion that it is nothing else than honour
and glory: thus, Cicero states (*De Repub.*): 'The ruler of a city should
be flattered with honours.' The reason for this seems to be indicated
by Aristotle in the *Ethics*, when he says, 'A prince who is not satisfied
with his honour and glory becomes a tyrant.' For there is within the
soul of all an urge to seek their own satisfaction. So, if a prince were
not satisfied with the honour and glory that was his, he would seek
further riches and pleasures, and so would become rapacious and
unjust towards his subjects.

But if we accept such an opinion, many unfortunate consequences
follow. In the first place it would be altogether too burdensome for a
king to undertake so great a task, and to be harried by so many cares,
for so fragile a reward. For in the whole range of human affairs
nothing would seem to be more uncertain than the glory and honour
of popular favour, since it depends upon human opinion, which is the
most changeable thing on earth. For this reason Isaias the prophet
likens such glory to the grass of the field (Chap. XX). Furthermore,
the desire of human glory destroys magnanimity of soul. For whoever
seeks favour of men must consider their desires in all that he says and
does: thus, because of his desire to please men he becomes the servant
of individuals. For this reason the same Cicero in his *De Officiis*,
warns us to beware the desire of glory. It is this in fact which destroys
that liberty of spirit which should be the greatest aspiration of the
magnanimous man: while there is nothing which befits a prince who
is elected to act with righteousness than this same magnanimity of
soul. We must conclude, then, that human glory is an insufficient
reward for the kingly office.

Not only is this the case, but it is also hurtful to the community
to set such a reward before princes: for it is the duty of a just man to
despise glory, together with all other temporal rewards. A virtuous

iustitia contemnere gloriam sicut et vitam: unde fit quiddam mirabile, ut quia virtuosos actus sequitur gloria, ipsa gloria virtuose contemnatur, et ex contemptu gloriae homo gloriosus reddatur, secundum sententiam Fabii dicentis: « *Gloriam qui spreverit, veram habebit* », et de Catone dixit Salustius: « *Quo minus petebat gloriam, tanto magis assequebatur illam* »; ipsique Christi discipuli se sicut Dei ministros exhibebant per gloriam et ignobilitatem, per infamiam et bonam famam. Non est igitur boni viri conveniens praemium gloria, quam contemnunt boni. Si igitur hoc solum bonum statuatur praemium principibus, sequetur bonos viros non assumere principatum, aut si assumpserint, impraemiatos esse.

Amplius: ex cupidine gloriae periculosa mala proveniunt. Multi enim dum immoderate gloriam in rebus bellicis quaerunt, se ac suos perdiderunt exercitus, libertate patriae sub hostili potestate redacta: unde Torquatus, Romanus princeps, in exemplo huius vitandi discriminis, filium, qui contra imperium suum provocatus ab hoste iuvenili ardore pugnavit, licet vicisset, occidit, ne plus mali esset in praesumptionis exemplo, quam utilitatis in gloria hostis occisi. Habet etiam cupido gloriae aliud sibi familiare vitium, simulationem videlicet. Quia enim difficile est, paucisque contingit veras virtutes assequi, quibus solis honor debetur, multi gloriam cupientes, virtutum simulatores fiunt. Propter quod, sicut dicit Salustius: « *Ambitio multos mortales falsos fieri coegit. Aliud clausum in pectore, aliud promptum habere in lingua, magisque vultum quam ingenium habere* ». Sed et Salvator noster eos, qui bona opera faciunt, ut ab hominibus videntur, hypocritas, id est simulatores, vocat. Sicut igitur periculosum est multitudini, si princeps voluptates et divitias quaerat pro praemio, ne raptor et contumeliosus fiat; ita periculosum est cum detinetur gloriae praemio, ne praesumptuosus et simulator existat. Sed, quantum ex dictorum sapientium intentione apparet, non ea ratione honorem et gloriam pro praemio principi decreverunt, tamquam ad hoc principaliter ferri debeat boni regis intentio; sed quia tolerabilius est si gloriam quaerat, quam si pecuniam cupiat, vel voluptatem sequatur. Hoc enim vitium virtuti propinquius est, cum gloria, quam homines cupiunt, ut ait Augustinus, nihil aliud sit, quam iudicium hominum bene de homini-

and high-souled man should despise glory and even life itself for the sake of justice. So it is a remarkable paradox that while glory follows virtuous action, there is virtue in despising glory. Thus, by holding glory in contempt, a man becomes the more renowned. As Fabius once said, 'He shall find true glory who spurns it'; and Sallust said of Cato, 'The less he sought after fame, the more renowned did he become.' And the disciples of Christ showed themselves to be ministers of God both in glory and in shame, through good report and evil report. A good man then, is not fittingly rewarded merely by that glory which the good avoid. And if this were the sole reward for ruling it would follow that good men would never accept such an office, or, accepting it, they would have to go unrewarded.

Furthermore, the love of glory leads to other and more dangerous evils. Many have been led to seek, too, great renown by making war; and, perishing with their whole army, have left the independence of their country at the mercy of an alien power. For this reason, Torquatus, King of the Romans, wishing to show how necessary it is to avoid such danger, slew his own son for allowing himself to be stung to act against orders by the jibes of the enemy, even though he did in his youthful zeal kill his adversary. So much did he fear the evil which might follow such an example of presumption, compared with the advantage gained from the death of an enemy.

There is another vice which is of like nature with the desire of glory, and that is deceit. For it is a difficult task, and one in which few succeed, to practise true virtue, which alone is honourable: but because many desire glory they are led to simulate virtue. So, as Sallust says, 'Ambition has made many false: having one sentiment in their hearts and another ready to the tongue, they are all appearance and no substance.' And our Saviour Himself calls them hypocrites and dissimulators who do good, only that they may be seen by men. So, just as it is perilous for the community if the ruler should seek pleasures and riches for his reward and thus become rapacious and overbearing; it is equally perilous if he be eaten up with desire of glory and thus become presumptuous and a deceiver. The intention, then, of the wise writers whom we first quoted was not to set the love of honour and glory as the true object of a good ruler and the main reward for good government; but rather to show that it is more tolerable for a ruler to seek glory than to be given over to the desire of riches and of pleasures. For, though a vice, it is a little nearer to virtue; since the glory which men seek, as Augustine tells us, is no more than the judgement of those

bus opinantium. Cupido enim gloriae aliquod habet virtutis vesti-
gium, dum saltem bonorum approbationem quaerit, et eis displicere
recusat. Paucis igitur ad veram virtutem pervenientibus tolerabilius
videtur, si praeferatur ad regimen qui, vel iudicium hominum metuens,
a malis manifestis retrahitur.

Qui enim gloriam cupit, aut vera via per virtutis opera nititur, ut ab
hominibus approbetur, vel saltem dolis ad hoc contendit atque fallaciis.
At qui dominari desiderat, si cupiditate gloriae carens non timeat bene
iudicantibus displicere, per apertissima scelera quaerit plerumque
obtinere, quod diligit, unde bestias superat sive crudelitatis, sive
luxuriae vitiis, sicut in Nerone Caesare patet, cuius, ut Augustinus
dicit, tanta luxuria fuit, ut nihil putaretur ab eo virile metuendum, tanta
crudelitas, ut nihil molle habere putaretur. Hoc autem satis exprimitur
per id quod Aristoteles de magnanimo in *Ethic.* dicit: quod non quaerit
honorem et gloriam quasi aliquid magnum, quod sit virtutis sufficiens
praemium, sed nihil ultra hoc ab hominibus exigit. Hoc enim inter
omnia terrena videtur esse praecipuum, ut homini ab hominibus
testimonium de virtute reddatur.

who think well of their fellows. So the desire of glory bears some traces of virtue, for it does at least seek the approval of the good and avoids giving them displeasure. And when so few attain true virtue it would seem more tolerable to chose for the kingly office one who at least fears the judgement of men and is, to that extent, prevented from open evil doing.

In fact, a man who desires glory is either driven along the true path of virtuous action to win the approval of men, or at least he tries for such approval by trickery and fraud. But one who desires only to dominate and cares nothing for glory will not fear the disapproval of right-thinking men, but will more often seek to obtain what he wants by open crimes, surpassing even the beasts in cruelty and debauchery. So Augustine says of Nero that he was too vicious for any manly action to be expected of him, and so cruel that not a trace of kindliness was left in his character. Aristotle's description of the magnanimous man, in the *Ethics*, puts the matter very clearly. Such a one does not seek honour and glory as though they were complete and sufficient reward for virtue; yet he is content to receive nothing more from men. For of all earthly rewards the highest, perhaps, is that a man's virtue should be publicly attested by his fellows.

Caput VIII.—Hic declarat Doctor, qualis est verus finis regis, qui movere ipsum debet ad bene regendum.

Quoniam ergo mundanus honor et hominum gloria regiae sollicitudini non est sufficiens praemium, inquirendum restat, quale sit eidem sufficiens. Est autem conveniens, ut rex praemium expectet a Deo. Minister enim pro suo ministerio praemium expectat a domino; rex autem, populum gubernando minister Dei est, dicente Apostolo, *Rom.* cap. XIII, 1 et 4, quod « *omnis potestas a Domino Deo est* », et quod « *est Dei minister vindex in iram ei qui male agit* », et in lib. *Sap.* reges Dei esse ministri describuntur. Debent igitur reges pro suo regimine praemium expectare a Deo. Remunerat autem Deus pro suo ministerio reges interdum temporalibus bonis, sed talia praemia sunt bonis malisque communia: unde Dominus *Ezech.* XXIX, 18, dicit: « *Nabuchodonosor rex Babylonis servire fecit exercitum suum servitute magna adversus Tyrum, et merces non est reddita ei, nec exercitui ejus de Tyro, pro servitute qua servivit mihi adversus eam* », ea scilicet servitute, qua potestas, secundum Apostolum, Dei minister est, vindex in iram ei qui male agit; et postea de praemio subdidit: « *Propterea haec dicit Dominus Deus: Ecce ego dabo Nabuchodonosor regem Babylonis in terra Aegypti, et diripiet spolia eius, et erit merces exercitui eius* ». Si ergo reges iniquos contra Dei hostes pugnantes, licet non intentione serviendi Deo, sed sua odia et cupiditates exequendi, tanta mercede Dominus remunerat, ut de hostibus victoriam tribuat, regna subiiciat, et spolia diripienda proponat, quid faciet bonis regibus, qui pia intentione Dei populum regunt et hostes impugnant? Non quidem terrenam, sed aeternam mercedem eis promittit, nec in alio quam in se ipso, dicente Petro pastoribus populi Dei, I *Petr.* cap. V: « *Pascite qui in vobis est gregem Domini, et cum venerit Princeps pastorum* », id est rex regum, Christus, « *percipietis immarcescibilem gloriae coronam* », de qua dicit *Isa.* XXVIII, 5: «*Erit Dominus sertum exultationis et diadema gloriae populo suo*».

Hoc autem ratione manifestatur. Est enim mentibus omnium ratione utentium inditum, virtutis praemium beatitudinem esse,

Chapter VIII.—THE TRUE AIM OF MONARCHICAL GOVERNMENT.

If, then, worldly honour and glory are no sufficient reward for the
cares of regal office, we are left with the task of deciding what is its
just reward. Now, it is right that a king should look to God for some
reward: for a minister expects the reward of his ministry from his
lord, and a king governing his people is a minister of God, as the
Apostle tells us (*Romans*, Chapter XIII, 1, 4), 'All power is from the
Lord God'; and again, 'He is the minister of God, terrible in his anger
against the evil-doer.' Or again, in the book of Wisdom, kings are
called the ministers of God. Kings, therefore, must expect recompense
from God in return for government. God does, on occasion, reward
the ministry of kings with worldly benefits, but such rewards are
common both to good and to bad kings. Thus, the Lord says (*Ezechiel*
XXIX, 18) 'Nabuchodonosor king of Babylon hath made his army
undergo hard service against Tyre: and there hath been no reward
given him, nor his army for Tyre, for the service that he rendered
me against it.' This is the service in virtue of which, according to
the Apostle, human power becomes the minister of God, taking
wrathful vengeance upon the evil-doer. And, with reference to a
reward, he later adds: 'Therefore, thus saith the Lord God, I will send
Nabuchodonosor king of Babylon into the land of Egypt and he will
divide its spoils and he and his army will be recompensed.' If, then, evil
kings who, though fighting against God's enemies, have no intention
of serving God but are spurred only by hatred and the desire of plunder,
are yet greatly rewarded by God with victory over their enemies,
the subjection of kingdoms to their arms, and much plunder to carry
off; what will be His reward for the good rulers who, with pious intention, minister to the people of God and oppose their enemies. To such
He promises not an earthly, but a heavenly reward; one which is to
be found in God alone, as St. Peter says to the pastors of God's people
(I *Peter*, V), 'Pasture God's flock which is entrusted to you: and when
the Prince of Pastors—that is the King of kings, Christ—shall come
you shall receive an incorruptible crown of glory.' And of this Isaias
says (XXVIII, 5), 'The Lord shall be a Throne of exultation and a
crown of glory for his people.'

This conclusion can also be demonstrated by reason. For there is a
firm conviction in the minds of all who think rationally that blessed-

Virtus enim uniuscuiusque rei describitur, quae bonum facit habentem, et opus eius bonum reddit. Ad hoc autem quisque bene operando nititur pervenire, quod est maxime desiderio inditum; hoc autem est esse felicem, quod nullus potest non velle. Hoc igitur praemium virtutis convenienter expectatur, quod hominem beatum facit. Si autem bene operari virtutis est opus, regis autem opus est bene regere subditos, hoc etiam erit praemium regis, quod eum faciat esse beatum. Quid autem hoc sit, hinc considerandum est. Beatitudinem quidem dicimus ultimum desideriorum finem. Neque enim desiderii motus usque in infinitum procedit; esset enim inane naturale desiderium, cum infinita pertransiri non possint. Cum autem desiderium intellectualis naturae sit universalis boni, hoc solum bonum vere beatum facere poterit, quo adepto nullum bonum restat quod amplius desiderari possit: unde et beatitudo dicitur bonum perfectum, quasi omnia desiderabilia in se comprehendens; tale autem non est aliquod bonum terrenum; nam qui divitias habent, amplius habere desiderant, et simile patet in caeteris. Et si ampliora non quaerunt, desiderant tamen ut ea permaneant, vel alia in locum eorum succedant. Nihil enim permanens invenitur in rebus terrenis, nihil igitur terrenum est quod quietare desiderium possit. Neque igitur terrenum aliquod beatum facere potest, ut possit esse regis conveniens praemium.

Adhuc: cuiuslibet rei finalis perfectio et bonum completum ab aliquo superiore dependet, quia et ipsa corporalia meliora redduntur ex adiunctione meliorum, peiora vero, si deterioribus misceantur. Si enim argento misceatur aurum, argentum fit melius, quod ex plumbi admixtione impurum efficitur. Constant autem terrena omnia esse infra mentem humanam; beatitudo autem est hominis finalis perfectio, et bonum completum, ad quod omnes pervenire desiderant: nihil igitur terrenum est quod hominem possit beatum facere; nec igitur terrenum aliquod est praemium regis sufficiens; non enim, ut Augustinus dicit, christianos principes ideo felices dicimus, quia diutius imperarunt, vel imperatores filios morte placida reliquerunt, vel hostes reipublicae domuerunt, vel cives adversum se insurgentes et cavere et opprimere potuerunt; sed felices eos dicimus, si iuste imperant, si malunt cupiditatibus potius quam gentibus quibuslibet imperare, si omnia faciunt non propter ardorem inanis gloriae, sed propter chari-

ness is the reward of virtue. Virtue in anything can, in fact, be described as that which perfects its possessor and renders action beneficent. But every one, when acting rightly, strives to achieve that which he most desires; that is, to be happy; for no one can desire otherwise than this. Consequently, one can rightly conclude that the reward of virtue is to make man happy. And since virtue has issue in right action and it is the duty of a king to govern his subjects aright, the reward of kingship also lies in happiness. We must now consider more closely what this means. Blessedness may be defined as the final aim of all desires; for the moving power of desire is not without limit. Otherwise such desire would be both natural and in vain; since the infinite is unattainable. But because an intellectual nature desires that which is universally good, it can be made truly happy only by the possession of such a good that its attainment leaves nothing further to be desired. For this reason blessedness is called the perfect good, as though containing in itself all that is desirable. But no earthly good can do this. Those who have riches will desire more; and similarly with other possessions: and even if they do not desire more, at least they will wish to retain what they have, or to replace their possessions with others. There is no permanence in earthly things and nothing earthly can, in consequence, fully satisfy desire. We must conclude, then, that there is no earthly satisfaction which could bring happiness to a king and adequately reward him.

Furthermore. The final perfection and complete good of anything comes from something which is of a superior order to it: just as bodies are rendered more precious by the admixture of finer bodies and more base by the admixture of those which are commoner. Silver becomes more precious when mixed with gold, but is debased by being mixed with lead. It is clear, however, that all earthly things are of a lesser order than the human mind; and, on the other hand, that blessedness is the final perfection of man and the complete good which all try to attain. There is nothing on earth, therefore, which could make a man blessed; nor, in consequence, is there any earthly reward sufficient for a king. As St. Augustine says, we do not hold that Christian rulers are the more happy the longer they reign, or because they are able to die in peace and leave the throne to their children, nor yet because of their success in defeating enemies or suppressing rebellion within the state. Rather, we consider them happy who rule wisely, who prefer the suppression of evil to the oppression of peoples, and who carry out their duties, not from a desire of empty glory but for love of eternal

tatem felicitatis aeternae. Tales imperatores christianos felices dicimus, interim spe, postea re ipsa futuros, cum id quod expectamus advenerit. Sed nec aliquid aliud creatum est, quod beatum hominem faciat et possit regi decerni pro praemio. Tendit enim uniuscuiusque rei desiderium in suum principium, a quo esse suum causatur. Causa vero mentis humanae non est aliud quam Deus, qui eam ad suam imaginem facit. Solus igitur Deus est qui hominis desiderium quietare potest, et facere hominem beatum, et esse regi conveniens praemium.

Amplius: mens humana universalis boni cognoscitiva est per intellectum, et desiderativa per voluntatem: bonum autem universale non invenitur nisi in Deo. Nihil ergo est quod possit hominem beatum facere, eius implendo desiderium, nisi Deus, de quo dicitur in *Psalm.* CII, 5: « *Qui replet in bonis desiderium tuum* »; in hoc ergo rex suum praemium statuere debet. Hoc igitur considerans David rex dicebat, *Ps.* LXXII, vers. 24: « *Quid mihi est in caelo et a te quid volui super terram?* » Cui quaestioni postea respondens, subiungit: « *Mihi autem adhaerere Deo bonum est et ponere in Domino Deo spem meam* ». Ipse enim est qui dat salutem regibus, non solum temporalem, qua communiter salvat homines et iumenta, sed etiam eam de qua, per *Isa.*, LI, 6, dicit: « *Salus autem mea in sempiternum erit* »; qua homines salvat, eos ad aequalitatem Angelorum perducens.

Sic igitur verificari potest, quod regis praemium est honor et gloria. Quis enim mundanus et caducus honor huic honori similis esse potest, ut homo sit civis et domesticus Dei, et inter Dei filios computatus, et haereditatem regni coelestis assequatur cum Christo? Hic est honor quem concupiscens et admirans rex David dicebat *Psalm.* CXXXVIII, 17: « *Nimis honorati sunt amici tui, Deus* ». Quae insuper humanae laudis gloria huic comparari potest, quam non fallax blandientium lingua, non decepta hominum opinio profert, sed ex interioris conscientiae testimonio producit, et Dei testimonio confirmatur, qui suis confessoribus repromittit, quod confiteatur eos in gloria Patris coram Angelis Dei? Qui autem hanc gloriam quaerunt eam inveniunt, et quam non querunt gloriam hominum, consequuntur, exemplo Salomonis, qui non solum sapientiam, quam quaesivit, accepit a Domino, sed factus est super reges alios gloriosus.

blessedness. We may say of such christian rulers that they are happy in this life by reason of their hope, and will be so hereafter, when all our hopes shall be fulfilled. Nor is there any other reward which could make a man happy or which could be considered a fitting recompense for kingship. For the desire which is in a thing leads it back always to its source and to that which is its cause. But the cause of the human spirit is none other than God who made it to His own image and likeness. God alone, therefore, can satisfy the desire which is in man and make him blessed. God alone is fitting reward for a king.

Again. The human soul is able, through intelligence, to know goodness in its universality, and through the will to desire it. But the universal good is nowhere found except in God. Nothing, therefore, can make man happy and satisfy all his desires but God; of Whom it is said in the Psalms (CII, 5) 'He fills with good things the desires of thy heart.' In Him then, a king must find his reward. King David, considering this point, said (*Psalm* LXXII, 24): 'What have I in heaven? and besides Thee what do I desire upon earth?' And later, replying to this question, he adds: 'It is good for me to cleave fast to God, and to put my hope in the Lord God.' He it is who grants to kings not only that temporal salvation which is commonly enjoyed by both men and beasts, but also that hope of which Isaias says (LI, 6): 'My salvation will be for all eternity.' This is His gift to men, which brings them to equality with the angels.

In this sense we may rightly conclude that the reward of a king lies in honour and glory. For what worldly and fleeting honour can equal that which makes a man a citizen and member of the household of God; by which he is numbered among the sons of God and becomes co-heir with Christ of the celestial kingdom? This is the honour which David desired and glorified, saying (*Psalm* CXXXVIII, 17): 'Thy friends, O God, are made exceedingly honourable.' What glory of human praise can be likened to this which springs, not from the flattery of deceitful tongues, nor from changing human opinion, but from the interior testimony of conscience; and is confirmed by the promise of God, to those who confess Him, that He will be their witness in the glory of the Father, before the angels of God. Those who seek such glory shall find it, and the glory of man which they seek not shall be given them; as we see from the example of Solomon, who not only received wisdom, which he sought from God, but was made renowned above all other kings.

Caput IX.—HIC DECLARAT SANCTUS DOCTOR, QUOD PRAEMIUM REGUM ET PRINCIPUM TENET SUPREMUM GRADUM IN BEATITUDINE COELESTI: ET HOC MULTIS RATIONIBUS OSTENDITUR ET EXEMPLIS.

Considerandum autem restat ulterius, quod et eminentem obtinebunt coelestis beatitudinis gradum, qui officium regium digne et laudabiliter exequuntur. Si enim beatitudo virtutis est praemium, consequens est ut maiori virtuti maior gradus beatitudinis debeatur. Est autem praecipua virtus, qua homo aliquis non solum se ipsum, sed etiam alios dirigere potest; et tanto magis, quanto plurium est regitiva; quia et secundum virtutem corporalem tanto aliquis virtuosior reputatur, quanto plures vincere potest, aut pondera plura levare. Sic igitur maior virtus requiritur ad regendum domesticam familiam, quam ad regendum se ipsum, multoque maior ad regimen civitatis et regni. Est igitur excellentis virtutis bene regium officium exercere; debetur igitur ei excellens in beatitudine praemium.

Adhuc: in omnibus artibus et potentiis laudabiliores sunt qui alios bene regunt, quam qui secundum alienam directionem bene se habent. In speculativis enim maius est veritatem aliis docendo tradere, quam quod ab aliis docetur capere posse. In artificiis etiam maius existimatur, maiorique conducitur pretio architector, qui aedificium disponit, quam artifex, qui secundum eius dispositionem manualiter operatur; et in rebus bellicis maiorem gloriam de victoria consequitur prudentia ducis, quam militis fortitudo. Sic autem se habet rector multitudinis in his quae a singulis secundum virtutem sunt agenda, sicut doctor in disciplinis et architector in aedificiis, et dux in bellis. Est igitur rex maiori praemio dignus, si bene subiectos gubernaverit, quam aliquis subditorum, si sub rege bene se habuerit.

Amplius: si virtutis est, ut per eam opus hominis bonum reddatur, maioris virtutis esse videtur quod maius bonum per eam aliquis operetur. Maius autem et divinius est bonum multitudinis quam bonum unius: unde interdum malum unius sustinetur, si in bonum multitudinis cedat, sicut occiditur latro, ut pax multitudini detur. Et ipse Deus mala

Chapter IX.—THE REWARD OF KINGSHIP IS THE HIGHEST BLESSEDNESS
OF HEAVEN.

It now remains for us to consider further the excellence of that state
of blessedness which will be the reward of those who fill the kingly
office worthily and with dignity. For if blessedness is the reward of
virtue it follows that a greater degree of blessedness will be owed to
greater virtue. But it requires outstanding virtue for a man to control
not only himself but others also; and such virtue will be the more
outstanding the greater the number of those to be governed: just as
in the case of bodily strength a man is reputed to be the more powerful
by reason of the numbers he can overcome, or the weight he is capable
of lifting. In similar manner greater virtue is required to control a
household than to discipline oneself; and far more again for the government of a city or a realm. The worthy exercise of the kingly office
requires, then, excelling virtue and must be requited by a high degree
of blessedness.

Again. In every art or science, those who can control others aright
are more praiseworthy than those who merely carry out the directions
of others with competence. In speculative science it is more important
to be able to expound the truth to others by teaching, than to be able
simply to understand what is taught by others. In the arts also, an
architect is more esteemed and is paid more highly because he plans
the house, compared with the builder who labours to construct what
the architect has designed. In war the glory of victory is reserved more
for the wise leadership of the general than for the steadfastness of the
soldier. But the ruler of a community is in the same position with
respect to the virtuous actions of the members of his community
as is the professor with respect to the sciences, or the architect with
respect to building, or the general with respect to war. For this reason
a king merits greater reward for ruling his subjects justly than does one
of his subjects for acting aright under his government.

Furthermore. If virtue is that quality which makes a man's actions
good it would seem that greater virtue is required for a greater act of
goodness. But the good of the community is greater and more divine
than the good of the individual. Thus the hurt of some individual is
sometimes to be tolerated, if it makes for the good of the community;
as, for instance, when a thief is put to death for the peace of the
community. God Himself would not permit evil in the world if

D

esse in mundo non sineret, nisi ex eis bona eliceret ad utilitatem et pulchritudinem universi. Pertinet autem ad regis officium, ut bonum multitudinis studiose procuret. Maius igitur praemium debetur regi pro bono regimine, quam subdito pro bona actione.

Hoc autem manifestius fiet si quis magis in speciali consideret. Laudatur enim ab hominibus quaevis privata persona et ei a Deo computatur in praemium, si egenti subveniat, si discordes pacificet, si oppressum a potentiore eripiat, denique si alicui qualitercumque opem vel consilium conferat ad salutem. Quanto igitur magis laudandus est ab hominibus, et praemiandus a Deo, qui totam provinciam facit pace gaudere, violentias cohibet, iustitiam servat, et disponit quid sit agendum ab hominibus suis legibus et praeceptis? Hinc etiam magnitudo regiae virtutis apparet, quod praecipue Dei similitudinem gerit, dum agit in regno, quod Deus in mundo; unde et in *Exod.* XXII, iudices multitudinis dii vocantur. Imperatores etiam apud romanos dii vocabantur. Tanto autem est aliquid Deo acceptius, quanto magis ad eius imitationem accedit: unde et apostolus monet *Ephes.* cap. V, 1: « *Estote imitatores Dei, sicut filii chrissimi* ». Sed si secundum sapientis sententiam, omne animal diligit simile sibi, secundum quod causae aliqualiter similitudinem habent causati, consequens igitur est bonos reges Deo esse acceptissimos, et ab eo maxime praemiandos. Simul etiam, ut Gregorii verbis utar: quid est tempestas maris, nisi tempestas mentis? Quieto autem mari recte navem etiam imperitus dirigit, turbato autem mari tempestatis fluctibus etiam peritus nauta confunditur: unde et plerumque in occupatione regiminis, ipse quoque boni operis usus perditur, qui in tranquillitate tenebatur. Valde enim difficile est si, ut Augustinus dicit, inter linguas sublimantium et honorantium, et obsequia nimis humiliter salutantium non extolluntur, sed se homines esse meminerint. Et in *Eccli.* capite XXXI: « *Beatus vir qui post aurum non abiit, nec speravit in pecuniae thesauris. Qui potuit* impune *transgredi, et non est transgressus, et facere mala, et non fecit* ». Ex quo quasi in virtutis opere probatus invenitur fidelis, unde secundum Biantis proverbium: « *Principatus virum ostendit* ». Multi enim, ad principatus culmen pervenientes, a virtute deficiunt, qui, dum in statu essent infimo, virtuosi videbantur.

good did not come of it, for the benefit and harmony of the universe. But it is the king's duty to foster the common good with all care. To a king, therefore, a greater reward is due for good rulership than to his subjects for right action.

This becomes even more clear when one considers the question in greater detail. For any one person is praised by men, and God considers him worthy of reward if he succours the needy, or brings peace to those in strife, or saves the weak from oppression by the strong—in a word if he benefits another by some assistance or counsel. How much more, then, does he deserve praise of men and reward of God who gladdens a whole country with peace, restrains the violent, preserves righteousness, and orders the actions of men by his laws and precepts?

The greatness of kingly virtue becomes further apparent from another fact; that is from a king's singular likeness to God; since a king does in his kingdom what God does in the universe. Hence in the book of Exodus, the judges of the community are called gods; and their emperors were called gods by the Romans. But a thing is the more acceptable to God the nearer it comes to imitating Him: so the Apostle warns the Ephesians (Chapter V, 1): 'Be ye imitators of God as most dear children.' And if, according to the opinion of the Wise Man, every animal has love for that which resembles it, according to the principle that causes have a certain similarity to that which they cause, it follows that good kings are most acceptable to God and worthy of great rewards from Him. Or again, to make use of the words of St. Gregory, what is a storm upon the sea if it be not also a storm for the mind? When the sea is calm, a landsman even can steer the ship, but when the sea is lashed by stormy waves, even the most skilled sailor may founder. So also in the exercise of government one can very often lose that constancy in right action which is attained in peaceful circumstances. As Augustine says, it is very difficult for kings in the midst of honours and of flattering tongues and of the obsequiousness of the over-humble to avoid being puffed up, and for them to remember that they are but men. We read in Ecclesiasticus (Chapter XXXI): 'Blessed is the man that hath not gone after gold, nor put his trust in money nor in treasures. He that could have transgressed, and hath not transgressed: and could do evil things and hath not done them.' This is a true test of virtuous action and by it one can recognize the faithful man. So, according to the proverb of Bias, 'Power proves a man.' For many, while they remain of humble station, have all the appearance of virtue, yet fall away from virtue so soon as they arrive at the height of power.

Ipsa igitur difficultas, quae principibus imminet ad bene agendum, eos facit maiori praemio dignos, et si aliquando per infirmitatem peccaverint, apud homines excusabiliores redduntur, et facilius a Deo veniam promerentur, si tamen, ut Augustinus ait, pro suis peccatis humilitatis, et miserationis, et orationis sacrificium Deo suo vero immolari non negligunt. In cuius rei exemplum de Achab, rege Israel, qui multum peccaverat, Dominus ad Heliam dixit (III *Reg.* XXI, 29): « *Quia humiliatus est mei causa, non inducam hoc malum in diebus suis* ».

Non autem solum ratione ostenditur quod regibus excellens praemium debeatur sed etiam auctoritate divina firmatur. Dicitur enim in *Zachar.* XII, quod in illa beatitudinis die, qua erit Dominus protector habitantibus in Hierusalem, id est in visione pacis aeternae, aliorum domus erunt sicut domus David, quia scilicet omnes reges erunt et regnabunt cum Christo, sicut membra cum capite; sed domus David erit sicut domus Dei, quia sicut regendo fideliter Dei officium gessit in populo, ita in praemio Deo propinquius erit et inhaerebit. Hoc etiam fuit apud gentiles aliqualiter somniatum, dum civitatum rectores atque servatores in deos transformari putabant.

This very difficulty, which confronts princes in acting aright, makes them worthy of a higher reward. And if, on occasion, they should err through frailty they are the more excusable before men and more easily obtain pardon from God; providing always, as Augustine says, they fail not to offer sacrifice of prayer and of humble repentance for their sins to the true God. As an example of this the Lord, speaking to Elias, said of Achab, king of Israel, who had sinned grievously, (III *Kings* XXI, 29) 'Because he hath humbled himself for my sake, I will not bring the evil in his days.'

But it is not only a conclusion of reason that kings should receive a high reward: there is divine authority also to confirm it. So we read in the prophecy of Zacharias (Chapter XII) that in the day of blessedness, when the Lord shall be the protector of those who dwell in Jerusalem—that is, in the vision of eternal peace—all houses shall be like to the house of David; for all will be kings, and will reign with Christ, as the members with the head. But the house of David will be like to the house of God because by wise government he faithfully carried out a divine task towards his people; and as a reward he will be nearer to God and joined to Him. This was, in some measure, foreseen also by the Gentiles, when they believed that rulers and liberators of the state were transformed into gods.

Caput X.—Quod rex et princeps studere debet ad bonum regimen propter bonum sui ipsius, et utile quod inde sequitur: cuius contrarium sequitur regimen tyrannicum.

Cum regibus tam grande in coelesti beatitudine praemium proponatur, si bene in regendo se habuerint, diligenti cura se ipsos observare debent, ne in tyrannidem convertantur. Nihil enim eis acceptabilius esse debet, quam quod ex honore regio, quo sublimantur in terris, in caelestis regni gloriam transferantur. Errant vero tyranni, qui propter quaedam terrena commoda iustitiam deserunt; qui tanto privantur praemio, quod adipisci poterant iuste regendo. Quod autem stultum sit pro huiusmodi parvis et temporalibus bonis maxima et sempiterna perdere bona, nullus, nisi stultus aut infidelis, ignorat.

Addendum est etiam, quod haec temporalia commoda, propter quae tyranni iustitiam deserunt, magis ad lucrum proveniunt regibus, dum iustitiam servant. Primo namque inter mundana omnia nihil est quod amicitiae digne praeferendum videatur. Ipsa namque est, quae virtuosos in unum conciliat, virtutem conservat atque promovet. Ipsa est, qua omnes indigent in quibuscumque negotiis peragendis, quae nec prosperis importune se ingerit, nec deserit in adversis. Ipsa est quae maximas delectationes affert, in tantum ut quaecumque delectabilia in taedium sine amicis vertantur. Quaelibet autem aspera facilia et prope nulla facit amor; nec est alicuius tyranni tanta crudelitas, ut amicitia non delectetur. Dionysius enim quondam Syracusanorum tyrannus cum duorum amicorum, qui Damon et Pythias dicebantur, alterum occidere vellet, is, qui occidendus erat, inducias impetravit, ut domum profectus res suas ordinaret: alter vero amicorum sese tyranno ob fidem pro eius reditu dedit. Appropinquante autem promisso die, nec illo redeunte, unusquisque fideiussorem stultitiae arguebat. At ille nihil se metuere de amici constantia praedicabat. Eadem autem hora, qua fuerat occidendus, rediit. Admirans autem amborum animum, tyrannus supplicium propter fidem amicitiae remisit, insuper rogans ut eum tertium reciperent in amicitiae gradu. Hoc autem amicitiae bonum, quamvis desiderent tyranni, consequi tamen non possunt. Dum enim commune bonum non quaerunt, sed proprium, fit parva vel nulla communio eorum ad subditos. Omnis autem

Chapter X.—THE AIM WHICH RULERS SHOULD SET BEFORE THEMSELVES IN THE EXERCISE OF POWER.

So great is the reward of heavenly blessedness promised to kings for the just exercise of their power, that they should strive with all care to avoid tyranny. Nothing, in fact, should be more dear to them than to be raised to glory in the heavenly kingdom with that same regal dignity which surrounds them on earth. Thus tyrants make a grave mistake by forsaking justice for some small earthly satisfaction; for so they deprive themselves of the highest reward which could be theirs in return for governing justly. Nobody, however foolish and unbelieving they may be, can fail to see the stupidity of losing so surpassing and eternal a reward for such fleeting and material satisfaction.

To this must be added the fact that these temporal advantages for which tyrants forsake justice are obtained by kings in greater abundance when they respect justice. Particularly, there is nothing on this earth to be preferred before true friendship. For friendship unites those who are virtuous and helps them to preserve and strengthen their virtue. We all of us, whatever our task in life, have need of it; steadfast alike in good times and in bad. Friendship is the source of the greatest pleasures, and without friends even the most agreeable pursuits become tedious. Love makes things which are difficult easy and almost unworthy of note. Nor was there ever a tyrant so cruel that he did not take delight in friendship. When Dionysius, the tyrant of Syracuse, was about to slay one of the two friends, Damon and Pythias, the one who had been condemned asked for a few days' grace to enable him to go home and put his affairs in order; and the other of the friends offered himself as a hostage against his return. But when the day of execution drew near, and the other did not return, every one laughed at the stupidity of the hostage. But he declared himself sure of his friend's fidelity: and, in fact, at the appointed hour of execution, his friend returned. The tyrant greatly admired the fortitude of spirit shown by both, and in recognition of such steadfast friendship revoked the sentence, asking moreover, that he might be admitted as a third within the bonds of such friendship. But, no matter how much they may desire it, tyrants can never win for themselves the joy of such friendship. Because they are concerned, not with the common good, but with their own satisfaction, there are few, if any, ties between them

amicitia super aliqua communione firmatur. Eos enim qui conveniunt
vel per naturae originem, vel per morum similitudinem, vel cuiuscumque societatis communionem, videmus amicitia coniungi. Parva
igitur, vel potius nulla est amicitia tyranni et subditi; simulque dum
subditi per tyrannicam iniustitiam opprimuntur, et se amari non sentiunt, sed contemni, nequaquam amant. Nec habent tyranni unde de
subditis conquerantur, si ab eis non diliguntur, quia nec ipsi tales se
ipsis exhibent, ut diligi ab eis debeant.

Sed boni reges, dum communi profectui studiose intendunt, et
eorum studio subditi plura commoda se assequi sentiunt, diliguntur
a plurimis, dum subditos se amare demonstrant: quia et hoc est maioris
malitiae, quam quod in multitudine cadat, ut odio habeantur amici, et
benefactoribus rependatur malum pro bono. Et ex hoc amore provenit,
ut bonorum regum regnum sit stabile, dum pro ipsis se subditi quibuscumque periculis exponere non recusant: cuius exemplum in Julio
Caesare apparet, de quo Suetonius refert, quod milites suos usque adeo
diligebat, ut, audita quorumdam caede, capillos et barbam ante non
dempserit quam vindicasset: quibus rebus devotissimos sibi et strenuis-
simos milites reddit, ita quod plerique eorum capti, concessam sibi sub
ea conditione vitam, si militare adversus Caesarem vellent, recusarent.
Octavianus etiam Augustus, qui modestissime imperio usus est, in
tantum diligebatur a subditis, ut plerique morientes, victimas quas
devoverant, immolari mandarent, quia eum superstitem reliquissent.

Non est ergo facile ut principis perturbetur dominium, quem tanto
consensu populus amat: propter quod Salomon dicit *Proverbiorum*
XXIX, 14: « *Rex, qui iudicat in iustitia pauperes, thronus eius in aeternum
firmabitur* ». Tyrannorum vero dominium diuturnum esse non potest,
cum sit multitudini odiosum. Non potest enim diu conservare, quod
votis multorum repugnat. Vix enim a quoquam praesens vita transigi-
tur, quin aliquas adversitates patiatur. Adversitatis autem tempore
occasio deesse non potest contra tyrannum insurgendi: et ubi adsit
occasio, non deerit ex multis vel unus qui occasione non utatur.
Insurgentem autem populus votive prosequitur: nec de facili carebit
effectu, quod cum favore multitudinis attentatur. Vix ergo potest
contingere, quod tyranni dominium protendatur in longum.

Hoc etiam manifeste patet, si quis consideret, unde tyranni dominium
conservatur. Non enim conservatur amore, cum parva vel nulla sit

and their subjects. The bonds of friendship, on the other hand, unite those who are connected either by ties of blood or by common custom or by some other common relationship. Consequently, any friendship between a tyrant and his subjects is slight or non-existent; for the citizens, being oppressed by the injustices of the tyrant, and feeling themselves despised rather than loved, can feel no love in return. Nor have tyrants just cause to deplore that they are not loved, for they do not act in a way which would win them affection.

Good kings, on the other hand, who dedicate themselves with all care to the common weal and who by their efforts bring their subjects to enjoy greater prosperity, are loved by most of their subjects in return for the love they have shown them: for no community is so faithless as to hate those who are its friends and return evil to its bene-factors. This is the reason for the stability of those kingdoms which are governed by good kings; for their subjects are willing on their account to run every risk. We have an example of such a one in Julius Caesar, of whom Suetonius tells us that he so loved his soldiers that, hearing of the death of some of them, he cut neither his beard nor his hair till he had avenged them: this made his soldiers so valiant and devoted to him that when some of them were made prisoners they refused to save their lives on condition of fighting against him. Octavius Augustus also, who was most moderate in his use of power, was so loved by his subjects that, when he lay dying, great numbers of them caused the victims which they had prepared for their own sacrifices to be offered instead for his safe recovery.

It is not easy, then, for the government of a prince who is so uni-versally loved to be subverted: for this reason Solomon says: (*Proverbs* XXIX, 14) 'The king that judgeth the poor in truth, his throne shall be established for ever.' A tyrant's rule, on the other hand, being hated by the community, cannot long endure; for that cannot last for long which is against the desire of many. Few tyrants, in fact, reach the end of their lives without meeting with some adversity. But in time of adversity there is no lack of opportunity to rise up against a tyrant, and, given the opportunity, there is sure to be some one out of the many who will make use of it. In such circumstances the people will support the rebel, and whoever acts thus with the favour of the people is unlikely to fail in his task. So it is difficult for tyrannical government to last very long.

This becomes still more evident when we consider how a tyrant keeps himself in power. He cannot do it through affection, for, as we

amicitia subiectae multitudinis ad tyrannum, ut ex praehabitis patet. De subditorum autem fide tyrannis confidendum non est. Non enim invenitur tanta virtus in multis, ut fidelitatis virtute reprimantur, ne indebitae servitutis iugum, si possint, excutiant. Fortassis autem nec fidelitati contrarium reputabitur secundum opinionem multorum, si tyrannicae nequitiae qualitercumque obvietur. Restat ergo ut solo timore tyranni regimen sustentetur, unde et timeri se a subditis tota intentione procurant. Timor autem est debile fundamentum. Nam qui timore subduntur, si occurrat occasio, qua possint impunitatem sperare, contra praesidentes insurgunt eo ardentius, quo magis contra voluntatem ex solo timore cohibebantur. Sicut si aqua per violentiam includatur, cum aditum invenerit, impetuosius fluit. Sed nec ipse timor caret periculo, cum ex nimio timore plerique in desperationem inciderint. Salutis autem desperatio audacter ad quaelibet attendenda praecipitat. Non potest igitur tyranni dominium esse diuturnum.

Hoc etiam non minus exemplis, quam rationibus apparet. Si quis enim antiquorum gesta, et modernorum eventus consideret, vix inveniet dominium tyranni alicuius diuturnum fuisse. Unde et Aristoteles, in sua *Politica*, multis tyrannis enumeratis, omnium demonstrat dominium brevi tempore fuisse finitum, quorum tamen aliqui diutius praefuerunt, quia non multum in tyrannide excedebant, sed quantum ad multa imitabantur regalem modestiam.

Adhuc autem hoc magis fit manifestum ex consideratione divini iudicii. Ut enim in *Job*, XXXIV, 30, dicitur: « *Regnare facit hominem hypocritam propter peccata populi* ». Nullus autem verius hypocrita dici potest, quam qui regis assumit officium, et exhibet se tyrannum. Nam hypocrita dicitur, qui alterius repraesentat personam, sicut in spectaculis fieri consuevit. Sic igitur Deus praefici permittit tyrannos ad puniendum subditorum peccata. Talis autem punitio in Scripturis ira Dei consuevit nominari. Unde per *Oseae*, cap. XIII, 11, Dominus dicit: « *Dabo vobis regem in furore meo* ». Infelix est autem rex, qui populo in furore Dei conceditur. Non enim eius stabile potest esse dominium: quia non obliviscetur misereri Deus, nec continebit in ira sua misericordias suas: quinimmo per *Joel*, II, 13, dicitur, quod « *est patiens, et multae misericordiae, et praestabilis super malitia* ». Non

have already seen, there is little or no love lost between a tyrant and the subject community. Nor can tyrants count upon the fidelity of their subjects. For the masses are not so virtuous as to think of fidelity when the chance presents itself to throw off the burden of unjust subjection. It is more likely that the general opinion will see no lack of faith in resistance by all means, against the malignity of a tyrant. In consequence tyrannical government is based exclusively upon fear; and tyrants seek by every means to make themselves feared by their subjects. But fear makes a weak foundation. For those who remain subject through fear will, when opportunity and the hope of success presents itself, rise up against those who command them: and the rising will be the more violent the more they have been constrained against their will and through fear alone. Just as water, when forcibly compressed, will gush out all the more violently when it finds an opening. Moreover, fear itself carries with it its own dangers; because, when excessive, it can drive many to desperation. And a desperate man will abandon himself all the more readily to any undertaking. Tyrannical government cannot last long.

This conclusion is just as clear from example as it is from reasoning. Whether we consider the tales of antiquity or modern events, it is difficult to find a tyrannical government which has lasted very long. For this reason Aristotle also, in his *Politics*, having named several tyrants, goes on to show how their rule was short-lived; and then points out that if some did reign for longer, it was because their tyranny was not over-harsh and because they did, in many respects, imitate the moderation of a true king.

Even more evident does this become when we consider the judgement of God. We read, for instance, in the *Book of Job* (XXXIV, 30): 'Who maketh a man that is a hypocrite to reign for the sins of the people.' No one could be more rightly called a hypocrite than the man who takes upon himself the task of kingship and then reveals himself a tyrant: for a hypocrite is one who pretends to take the part of another, as in a play. God, then, permits tyrants to rule in punishment for the sins of their subjects, and such punishment is commonly called in the scriptures the anger of God. So the Lord says through *Hosea* (XIII, 11) 'I will give thee a king in my wrath.' But unhappy is the king inflicted by God in His wrath upon His people; nor can His dominion be lasting. For God will not fail to pardon and to show mercy, despite His anger: as we read in *Joel* (II, 13) 'He is gracious and merciful and ready to repent of the evil.' God, then,

igitur permittit Deus diu regnare tyrannos, sed post tempestatem per
eos inductam populo, per eorum deiectionem tranquillitatem inducet.
Unde, *Eccli.* X, 17, dicitur: « *Sedes ducum superborum destruxit Deus, et
sedere fecit mites pro eis* ».

Experimento etiam magis apparet, quod reges per iustitiam adipi-
scuntur divitias, quam per rapinam tyranni. Quia enim dominium
tyrannorum subiectae multitudini displicit, ideo opus habent tyranni
multos habere satellites, per quos contra subditos tuti reddantur, in
quibus necesse est plura expendere, quam a subditis rapiant. Regum
autem dominium, quod subditis placet, omnes subditos pro satellitibus
ad custodiam habet in quibus expendere opus non est; sed interdum in
necessitatibus plura regibus sponte donant, quam tyranni diripere
possint, et sic impletur quod Salomon dicit, *Proverbiorum* XI, 24: « *Alii
— scilicet reges — dividunt propria benefaciendo subiectis, et ditiores fiunt.
Alii — scilicet tyranni — rapiunt non sua, et semper in egestate sunt* ».
Similiter autem iusto dei contingit iudicio, ut qui divitias iniuste
congregant, inutiliter eas dispergant, aut etiam iuste auferantur ab eis.
Ut enim Salomon dicit, *Ecclesiastes,* V, 9: « *Avarus non implebitur
pecunia, et qui amat pecunias, fructum non capiet ex eis* »; quinimmo ut
Proverbiorum, XV, 27, dicit: « *Conturbat domum suam, qui sectatur ava-
itiam* ». Regibus vero, qui iustitiam quaerunt, divitiae adduntur a
Deo, sicut Salomon, qui, dum sapientiam quaesivit ad faciendum
iudicium, promissionem de abundantia divitiarum accepit.

De fama vero superfluum videtur dicere. Quis enim dubitet bonos
reges non solum in vita, sed magis post mortem quodammodo laudibus
hominum vivere, et in desiderio haberi; malorum vero nomen aut
statim deficere, vel si excellentes in malitia fuerint, cum detestatione
eorum rememorari? Unde Salomon dicit, *Proverbiorum,* X, 7:
« *Memoria iusti cum laudibus, nomen autem impiorum putrescet* », quia vel
deficit, vel remanet cum foetore.

does not allow tyrants to reign overlong; but having made use of them to let loose a storm upon His people, He sweeps them away and restores calm. So we read in *Ecclesiasticus* (X, 17): 'God hath overturned the thrones of proud princes, and hath set up the meek in their stead.'

Even more clearly we see from experience that kings gain greater riches through justice than do tyrants by rapacity. For the rule of a tyrant is hated by all, so that he needs a numerous bodyguard to keep him safe from his people; and this costs him far more than he can wring from his subjects. A king's government, on the other hand, being pleasing to his subjects, is guarded by the citizens themselves, for no love of gain; indeed, in times of necessity, they will give freely to their king far more than any tyrant can exact. This brings out the truth of what Solomon says (*Proverbs*, XI, 24): 'Some (that is, kings) distribute their own goods, and grow richer: others (that is, tyrants) take away what is not their own, and are always in want.' So it comes about through the just judgement of God that those who store up to themselves riches unjustly, squander them as uselessly, thus seeing themselves constrained to make recompense. As Solomon says in *Ecclesiastes* (V, 9): 'A covetous man shall not be satisfied with money: and he that loveth riches shall reap no fruit from them.' And again (*Proverbs* XV, 27): 'He that is greedy of gain troubleth his own house.' But to kings who follow the way of justice, God Himself makes increase of riches, as He did to Solomon who followed after wisdom in judgement, and who received also a promise of abundant riches.

As for fame, it is a waste of time to speak of it. Who can doubt that good kings, not only during life, but more so after their death, live on in a certain way in the good estimation of men and are mourned: while the name of the evil is soon forgotten, or, if they have been particularly distinguished for their crimes, they are remembered only with detestation? Thus Solomon says (*Proverbs* X, 7): 'The memory of the just is with praises: and the name of the wicked shall rot.' Either he is forgotten or only a stench remains.

Caput XI.—Quod bona etiam mundialia, ut sunt divitiae, potestas, honor, et fama, magis proveniunt regibus quam tyrannis, et de malis in quae incurrunt tyranni etiam in hac vita.

Ex his ergo manifestum est, quod stabilitas potestatis, divitiae, honor et fama magis regibus quam tyrannis ad votum proveniunt, propter quae indebite adipiscenda declinat in tyrannidem princeps. Nullus enim a iustitia declinat nisi cupiditate alicuius commodi tractus. Privatur insuper tyrannus excellentissima beatitudine, quae regibus debetur pro praemio, et, quod est gravius, maximum tormentum sibi acquirit in poenis. Si enim qui unum hominem spoliat, vel in servitutem redigit, vel occidit, maximam poenam meretur, quantum quidem ad iudicium hominum mortem, quantum vero ad iudicium Dei damnationem aeternam; quanto magis putandum est tyrannum deteriora mereri supplicia, qui undique ad omnibus rapit, contra omnium libertatem laborat, pro libito voluntatis suae quoscumque interficit? Tales insuper raro poenitent, vento inflati superbiae, merito peccatorum a Deo deserti, et adulationibus hominum delibuti, rarius digne satisfacere possunt. Quando enim restituent omnia, quae praeter iustitiae debitum abstulerunt? Ad quae tamen restituenda nullus dubitat eos teneri. Quando recompensabunt eis quos oppresserunt, et iniuste qualitercumque laeserunt? Adiicitur autem ad eorum impoenitentiam, quod omnia sibi licita existimant, quae impune sine resistentia facere potuerunt: unde non solum emendare non satagunt quae male fecerunt, sed sua consuetudine pro auctoritate utentes, peccandi audaciam transmittunt ad posteros, et sic non solum suorum facinorum apud Deum rei tenentur, sed etiam eorum, quibus apud Deum peccandi occasionem reliquerunt. Aggravatur etiam eorum peccatum ex dignitate suscepti officii. Sicut enim terrenus rex gravius punit suos ministros, si invenit eos sibi contrarios; ita Deus magis puniet eos, quos sui regiminis executores et ministros facit, si nequiter agant, dei iudicium in amaritudinem convertentes. Unde et in libro *Sapientiae*, VI, 5, ad reges iniquos dicitur: « *Quoniam, cum essetis ministri regni illius, non recte iudicastis, neque custodistis legem iustitiae*

Chapter XI.—THE MATERIAL BENEFITS OF GOOD GOVERNMENT, AND THE DAMAGING EFFECTS OF TYRANNY.

From what we have said it is, then, evident, that stability in government, riches, and honour and glory, are all more surely attained by kings than by tyrants; and that a prince who would gain these ends by dishonest means risks becoming a tyrant. No one will leave the path of justice if he is kept to it by the hope of some gain. But furthermore, a tyrant is deprived of that supreme blessedness which is the reward of a good king; and, what is worse, brings down upon himself the most terrible penalties. If a man who robs or enslaves or kills another merits the maximum penalty, death from the tribunal of man and eternal damnation before the tribunal of God, how much more reason have we for saying that a tyrant deserves the most terrible penalties; when he has despoiled every one, and everywhere trampled on the liberties of all, and taken life at a mere whim? To this we must add that men of this sort rarely repent: puffed up with pride, abandoned by God for their sins, hardened by adulation, it is seldom indeed that they are capable of due reparation. When, indeed, could they restore all they have gained above what was due to them in justice? Yet it is not to be doubted that they are bound to make restitution. When could they do justice to those whom they have oppressed or otherwise ill-treated? We must further consider, besides their impenitence, the fact that they begin to think legitimate all that they have been able to do with impunity and without encountering resistance, so that, far from seeking to repair the evil they have done, they make evil a habit and an example which leads their successors to even more flagrant wrongdoing. So they become responsible before God not only for their own crimes but also for the crimes of those to whom they have given the occasion of sin. Their guilt is further aggravated by the dignity of the office they fill. Just as a king on this earth punishes his ministers more severely if he should find them rebelling against him, so also God has heavier punishments for those whom He has destined as His ministers and the dispensers of His authority, if they act evilly and pervert His judgements. So in the *Book of Wisdom* (VI, 5–7), it is said of evil kings: 'Because being ministers of his kingdom, you have not judged rightly, nor kept the law of justice, nor walked according to the will of

*nostrae, nec secundum voluntatem Dei ambulastis, horrende et cito apparebit
vobis quoniam indicium durissimum his qui praesunt fiet. Exiguo enim
conceditur misericordia, potentes autem potenter tormenta patientur* ».
Et Nabuchodonosor per *Isa.*, XIV, 15 dicitur: « *Ad infernum detraheris
in profundum laci. Qui te viderint, ad te inclinabuntur, teque prospicient* »,
quasi profundus in poenis submersum. Si igitur regibus abundant
temporalia bona et proveniunt, et excellens beatitudinis gradus prae-
paratur a Deo, tyranni autem a temporalibus bonis quae cupiunt
plerumque frustrantur, multis insuper periculis subiacentes, et, quod est
amplius, bonis aeternis privantur ad poenas gravissimas reservati,
vehementer studendum est his, qui regendi officium suscipiunt, ut
reges se subditis praebeant, non tyrannos.

De rege autem quid sit, et quod expediat multitudini regem habere:
adhuc autem, quod praesidi expediat se regem multitudini exhibere
subiectae, non tyrannum, tanta a nobis dicta sint.

the Lord: horribly and speedily will he appear to you: for a most severe judgement shall be for them that bear rule. For to him that is little, mercy is granted: but the mighty shall be mightily tormented.' And *Isaias* (XIV, 15–16), says to Nabuchodonosor: 'Thou shalt be brought down to hell, into the depth of the pit. They that shall see thee, shall turn toward thee, and behold thee,' as though to one who is engulfed in tribulation. If, then, kings receive temporal benefits in abundance, and God prepares for them a surpassing degree of blessedness; while tyrants are for the most part deprived of even those worldly satisfactions which they seek so eagerly, besides running many risks and, what is worse, being deprived of eternal benefits and condemned to most grievous pain; it is clear that those who assume the office of government must take every care to act as true kings to their subjects and not as tyrants.

We have now said sufficient about the powers of a king; about the advantages of a monarchy for the community, and about the importance of a ruler's bearing himself as a true king towards the community and not as a tyrant.

Caput XII.—Procedit ad ostendendum regis officium, ubi secundum viam naturae ostendit regem esse in regno, sicut anima est in corpore, et sicut Deus est in mundo.

Consequens autem ex dictis est considerare, quod sit regis officium, et qualem oporteat esse regem. Quia vero ea, quae sunt secundum artem, imitantur ea, quae sunt secundum naturam, ex quibus accipimus, ut secundum rationem operari possimus, optimum videtur regis officium a forma regiminis naturalis assumere. Invenitur autem in rerum natura regimen et universale et particulare. Universale quidem, secundum quod omnia sub Dei regimine continentur, qui sua providentia universa gubernat. Particulare autem regimen maxime quidem divino regimini simile est, quod invenitur in homine, qui ob hoc minor mundus appellatur, quia in eo invenitur forma universalis regiminis. Nam sicut universa creatura corporea et omnes spirituales virtutes sub divino regimine continentur, sic et corporis membra et caeterae vires animae a ratione reguntur, et sic quodammodo se habet ratio in homine, sicut Deus in mundo. Sed quia, sicut supra ostendimus, homo est animal naturaliter sociale in multitudine vivens, similitudo divini regiminis invenitur in homine non solum quantum ad hoc, quod per rationem regitur unus homo, sed etiam quantum ad hoc, quod per rationem unius hominis regitur multitudo: quod maxime pertinet ad officium regis, dum et in quibusdam animalibus, quae socialiter vivunt, quaedam similitudo invenitur, huius regiminis: sicut in apibus, in quibus et reges esse dicuntur, non quod in eis per rationem sit regimen, sed per instinctum naturae inditum a summo regente, qui est auctor naturae. Hoc igitur officium rex suscepisse cognoscat, ut sit in regno sicut in corpore anima, et sicut Deus in mundo. Quae si diligenter recogitet, ex altero iustitiae in eo zelus accenditur, dum considerat ad hoc se positum, ut, loco Dei, iudicium regno exerceat; ex altero vero mansuetudinis et clementiae lenitatem acquirit, dum reputat, singulos, quo suo subsunt regimini, sicut propria membra.

Chapter XII.—THE DUTIES OF A KING: THE SIMILARITY BETWEEN ROYAL POWER AND THE POWER OF THE SOUL OVER THE BODY AND OF GOD OVER THE UNIVERSE.

To complete what we have so far said it remains only to consider what is the duty of a king and how he should comport himself. And since art is but an imitation of nature, from which we come to learn how to act according to reason, it would seem best to deduce the duties of a king from the examples of government in nature. Now in nature there is to be found both a universal and a particular form of government. The universal is that by which all things find their place under the direction of God, who, by His providence, governs the universe. The particular is very similar to this divine control, and is found within man himself; who, for this reason, is called a microcosm, because he provides an example of universal government. Just as the divine control is exercised over all created bodies and over all spiritual powers, so does the control of reason extend over the members of the body and the other faculties of the soul: so, in a certain sense, reason is to man what God is to the universe. But because, as we have shown above, man is by nature a social animal living in community, this similarity with divine rule is found among men, not only in the sense that a man is directed by his reason, but also in the fact that a community is ruled by one man's intelligence; for this is essentially the king's duty. A similar example of such control is to be found among certain animals which live in community, such as bees, which are said to have a king. But in their case, of course, the control has no rational foundation, but springs from an instinct of their nature, given them by the supreme ruler who is the author of nature. A king, then, should realize that he has assumed the duty of being to his kingdom what the soul is to the body and what God is to the universe. If he thinks attentively upon this point he will, on the one hand, be fired with zeal for justice, seeing himself appointed to administer justice throughout his realm in the name of God, and, on the other hand, he will grow in mildness and clemency, looking upon the persons subject to his government, as the members of his own body.

Caput XIII.—Assumit ex hac similitudine modum regiminis, ut sicut Deus unamquamque rem distinguit quodam ordine, et propria operatione, et loco, ita rex subditos suos in regno: et eodem modo de anima.

Oportet igitur considerare, quid Deus in mundo faciat: sic enim manifestum erit quid immineat regi faciendum. Sunt autem universaliter consideranda duo opera Dei in mundo. Unum quo mundo instituit, alterum quo mundum institutum gubernat. Haec etiam duo opera anima habet in corpore. Nam primo quidem virtute animae informatur corpus, deinde vero per animam corpus regitur et movetur. Horum autem secundum quidem magis proprie pertinet ad regis officium. Unde ad omnes reges pertinet gubernatio, et a gubernationis regimine regis nomen accipitur. Primum autem opus non omnibus regibus convenit. Non enim omnes regnum aut civitatem instituunt, in quo regnant, sed regno ac civitati iam institutis regiminis curam impendunt. Est autem considerandum, quod nisi praecessisset qui institueret civitatem aut regnum, locum non haberet gubernatio regni. Sub regis enim officio comprehenditur etiam institutio civitatis et regni. Nonnulli enim civitates instituerunt, in quibus regnarent, ut Ninus Ninivem, et Romulus Romam. Similiter etiam ad gubernationis officium pertinet, ut gubernata conservet, ac eis utatur, ad quod sunt constituta. Non igitur gubernationis officium plene cognosci poterit, si institutionis ratio ignoretur. Ratio autem institutionis regni ab exemplo institutionis mundi sumenda est: in quo primo consideratur ipsarum rerum productio, deinde partium mundi ordinata distinctio. Ulterius autem singulis mundi partibus diversae rerum species distributae videntur, ut stellae coelo, volucres aeri, pisces aquae, animalia terrae: deinde singulis ea, quibus indigent, abundanter divinitus provisa videntur. Hanc autem institutionis rationem Moyses subtiliter et diligenter expressit.

Primo enim rerum productionem proponit, dicens: « *In principio creavit Deus coelum et terram* »; deinde secundum ordinem convenientem omnia divinitus distincta esse denuntiat, videlicet diem a nocte,

Chapter XIII.—FURTHER DEVELOPMENT OF THIS ANALOGY AND OF THE
CONCLUSIONS TO BE DRAWN FROM IT.

We must now consider what God does in the universe, and thus we
shall see what a king should do. There are, in general, two aspects of
the work of God in the world. The first is the act of creation; the
second His governance of it once He has created it. Similarly, the
action of the soul upon the body presents two aspects. In the first
place it is the soul which gives form to the body and secondly it is
by the soul that the body is controlled and moved. It is the second of
these two operations which pertains more particularly to the king's
office; for all kings are bound to govern, and it is from this process of
directing the government that the term king [*rex*] is derived. The
former task, however, does not fall to all kings; for not every king
founds the city or kingdom over which he rules; many fulfil their
duties in cities or kingdoms which are already flourishing. It must
not, however, be forgotten that if there had been no one in the first
place to establish a city or a kingdom, there would be nothing to
govern: so that the kingly office must also cover the founding of a city
or a kingdom. Some kings have, in fact, founded the cities over which
they afterwards ruled, as Ninus founded Nineveh, and Romulus
Rome. It is furthermore the ruler's duty to protect what he governs
and to make use of it for the ends for which it was intended: but he
cannot be fully aware of the duties of his office if he fails to acquaint
himself with the reasons for government. Now the reason for the
foundation of a kingdom is to be found in the example provided by
the creation of the world: in this we must first consider the creation
of things themselves, and then their orderly distribution throughout
the universe. Then we see how things are distributed in the various
parts of the universe according to their different species; the stars in
the heavens, birds in the air, fishes in the sea and animals upon the earth.
Finally we note how abundantly divine providence furnishes each
species with all that is necessary to it. Moses has described this orderli-
ness shown in creation with great care and subtlety.

He first considers the creation of things by the words: 'In the
beginning God created heaven and earth'; then he notes that all things
became, by divine command, distinct according to their appropriate

a superioribus inferiora, mare ab arida. Hinc coelum luminaribus, avibus aerem, mare piscibus, animalibus terram ornatam refert: ultimo assignatum hominibus terrae animaliumque dominium. Usum vero plantarum tam ipsis quam animalibus caeteris ex providentia divina denuntiat. Institutor autem civitatis et regni de novo producere homines, et loca ad inhabitandum, et caetera vitae subsidia non potest, sed necesse habet his uti quae in natura praeexistunt. Sicut etiam caeterae artes operationis suae materiam a natura accipiunt, ut fabri ferrum, aedificator ligna et lapides in artis usum assumunt. Necesse est igitur institutori civitatis et regni primum quidem congruum locum eligere, qui salubritate habitatores conservet, ubertate ad victum sufficiat, amoenitate delectet, munitione ab hostibus tutos reddat. Quod si aliquid de dicta opportunitate deficiat, tanto locus erit convenientior quanto plura vel magis necessaria de praedictis habuerit. Deinde necesse est ut locum electum institutor civitatis aut regni distinguat secundum exigentiam eorum, quae perfectio civitatis aut regni requirit. Puta, si regnum instituendum, sit, oportet providere quis locus aptus sit urbibus constituendis, quis villis, quis castris, ubi constituenda sint studia litterarum, ubi exercitia militum, ubi negotiatorum conventus, et sic de aliis, quae perfectio regni requirit. Si autem institutioni civitatis opera detur, providere oportet, quis locus sit sacris, quis iuri reddendo, quis artificibus singulis deputandus. Ulterius autem oportet homines congregare, qui sunt congruis locis secundum sua officia deputandi. Demum vero providendum est, ut singulis necessaria suppetant secundum uniuscuiusque constitutionem et statum: aliter enim nequaquam posset regnum vel civitas commanere. Haec igitur sunt, ut summarie dicatur, quae ad regis officium pertinent in institutione civitatis aut regni, ex similitudine institutionis mundi assumpta.

order, as day from night, the heights from the depths, and the waters from dry land. Then he tells how the heavens were adorned with stars, the air with birds, the sea with fishes, and the earth with animals. Finally, he tells how dominion was given to men over the whole earth and the animals thereon. As for plant life, he says that it was given by providence for the use of both animals and men. Now the founder of a city or of a kingdom cannot create out of nothing the men or the dwelling places or all the other things necessary to life: he must use instead what nature has already provided. Just as all other arts find their materials from natural sources; the smiths working with iron and the builder with wood and stone. So one who is about to establish a city or a realm must, in the first place, choose a suitable site; healthy, to ensure the health of the inhabitants; fertile, to provide for their sustenance; one which will delight the eye with its loveliness and give natural security against hostile attack. Where any of these advantages are lacking, the site chosen will be the more suitable to the extent that such conditions, or at least the more indispensible of them, are fulfilled. Having chosen the site, the next task which confronts the founder of a city or of a kingdom is to plan the area to meet all the requirements of a civic life. When founding a kingdom, for example, one must decide where to build the towns and where to leave the countryside open, or to construct fortifications: centres of study, open places for military training, and markets, all have to be taken into consideration: and similarly for every other activity which goes to make up the life of a kingdom. If it is a city which is to be established, sites must be assigned to churches, to administrative. offices, and to the workshops of various trades. The citizens then have to be grouped in various quarters of the city according to their calling. Finally, provision must be made so that no person goes in want, according to his condition and calling: otherwise neither city nor kingdom would long endure. Such, very briefly, are the points a king must consider when establishing a city or a kingdom, and they can all be arrived at by analogy with the creation of the world.

Caput XIV.—Quis modus gubernandi competat regi, quia secundum modum gubernationis divinae: qui quidem modus gubernandi a gubernatione navis sumpsit initium, ubi et ponitur
comparatio sacerdotalis dominii et regalis.

Sicut autem institutio civitatis aut regni ex forma institutionis
mundi convenienter accipitur, sic et gubernationis ratio ex gubernatione sumenda est. Est tamen praeconsiderandum, quod gubernare
est, id quod gubernatur convenienter ad debitum finem perducere. Sic
etiam navis gubernari dicitur, dum per nautae industriam recto itinere
ad portum illaesa perducitur. Si igitur aliquid ad finem extra se ordinetur, ut navis ad portum, ad gubernatoris officium pertinebit non solum,
ut rem in se conservet illaesam, sed quod ulterius ad finem perducat.
Si vero aliquid esset, cuius finis non esset extra ipsum, ad hoc solum
intenderet gubernatoris intentio, ut rem illam in sua perfectione con-
servaret illaesam. Et quamvis nihil tale inveniatur in rebus post ipsum
Deum, qui est omnibus finis, erga id tamen, quod ad extrinsecum
ordinatur, multipliciter cura impeditur a diversis. Nam forte alius
erit qui curam gerit, ut res in suo esse conservetur; alius autem, ut ad
altiorem perfectionem perveniat, ut in ipsa navi, unde gubernationis
ratio assumitur, manifeste apparet. Faber enim lignarius curam habet
restaurandi, si quid collapsum fuerit in navi, sed nauta sollicitudinem
gerit, ut navem perducat ad portum; sic etiam contingit in homine.
Nam medicus curam gerit ut vita hominis conservetur in sanitate;
oeconomus, ut suppetant necessaria vitae; doctor autem curam gerit
ut veritatem cognoscat; institutor autem morum, ut secundum
rationem vivat. Quod si homo non ordinaretur ad aliud exterius
bonum, sufficerent homini curae praedictae.

Sed est quoddam bonum extraneum homini quam diu mortaliter
vivit, scilicet ultima beatitudo, quae in fruitione Dei expectatur post
mortem. Quia, ut Apostolus ait, II *ad Cor.*, V, 6: « *Quamdiu sumus in
corpore, peregrinamur a Domino* ». Unde homo Christianus, cui beatitudo
illa est per Christi sanguinem acquisita, et qui pro ea assequenda Spiritus
Sancti arrham accepit, indiget alia spirituali cura per quam dirigatur
ad portum salutis aeternae; haec autem cura per ministros Ecclesiae
Christi fidelibus exhibetur.

Idem autem oportet esse iudicium de fine totius multitudinis et

Chapter XIV.—COMPARISON BETWEEN THE PRIESTLY POWER AND THAT OF A KING.

Just as the creation of the world serves as a convenient model for the establishment of a city or a kingdom, so does its government allow us to deduce the principle of civil government. We must first have in mind that to govern is to guide what is governed to its appointed end. So we say that a ship is under control when it is sailed on its right course to port by the skill of a sailor. Now when something is ordered to an end which lies outside itself, as a ship is to harbour, it is the ruler's duty not only to preserve its integrity, but also to see that it reaches its appointed destination. If there were anything with no end beyond itself, then the ruler's sole task would be to preserve it unharmed in all its perfection. But though there is no such example to be found in creation, apart from God who is the end of all things, care for higher aims is beset with many and varied difficulties. For it is very clear that there may be one person employed about the preservation of a thing in its present state, and another concerned with bringing it to higher perfection; as we see in the case of a ship, which we have used as an example of government. Just as it is the carpenter's task to repair any damage which may occur and the sailor's task to steer the ship to port, so also in man himself the same processes are at work. The doctor sets himself to preserve man's life and bodily health; the economist's task is to see that there is no lack of material goods; the learned see to it that he knows the truth; and the moralist that he should live according to reason. Thus, if man were not destined to some higher end, these attentions would suffice.

But there is a further destiny for man after this mortal life; that final blessedness and enjoyment of God which he awaits after death. For, as the Apostle says (II *Corinthians* V, 6): 'While we are in the body we are absent from God.' So it is that the Christian, for whom that blessedness was obtained by the blood of Christ, and who is led to it through the gift of the Holy Ghost, has need of another, spiritual, guide to lead him to the harbour of eternal salvation: such guidance is provided for the faithful by the ministers of the Church of Christ.

Our conclusion must be the same, whether we consider the destiny of one person or of a whole community. Consequently, if the end of

unius. Si igitur finis hominis esset bonum quodcumque in ipso existens, et regendae multitudinis finis ultimus esset similiter ut tale bonum multitudo acquireret, et in eo permaneret; et siquidem talis ultimus sive unius hominis, sive multitudinis finis esset corporalis, vita et sanitas corporis, medici esset officium. Si autem ultimus finis esset divitiarum affluentia, oeconomus rex quidam multitudinis esset. Si vero bonum cognoscendae veritatis tale quid esset, ad quod posset multitudo pertingere, rex haberet doctoris officium. Videtur autem finis esse multitudinis congregatae vivere secundum virtutem. Ad hoc enim homines congregantur, ut simul bene vivant, quod consequi non posset unusquisque singulariter vivens; bona autem vita est secundum virtutem; virtuosa igitur vita est congregationis humanae finis.

Huius autem signum est, quod hi soli partes sint multitudinis congregatae, qui sibi invicem communicant in bene vivendo. Si enim propter solum vivere homines convenirent, animalia et servi essent pars aliqua congregationis civilis. Si vero propter acquirendas divitias, omnes simul negotiantes ad unam civitatem pertinerent: sicut videmus eos solos sub una multitudine computari, qui sub eisdem legibus et eodem regimine diriguntur ad bene vivendum. Sed quia homo vivendo secundum virtutem ad ulteriorem finem ordinatur, qui consistit in fruitione divina, ut supra iam diximus, oportet eumdem finem esse multitudinis humanae, qui est hominis unius. Non est ergo ultimus finis multitudinis congregatae vivere secundum virtutem, sed per virtuosam vitam pervenire ad fruitionem divinam. Siquidem autem ad hunc finem perveniri posset virtute humanae naturae, necesse esset ut ad officium regis pertineret dirigere homines in hunc finem. Hunc enim dici regem supponimus, cui summa regiminis in rebus humanis committitur. Tanto autem est regimen sublimius, quanto ad finem ulteriorem ordinantur. Semper enim invenitur ille, ad quem pertinet ultimus finis, imperare operantibus ea quae ad finem ultimum ordinantur; sicut gubernator, ad quem pertinet navigationem disponere, imperat ei, qui navem constituit, qualem navem navigationi aptam facere debeat; civilis autem qui utitur armis, imperat fabro, qualia arma fabricet. Sed quia finem fruitionis divinae non consequitur homo per virtutem humanam, sed virtute divina, iuxta illud Apostoli, *Rom.* VI, 23: « *Gratia Dei, vita aeterna* », perducere ad illum finem non humani erit, sed divini regiminis. Ad illum igitur regem huiusmodi

man were to be found in any perfection existing in man himself, the final object of government in a community would lie in the acquisition of such perfection and in its preservation once acquired. So that if such an end, whether of an individual or of a community, were life and bodily health, doctors would govern. If, on the other hand, it were abundance of riches, the government of the community could safely be left in the hands of the economist. If it were knowledge of truth, the king, whose task it is to guide the community, would have the duties of a professor. But the object for which a community is gathered together is to live a virtuous life. For men consort together that they may thus attain a fullness of life which would not be possible to each living singly: and the full life is one which is lived according to virtue. Thus the object of human society is a virtuous life.

A proof of this lies in the fact that only those members may be considered part of the community who contribute jointly to the fullness of social life. If men consorted together for bare existence, both animals and slaves would have a part in civil society. If for the multiplication of riches, all who had common commercial ties would belong to one city. But it is those who obey the same laws, and are guided by a single government to the fullness of life, who can be said to constitute a social unit. Now the man who lives virtuously is destined to a higher end, which consists, as we have already said, in the enjoyment of God: and the final object of human association can be no different from that of the individual man. Thus the final aim of social life will be, not merely to live in virtue, but rather through virtuous life to attain to the enjoyment of God. If, indeed, it were possible to attain this object by natural human virtue, it would, in consequence, be the duty of kings to guide men to this end. We believe, however, that it is the supreme power in temporal affairs which is the business of a king. Now government is of a higher order according to the importance of the ends it serves. For it is always the one who has the final ordering of affairs who directs those who carry out what pertains to the attainment of the final aim: just as the sailor who must navigate the ship advises the shipwright as to the type of ship which will suit his purpose; and the citizen who is to bear arms tells the smith what weapons to forge. But the enjoyment of God is an aim which cannot be attained by human virtue alone, but only through divine grace, as the Apostle tells us (*Romans*, VI, 23): 'The grace of God is eternal life.' Only a divine rule, then, and not human government, can lead us to this end. Such government belongs only to that King who is

regimen pertinet, qui non est solum homo, sed etiam Deus, scilicet
ad Dominum nostrum Jesum Christum, qui homines filios Dei faciens
in coelestem gloriam introduxit.

Hoc igitur est regimen ei traditum, quod non corrumpetur, propter
quod non solum sacerdos, sed rex in Scripturis sacris nominatur,
dicente Jer. XXIII, vers. 5: « *Regnabit rex, et sapiens erit* »; unde ab eo
regale sacerdotium derivatur. Et, quod est amplius, omnes Christi
fideles, in quantum sunt membra eius, reges et sacerdotes dicuntur.
Huius ergo regni ministerium, ut a terrenis essent spiritualia distincta,
non terrenis regibus, sed sacerdotibus est commissum, et praecipue
Summo Sacerdoti, successori Petri, Christi Vicario, Romano Pontifici,
cui omnes reges populi christiani oportet esse subditos, sicut ipsi
Domino Jesu Christo. Sic enim ei, ad quem finis ultimi cura pertinet,
subdi debent illi, ad quos pertinet cura antecedentium finium, et eius
imperio dirigi. Quia igitur sacerdotium gentilium et totus divinorum
cultus erat propter temporalia bona conquirenda, quae omnia ordinantur ad multitudinis bonum commune, cuius regi cura incumbit,
convenienter sacerdotes gentilium regibus subdebantur. Sed et quia in
veteri lege promittebantur bona terrena non a daemonibus, sed a Deo
vero religioso populo exhibenda, inde et in lege veteri sacerdotes
regibus leguntur fuisse subiecti. Sed in nova lege est sacerdotium altius,
per quod homines traducuntur ad bona coelestia: unde in lege Christi
reges debent sacerdotibus esse subiecti.

Propter quod mirabiliter ex divina providentia factum est, ut in
Romana urbe, quam Deus praeviderat christiani populi principalem
sedem futuram, hic mos paulatim inolesceret, ut civitatum rectores
sacerdotibus subiacerent. Sicut enim Valerius Maximus refert « *omnia
post religionem ponenda semper nostra civitas duxit etiam in quibus summae
maiestatis decus conspici voluit. Quapropter non dubitaverunt sacris imperia
servire, ita se humanarum rerum habitura regimen existimantia, si divinae
potentiae bene atque constanter fuissent famulata* ». Quia vero etiam
futurum erat, ut in Gallia Christiani sacerdotii plurimum vigeret
religio, divinitus est permissum, ut etiam apud Gallos gentiles sacerdotes, quod Druidas nominabant, totius Galliae ius definirent, ut refert
Julius Caesar in libro, quem de bello Gallico scripsit.

both man, and also God: that is to Jesus Christ, our Lord, Who, making men to be Sons of God has led them to the glory of heaven.

This, then, is the government entrusted to Him: a dominion which shall never pass away, and in virtue of which He is called in the Holy Scriptures, not only a priest but a king; as *Jeremias* says (XXIII, 5): 'A king shall reign and shall be wise.' It is from Him that the royal priesthood derives; and, what is more, all the Faithful of Christ, being members of Him, become thus, priests and kings. The ministry of this kingdom is entrusted not to the rulers of this earth but to priests, so that temporal affairs may remain distinct from those spiritual: and, in particular, it is delegated to the High Priest, the successor of Peter and Vicar of Christ, the Roman Pontiff; to whom all kings in Christendom should be subject, as to the Lord Jesus Christ Himself. For those who are concerned with the subordinate ends of life must be subject to him who is concerned with the supreme end and be directed by his command. And because the pagan priesthood and everything connected with the cult of pagan gods was directed to the attainment of temporal benefits, which form part of the common weal of the community, and which lie within the king's competence, it was right that pagan priests should be subject to their kings. Similarly in the Old Testament, temporal benefits were promised to the people in reward for their faith, though these promises were made by the true God and not by demons; so that under the Old Law we read that the priesthood was subject to kings. But under the New Law there is a higher priesthood through which men are led to a heavenly reward: and under Christ's Law, kings must be subject to priests.

For this reason it came about by the admirable dispensation of divine providence, that in the city of Rome which God chose to be the main centre of Christendom, it gradually became the custom for the rulers of the city to be subject to the pontiffs. So Valerius Maximus relates: 'It has been the custom in our city always to subordinate all things to religion, even in matters which concerned the dignity of the supreme power. So the authorities have never hesitated to place themselves at the service of the altar; thus showing their belief that only by good and faithful service of divine authority can temporal government be rightly exercised.' And because it was to come about that in Gaul Christian priesthood would be more highly respected, providence permitted that the pagan priests of the Gauls, who were called Druids, should establish their authority, throughout the country; as Caesar tells us in his book, *De Bello Gallico*.

Caput XV.—QUOD SICUT AD ULTIMUM FINEM CONSEQUENDUM RE-
QUIRITUR UT REX SUBDITOS SUOS AD VIVENDUM SECUNDUM VIRTUTEM
DISPONAT, ITA AD FINES MEDIOS. ET PONUNTUR HIC, QUAE SUNT ILLA
QUAE ORDINANT AD BENE VIVENDUM ET QUAE IMPEDIUNT, ET QUOD
REMEDIUM REX APPONERE DEBET CIRCA DICTA IMPEDIMENTA.

Sicut autem ad vitam, quam in coelo speramus beatam, ordinatur,
sicut ad finem, vita qua hic homines bene vivunt; ita ad bonum
multitudinis ordinantur, sicut ad finem, quaecumque particularia bona
per hominem procurantur, sive divitiae, sive lucra, sive sanitas, sive
facundia vel eruditio. Si igitur, ut dictum est, qui de ultimo fine curam
habet, praeesse debet his, qui curam habent de ordinatis ad finem, et
eos dirigere suo imperio, manifestum ex dictis fit, quod rex, sicut dominio et regimini, quod administratur per sacerdotis officium, subdi
debet, ita praeesse debet omnibus humanis officiis, et ea imperio sui
regiminis ordinare. Cuicumque autem incumbit aliquid perficere, quod
ordinatur in aliud, sicut in finem, hoc debet attendere ut suum opus sit
congruum fini. Sicut faber sic facit gladium ut pugnae conveniat, et
aedificator sic debet domum disponere ut ad habitandum sit apta.
Quia igitur vitae, qua in praesenti bene vivimus, finis est beatitudo
coelestis, ad regis officium pertinet ea ratione vitam multitudinis
bonam procurare, secundum quod congruit ad coelestem beatitudinem consequendam, ut scilicet ea praecipiat, quae ad coelestem
beatitudinem ducunt, et eorum contraria, secundum quod fuerit
possibile, interdicat. Quae autem sit ad veram beatitudinem via, et
quae sint impedimenta eius, ex lege divina cognoscitur, cuius doctrina
pertinet ad sacerdotum officium, secundum illud *Malach.* cap. II, 7:
« *Labia sacerdotis custodient scientiam, et legem requirent de ore eius* ». Et
ideo in *Deut.* XVII, 18, Dominus praecipit: « *Postquam sederit rex in
solio regni sui, describet sibi Deuteronomium legis huius in volumine, accipiens
exempla a sacerdote Leviticae tribus, et habebit secum, legetque illud omnibus
diebus vitae suae, ut discat timere Dominum Deum suum et custodire verba
et caeremonias eius, quae in lege praecepta sunt* ». Rex legem igitur
divinam edoctus, ad hoc praecipuum studium debet intendere, qualiter
multitudo sibi subdita bene vivat: quod quidem studium in tria dividitur, ut primo quidem in subiecta multitudine bonam vitam instituat;

Chapter XV.—How to attain the aim of a good life in the
political community.

Just as the good life of men on this earth is directed, as to its end,
to the blessed life which is promised us in heaven, so also all those
particular benefits which men can procure for themselves, such as
riches, or gain, or health, or skill, or learning, must be directed to the
good of the community. But, as we have said, he who has charge of
supreme ends must take precedence over those who are concerned
with aims subordinate to these ends, and must guide them by his
authority; it follows, therefore, that a king, though subject to that power
and authority must, nevertheless, preside over all human activities,
and direct them in virtue of his own power and authority. Now,
whoever has a duty of completing some task, which is itself connected
with some higher aim, must satisfy himself that his action is rightly
directed towards that aim. Thus the smith forges a sword which is
fit to fight with; and the builder must construct a house so that it is
habitable. And because the aim of a good life on this earth is blessedness in heaven, it is the king's duty to promote the welfare of the
community in such a way that it leads fittingly to the happiness of
heaven; insisting upon the performance of all that leads thereto, and
forbidding, as far as is possible, whatever is inconsistent with this
end. The road to true blessedness and the obstacles which may be
found along it, are learnt through the medium of the divine law; to
teach which is the duty of priests, as we read in *Malachy* (Chapter II, 7):
'The lips of the priest shall keep knowledge, and they shall seek the
law at his mouth.' So the Lord commands (*Deuteronomy* XVII, 18):
'But after he is raised to the throne of his kingdom, he shall copy
out to himself the Deuteronomy of this law in a volume, taking
the copy of the priests of the Levitical tribe, and he shall have it with
him and shall read it all the days of his life, that he may learn to fear
the Lord his God, and keep his words and ceremonies, that are commanded in the law.' A king then, being instructed in the divine law,
must occupy himself particularly with directing the community
subject to him to the good life. In this connection he has three tasks.
He must first establish the welfare of the community he rules; secondly,

secundo, ut institutam conservet; tertio, ut conservatam ad meliora promoveat.

Ad bonam autem unius hominis vitam duo requiruntur: unum principale, quod est operatio secundum virtutem, (virtus enim est qua bene vivitur); aliud vero secundarium et quasi instrumentale, scilicet corporalium bonorum sufficientia, quorum usus est necessarius ad actum virtutis. Ipsa tamen hominis unitas per naturam causatur, multitudinis autem unitas, quae pax dicitur, per regentis industriam est procuranda. Sic igitur ad bonam vitam multitudinis instituendam tria requiruntur. Primo quidem, ut multitudo in unitate pacis constituatur. Secundo, ut multitudo vinculo pacis unita dirigatur ad bene agendum. Sicut enim homo nihil bene agere potest nisi praesupposita suarum partium unitate, ita hominum multitudo pacis unitate carens dum impugnat se ipsam, impeditur a bene agendo. Tertio vero requiritur, ut per regentis industriam necessariorum ad bene vivendum adsit sufficiens copia. Sic igitur bona vita per regis officium in multitudine constituta, consequens est ut ad eius conservationem intendat.

Sunt autem tria, quibus bonum publicum permanere non sinitur, quorum quidem unum est a natura proveniens. Non enim bonum multitudinis ad unum tantum tempus institui debet, sed ut sit quodammodo perpetuum. Homines autem cum sint mortales, in perpetuum durare non possunt. Nec, dum vivunt, semper sunt in eodem vigore, quia multis variationibus humana vita subiicitur, et sic non sunt homines ad eadem officia peragenda aequaliter per totam vitam idonei. Aliud autem impedimentum boni publici conservandi ab interiori proveniens in perversitate voluntatum consistit, dum vel sunt desides ad ea peragenda quae requirit respublica, vel insuper sunt paci multitudinis noxii, dum transgrediendo iustitiam aliorum pacem perturbant. Tertium autem impedimentum reipublicae conservandae ab exteriori causatur, dum per incursum hostium pax dissolvitur, et interdum regnum, aut civitas funditus dissipatur. Igitur circa tria praedicta triplex cura imminet regi. Primo quidem de successione hominum, ut substitutione illorum qui diversis officiis praesunt, ut sicut per divinum regimen in rebus corruptibilibus, quia semper eadem durare non possunt, provisum est, ut per generationem alia in locum aliorum succedant, ut vel sic conservetur integritas universi, ita per regis studium conservetur subiectae multitudinis bonum, dum sollicite curat qualiter alii in deficientium locum succedant. Secundum autem

he must ensure that nothing undermines the well-being thus established; and thirdly he must be at pains continually to extend this welfare.

For the well-being of the individual two things are necessary: the first and most essential is to act virtuously (it is through virtue, in fact, that we live a good life); the other, and secondary requirement, is rather a means, and lies in a sufficiency of material goods, such as are necessary to virtuous action. Now man is a natural unit, but the unity of a community, which is peace, must be brought into being by the skill of the ruler. To ensure the well-being of a community, therefore, three things are necessary. In the first place the community must be united in peaceful unity. In the second place the community, thus united, must be directed towards well-doing. For just as a man could do no good if he were not an integral whole, so also a community of men which is disunited and at strife within itself, is hampered in well-doing. Thirdly and finally, it is necessary that there be, through the ruler's sagacity, a sufficiency of those material goods which are indispensable to well-being. Once the welfare of the community is thus ensured, it remains for the king to consider its preservation.

Now there are three things which are detrimental to the permanence of public welfare and one of these springs from the nature of things. For the common prosperity should not be for any limited period, but should endure, if possible, in perpetuity. But men, being mortal, cannot live for ever. Nor, even while they are still alive, have they always the same vigour; for human life is subject to many changes, and a man is not always capable of fulfilling the same tasks throughout the span of his lifetime. Another obstacle to the preservation of public welfare is one which arises from within, and lies in the perversity of the will; for many are inattentive in carrying out duties necessary to the community, or even harm the peace of the community by failing to observe justice and disturbing the peace of others. Then there is a third obstacle to the preservation of the community which comes from without: when peace is shattered by hostile invasion, and sometimes the kingdom or city itself is entirely destroyed. Corresponding to these three points, the task of a king has a threefold aspect. The first regards the succession and substitution of those who hold various offices: just as divine providence sees to it that corruptible things, which cannot remain unchanged for ever, are renewed through successive generations, and so conserves the integrity of the universe, it is the king's duty also to preserve the well-being of the community subject to him, by providing successors for those who are failing.

F

ut suis legibus et praeceptis, poenis et praemiis homines sibi subiectos ab iniquitate coerceat, et ad opera virtuosa inducat, exemplum a Deo accipiens, qui hominibus legem dedit, observantibus quidem mercedem, transgredientibus poenas retribuens. Tertio imminet regi cura, ut multitudo sibi subiecta contra hostes tuta reddatur. Nihil enim prodesset interiora vitare pericula, si ab exterioribus defendi non posset.

Sic igitur bonae multitudinis institutioni tertium restat ad regis officium pertinens, ut sit de promotione sollicitus, quod fit dum in singulis quae praemissa sunt, si quid inordinatum est, corrigere, si quid deest supplere, si quid melius fieri potest, studet perficere. Unde et Apostolus, I *Corinth.*, XII, fideles monet, ut semper aemulentur charismata meliora.

Haec igitur sunt quae ad regis officium pertinent, de quibus per singula diligentius tractare oportet.

Secondly he must, in governing, be concerned, by laws and by advice, by penalties and by rewards, to dissuade men from evildoing and to induce them to do good; following thus the example of God, who gave to men a law, and rewards those who observe it but punishes those who transgress. Thirdly it is a king's duty to make sure that the community subject to him is made safe against its enemies. There is no point in guarding against internal dangers, when defence from enemies without is impossible.

So, for the right ordering of society there remains a third task for the king: he must be occupied with its development. This task is best fulfilled by keeping in mind the various points enumerated above; by attention to what may be a cause of disorder, by making good whatever is lacking and by perfecting whatever can be better done. Therefore the Apostle (I *Corinthians*, XII), warns the faithful always to prize the better gifts.

These, then, are the things which go to make up the duty of a king: but each should be treated in much greater detail.

DE REGIMINE JUDAEORUM

AD DUCISSAM BRABANTIAE

Excellentiae vestrae recepi literas, ex quibus et piam solicitudinem circa regimen subditorum vestrorum, et devotam dilectionem quam habetis ad fratres nostri ordinis plenarie intellexi, Deo gratias agens qui vestro cordi tantarum virtutum semina inspiravit. Quod tamen in eisdem a me requirebatis literis, ut vobis super quibusdam articulis responderem, utique mihi dificile fuit: tum propter occupationes meas, quas requirit operatio lectionis: tum quia mihi placeret, ut super his requireretis aliorum consilium magis in talibus peritorum. Verum quia indecens reputavi ut vestrae solicitudini neglegens coadiutor inveniar, aut dilectioni ingratus existam, super propositis articulis vobis ad praesens respondere curavi, absque praeiudicio sententiae melioris.

Primo ergo vestra requirebat excellentia, « Si liceat vobis aliquo tempore, et quo exactionem facere in Judaeos »: ad quam quaestionem sic absolute propositam responderi potest, quia licet, ut iura dicunt, Judaei merito culpae suae sint, vel essent perpetuae servituti addicti, et sic eorum res terrarum domini possint accipere tamquam suas: hoc tamen servato moderamine, ut necessaria vitae subsidia eis nullatenus subtrahantur. Quia tamen oportet nos honeste ambulare etiam ad eos qui foris sunt, ne nomen Domini blasphemetur, ut Apost. fideles admonet suo exemplo, ut sine offensione simus Judaeis ac Gentibus et Ecclesiae Dei; hoc servandum videtur ut, sicut iura determinant, ab eis coacta servitia non exigantur, quae ipsi praeterito tempore facere non consueverunt: quia ea, quae sunt insolita, magis solent animos hominum perturbare. Secundum igitur huiusmodi rationis sententiam potestis secundum consuetudinem praedecessorum vestrorum exactionem in Judaeos facere, si tamen aliud non obsistat. Videtur autem, quantum coniicere potui, circa hoc dubitatio vestra augeri ex his quae consequenter inquiritis, quod Judaei terrae vestrae nihil videntur habere nisi quod acquisierunt per usurariam pravitatem; unde conse-

ON THE GOVERNMENT OF JEWS

TO THE DUCHESS OF BRABANT

I have received your Excellency's letter, and fully understand from it your pious solicitude for the government of your subjects and the devout affection you bear towards the brothers of our order: I thank God who has moved your heart to such great virtue. In truth, I find myself in some difficulty in meeting your request for advice on certain points: partly because I am fully occupied in lecturing, and partly because I would have preferred that you had addressed your questions on these matters to others, more versed in them than I. It would be ill-befitting of me, however, should I fail to give you what help I can in your difficulties, and a poor requital of your affection. Thus I have attempted, in what follows, to answer the questions you have raised; but without prejudice to any better opinion.

In the first place, then, Your Excellency asked, 'whether at any time, and if so when, it is permissible to exact tribute of the Jews.' To such a question, put thus in general terms, one may reply that it is true, as the Law declares, that Jews, in consequence of their sin, are or were destined to perpetual slavery; so that sovereigns of states may treat their goods as their own property; with the sole proviso that they do not deprive them of all that is necessary to sustain life. But because we must bear ourselves honestly, even to those who are outcasts, lest the name of Christ be blasphemed, (as the Apostle warns us by his own example, to give no offence either to Jews or to Gentiles or to the church of God), it would seem more correct to forego what is permitted by the law, and to abstain from forced loans which it has not been the custom to exact in the past; for what is unaccustomed always rankles more deeply in men's minds. According to this opinion, therefore, you may exact tribute of the Jews according to the custom established by your predecessors, and where there are no other considerations to be taken into account. But, from what I have been able to conjecture, it would seem that your doubts upon this point are heightened by the question you proceed to ask: by the fact, that is, that the Jews in your country appear to possess nothing but what they have acquired by the evil practice of usury. You ask whether it is right to exact

quenter quaeritis, si liceat aliquid ab eis exigere, cum restituenda sint
sic extorta. Super hoc ergo sic respondendum videtur, quod cum ea
quae Judaei per usuras ab aliis [extorserunt], non possint licite retinere,
consequens est ut, si etiam vos haec acceperitis ab eis, non possetis licite
retinere, nisi forsan essent talia quae a vobis, vel antecessoribus vestris
hactenus extorsissent. Si qua vero habent quae extorserunt ab aliis,
haec ab eis exacta illis debetis restituere, quibus Judaei restituere tenebantur: unde si inveniuntur certae personae a quibus extorserunt
usuras, debet eis restitui, alioquin debet in pios usus secundum consilium dioecesani episcopi, et aliorum proborum, vel etiam in communem utilitatem terrae, si necessitas immineat, vel exposcat communis utilitas, erogari: nec esset illicitum, si a Judaeis exigeretis talia
de novo, servata consuetudine praedecessorum vestrorum, hac intentione, ut in praedictos usus expenderentur.

Secundo vero requirebatis, si peccaverit Judaeus, utrum sit poena
pecuniaria puniendus, cum nihil habeat praeter usuras. Respondendum
videtur secundum praedicta, quod expedit eum pecuniaria poena
puniri, ne ex sua iniquitate commodum reportet. Videtur etiam mihi
quod esset maiori poena puniendus Judaeus, vel quicumque alius
usurarius, quam aliquis alius, quantum pecunia, quae aufertur ei,
minus ad eum noscitur pertinere. Potest etiam pecuniariae alia poena
superaddi, ne hoc solum ad poenam sufficere videatur, quod pecuniam
aliis debitam desinit possidere. Pecunia autem poenae nomine ab
usurariis ablata retineri non potest, sed in usos praedictos debet
expendi, si nihil aliud habeant quam usuras. Si vero dicatur, quod ex
hoc principes terrarum damnificantur, hoc damnum sibi imputent,
utpote ex negligentia eorum proveniens. Melius enim esset ut Judaeos
laborare compellerent ad proprium victum lucrandum, sicut in partibus Italiae faciunt, quam quod otiosi viventes solis usuris ditentur, et
sic eorum domini suis reditibus defraudentur. Ita enim et per suam
culpam principes defraudarentur reditibus propriis, si permitterent
suos subditos ex solo latrocinio, vel furto lucrari. Tenerentur nam ad
restitutionem eius quodcumque ab eis exigerent.

Tertio quaerebatur, si ultro offerant pecuniam, vel aliquod encenium,

from them monies, which in any case should be restored, owing
to the way in which they were extorted. The reply to this question
would seem to be that although the Jews have no right to retain the
money they have extorted from others by usury, neither have you
any right to retain it if you take it back from the Jews; except, perhaps,
in the case of goods they may have extorted from you yourself or from
your predecessors. If they possess goods which they have extorted from
others, it is your duty to restore them to those persons to whom the
Jews are obliged to make restitution. So if you can find with certainty
those of whom usury was extorted, you must make restitution to
them. Otherwise, such money must be put to pious use, according to
the advice of diocesan bishops and of other upright men; or used
for the public benefit of your kingdom, to relieve want or serve the
interest of the community. Nor will you be doing wrong by exacting
such goods back from the Jews; providing always that you observe
the customs of your predecessors, and have the intention of using
them in the manner prescribed.

Secondly, you asked whether Jews should be punished by fines for
breaking the law, since they possess nothing but the proceeds of their
usury. The reply to this, on the lines already given, would seem to be
that it is quite right to inflict a monetary penalty to ensure that no
profit is obtained from dishonesty. And I am also of the opinion
that a Jew, or any other usurer, should be punished by heavier fines
than other malefactors, since they are known to have less title to the
money which is thus taken from them. In addition to fines other
penalties may also be inflicted, lest it should be thought sufficient
punishment to restore what is already owed to others. But money
which is the proceeds from fines upon usurers may not be retained:
it must be employed in the manner already indicated when it comes
entirely from usury. Nor may rulers of countries object that they
suffer loss of revenue by so acting, because they are themselves responsible for such loss. They would do better to compel the Jews to work
for their living, as is done in parts of Italy; rather than to allow them
to live in idleness and grow rich by usury. It is because of this that they
suffer loss. In the same way, and for the very same reason, princes
would suffer loss of revenue if they were to allow their subjects to
enrich themselves by fraud and piracy. They would be equally bound
to make restitution from any of the proceeds they obtained in consequence.

In the third place, you asked whether it is permissible to accept

an recipere liceat. Ad quod respondendum videtur, quod licet recipere, sed expedit quod sic acceptum reddatur his quibus debetur, vel aliter, ut supra dictum est, expendatur, si nihil aliud habeant quam usuras.

Quarto quaeritur, si plus accipitur a Judaeo, quam ab eo Christiani requirant, quid sit de residuo faciendum. Ad quod patet responsio ex iam dictis. Quod enim Christiani minus requirunt, potest esse propter duo. Vel quia forte Judaeus aliquid habeat praeter usurarium lucrum, et in tali casu licet nobis illud retinere servato moderamine supradicto: et idem videtur dicendum, si illi extorserint usuras eis qui postea bona voluntate donaverunt, cum tamen Judaei prompte se offerent ad restituendum usuras. Vel potest contingere, quod illi, a quibus acceperunt, sunt sublati de medio vel per mortem, vel in terris aliis morantes; et tunc ipsi debent restituere. Si tamen non apparent certae personae quibus restituere teneantur, procedendum est ut supra.

Quod autem de Judaeis dictum est, intelligendum est et de cavorsinis, vel quibuscumque aliis insistentibus usurariae pravitati.

Quinto quaerebatis de balivis et officialibus vestris, si liceat eis officia vendere, vel mutuo ab eis accipere aliquid certum, donec tantum recipiant ex officiis. Ad quod dicendum videtur, quod quaestio ista duas difficultates habere videtur: quarum prima est de officiorum venditione. Circa quam considerandum videtur, quod Apost. dicit, quod multa licent, quae non expediunt. Cum autem balivis et officialibus vestris nihil committatis nisi temporalis officium potestatis, non video quare huiusmodi officia non liceat vobis vendere, dummodo talibus vendatis, de quibus possit praesumi, quod sint utiles ad talia officia exercenda, et non tanto pretio venumdantur officia, quod recuperari non possint sine gravamine vestrorum subditorum. Sed tamen talis venditio expediens non videtur. Primo quidem, quia contingit frequenter quod illi, qui essent magis idonei ad huiusmodi officia exercenda, sunt pauperes, ut emere non possint; et si etiam sunt divites illi qui meliores sunt, talia officia non ambiunt, nec inhiant ad lucra ex officio acquirenda. Sequitur igitur quod ut plurimum illi

from them some gift, or token, if it be offered. To which the reply would seem to be that it is quite permissible to accept such gifts; but that it would be wise to restore what is thus received to its rightful owners, or to put it to one of the uses already mentioned—since the donors possess nothing but the proceeds of usury.

Fourthly, you ask what should be done with the surplus if more is taken from a Jew than is owed as restitution to Christians. The reply to this is obvious from what has already been said. Such surplus may arise from two causes. Either the Jew may have some other possessions besides the proceeds of usury: and in this case we may retain what is given up, keeping always to the proviso mentioned above. The same holds true if the surplus come from a free gift made to a Jew in addition to the payment of usury; provided that the proceeds of the usury are first repaid. It may, on the other hand, happen that those who have suffered usury are no longer within the realm, being either dead or living in some other country. In this case restitution must be made. But if it cannot be known for certain the precise person to whom restitution is to be made, you must act as already advised.

Whatever has been said about Jews must be understood to apply equally to the money-dealers of Cahors or to any others who practise the evil custom of usury.

Fifthly, you ask with regard to your bailiffs and other officers, whether it is permissible to put up their offices for sale, or to accept from them a deposit in anticipation, which they will afterwards recover from the proceeds of their office. The answer is that this question raises two difficulties. The first concerns the sale of offices. On this point we must keep in mind what the Apostle says, that there are many things which are permissible but which are not always expedient. Since it is only a civil office which you confer upon your bailiffs and other functionaries, I see nothing wrong in your offering such offices for sale: providing always that you sell them to such as are capable of fulfilling their duties usefully, and do not merely offer them to the highest bidder, who will then recoup himself at the expense of your subjects. On the other hand, the sale of offices is not advisable. In the first place those who are best fitted for such offices are frequently poor, and so cannot buy them; and even if they were rich, the best candidates often have no wish to undertake such activities, or to profit from the occasions they offer. In consequence it would frequently

officia in terra vestra suscipiant, qui sunt peiores, ambitiosi, et pecuniae amatores; quos etiam probabile est subditos vestros opprimere, et vestra etiam commoda non sic fideliter procurare. Unde magis videtur expediens ut bonos homines et idoneos ad suscipiendum vestra officia eligatis, quos etiam invitos, si necesse fuerit, compellatis: quia per eorum bonitatem et industriam maiora accrescent vobis et subditis vestris, quam de praedicta officiorum venditione acquirere valeatis: et hoc consilium dedit Moysi eius cognatus. « *Provide* — inquit — *de omni plebe viros sapientes et timentes Deum, in quibus sit charitas, et qui oderint avaritiam: et constitue ex eis tribunos, et centuriones, et quinquagenarios, et decanos qui iudicent populum omni tempore* ». Secunda vero dubitatio circa hunc articulum potest esse de mutuo. Circa quod dicendum videtur, quod si hoc pacto mutuum daret, ut officium accipiant, absque dubio pactum est usurarium, quia pro mutuo accipiunt officii potestatem: unde in hoc datis eis occasionem peccandi, et ipsi etiam tunc tenerentur resignare officio taliter acquisito. Si tamen gratis officia dederitis, et post ab eis mutuum acceperitis, quod de suo officio possint recipere, hoc absque omni peccato fieri potest.

Sexto quaerebatis, si liceat vobis exactiones facere in vestros subditos Christianos: in quo considerare debetis, quod principes terrarum sunt a Deo instituti non quidem ut propria lucra quaerant, sed ut communem populi utilitatem procurent. In reprehensione enim quorundam principum dicitur in *Ezech.* XXII: « *Principes eius in medio eius quasi lupi rapaces, positi ad effundendum sanguinem, et ad quaerendas animas, et avaritiae lucra sequenda* »: et alibi dicitur per quemdam prophetam: « *Vae pastoribus Israel, qui pascebant semetipsos. Nonne greges pascuntur a pastoribus? Lac comedebatis, et lanis cooperiebamini! quidquid crassum erat, occidebatis; gregem autem meum non pascebatis* ». Unde constituti sunt reditus terrarum principibus, ut ex illis viventes a spoliatione subditorum abstineant. Unde in eodem Propheta Domino mandante dicitur, quod « *principi erit possessio in Israel, et non depopulabuntur ultra principes populum meum* ». Contingit tamen aliquando, quod principes

happen that such offices in your domain would be filled by the worst elements, who are both ambitious and avaricious: with the further consequence that they would probably oppress your subjects and take no account of your true interests. So it would seem to be much the wisest course to chose good and capable men to act in your service, even obliging them to do so, if they prove unwilling. Both you and your subjects will receive much greater return from their industry and fidelity than you would possibly obtain through the sale of such offices. This was the advice which Moses gave to his kinsman, when he said: 'Seek out from among the people wise men who fear God, in whom there is charity and who despise the love of money: and appoint from them leaders of thousands and of hundreds and of fifties and of tens, to judge the people at all times.' Then there is a second difficulty which here arises from the question of a deposit. On this point it should be said that if the appointment is made contingent upon such a deposit, then, without doubt, such an agreement would be usurious; because appointment to the office is obtained in virtue of a loan. In such a case you would be providing them with an occasion of sin, and they would also be obliged to resign from the appointment so obtained. If, on the other hand, you were to confer the office upon them freely, and afterwards were to accept a loan which could be recovered by them in the course of their duties, this can be done without any sin.

Sixthly, you asked whether it were permissible to levy tribute of your Christian subjects. In this matter you must remember that rulers of countries are appointed by God, not that they may seek their own gain, but that they may prosper the common welfare. Avaricious rulers are reprehended by what is said in *Ezechiel* (XXII) 'Her princes in the midst of her are like wolves ravening the prey to shed blood and to destroy souls, and to run after gains through covetousness.' And elsewhere, one of the prophets says: 'Woe to the pastors of Israel who have fed only themselves. Is it not the shepherds' duty to feed their flocks? You have drunk your fill of milk, and have covered yourselves with fine wool. You have slain the fattest of the flocks; but my sheep you have not pastured.' For this reason, the rulers of countries are appointed a pension which should suffice for their needs, and which removes any excuse for the spoliation of their subjects. Thus, in the same prophecy it is said by the Lord's command: 'To the king shall be given a certain possession in Israel: and princes shall no more prey upon my people.' It sometimes happens, however,

non habent sufficientes reditus ad custodiam terrae, et ad alia quae imminent rationabiliter principibus expetenda: et in tali casu iustum est ut subditi exhibeant unde possit communis eorum utilitas procurari. Et inde est, quod in aliquibus terris ex antiqua consuetudine domini suis subditis certas collectas imponunt, quae, si non sunt immoderatae, absque peccato exigi possunt, quia secundum Apostolum: « *Nullus militat stipendiis suis* ». Unde princeps, qui militat utilitati communi, potest de communibus vivere, et communia negotia procurare vel per reditus deputatos, vel si huiusmodi desint, aut sufficientes non fuerint, per ea quae a singulis colliguntur. Et similis ratio esse videtur si aliquis casus emergat de novo, in quo oportet plura expendere pro utilitate communi, vel pro honesto statu principis conservando, ad quae non sufficiunt reditus proprii, vel exactiones consuetae; puta, si hostes terram invadant, vel aliquis similis casus emergat. Tunc enim et praeter solitas exactiones possent licite terrarum principes a suis subditis aliqua exigere pro utilitate communi. Si vero velint exigere ultra id quod est institutum, pro sola libidine habendi, aut propter inordinatas et immoderatas expensas: hoc eis omnino non licet. Unde Joannes Baptista militibus ad se venientibus dixit: « *Neminem concutiatis, nec calumniam faciatis, et contenti estote stipendiis vestris* ». Sunt enim quasi stipendia principum eorum reditus, quibus debent esse contenti, ut ultra non exigant, nisi secundum rationem praedictam, et si utilitas est communis.

Septimo quaerebatis, si officiales vestri absque iuris ordine aliquid a subditis extorserint, quod ad manus vestras devenerit, vel non forte, quid circa hoc facere debeatis. Super quo plana est responsio: quia si ad manus vestras devenerint, debetis restituere vel certis personis, si potestis, vel in pios usus expendere, sive pro utilitate communi, si personas certas non potestis invenire. Si autem ad manus vestras non devenerint, debetis compellere officiales vestros ad consimilem restitutionem, etiam si non fuerint notae vobis aliquae certae personae, a quibus exegerint, ne a sua iniustitia commodum reportent: quinimmo sunt a vobis super hoc gravius puniendi, ut ceteri a similibus abstineant

that princes do not possess sufficient means to provide against hostile attack or for other tasks which they may reasonably take upon themselves. In such a case it is just that the citizens should contribute what is necessary to promote the common interest. For this reason it is an ancient custom in some countries, for the rulers to exact certain contributions from their subjects: and if these be not excessive, such a course may be followed without sin. For, as the Apostle says, 'Nobody fights at his own expense.' So a prince who fights for the interests of his country may make use of the resources of the community and make a charge upon the common business, either through the normal forms of taxation or, if such do not exist or are insufficient, through individual contribution. The same conclusions hold good when some unforeseen situation arises, and it is necessary to increase expenditure in the common interest, or to preserve the dignity of the court, and when the normal returns to the royal exchequer and ordinary taxes are not sufficient; as, for example, when hostile invasion takes place, or in similar circumstances. In such a case it is permissible for sovereign princes to exact special levies from their citizens, above the normal taxation, for this is in the interest of all. It is never, however, permissible to exact more than the accustomed taxes merely from the love of money or because of inordinate and immoderate expenditure. So John the Baptist told the soldiers who came to him (*Luke*, III, 14): 'Do violence to no man, neither calumniate any man; and be content with your pay.' The pensions of princes are in a way their pay, and with these they should remain content. Nor should they demand more, except for the reasons already given and in the common interest.

Seventhly, you ask what action you should take in the case that your ministers have extorted money from your subjects beyond the provision of the law: whether or no the proceeds have come into your hands. On this point the reply is easy. If the proceeds of such exaction have come into your hands, you are bound to restore them to the persons from whom they were taken; if this is possible: and where it is not possible to find the owners with certainty, you must use them for some pious object, or in the interest of the whole community. If, on the other hand, the proceeds have not reached you, you must compel your officers to make restitution, lest they benefit from their injustices; even when the persons who have suffered from their extortions cannot be known for certain. You should, in fact, be particularly severe in your punishment of such offences, to dissuade others from

in futurum: quia, sicut Salomon dicit, « *pestilente flagellato stultus sapientior fit* ».

Ultimo quaeritis, si bonum est, ut per provinciam vestram Judaei signum distinctivum a Christianis deportare cogantur. Ad quod plana est responsio, et secundum statum concilii generalis, Judaei utriusque sexus in omni Christianorum provincia, et in omni tempore aliquo habitu ab aliis populis debent distingui. Hoc eis etiam in lege eorum mandatur, ut scilicet faciant fimbrias per quatuor angulos palliorum, per quos ab aliis discernantur.

Haec sunt, illustris et religiosa Domina, quae vestris quaestionibus ad praesens respondenda occurrunt: in quibus vobis non sic meam sententiam ingero, quin magis suadeam peritiorum sententiam esse tenendam. Valeat dominatio vestra per tempora longiora.

following their example: for, as Solomon says: 'The wicked man being scourged, the fool shall be wiser' (*Proverbs*, XIX, 25).

So, to your last question; whether it is correct that all Jews in your realm should be obliged to bear some special sign to distinguish them from Christians. To this the answer is easy and in conformity with the decision given by the General Council. Jews of both sexes and in all Christian lands should on all occasions be distinguished from other people by some particular dress. This is, in any case, imposed upon them by their own law, which ordains that they shall wear a fringe at the four corners of their cloaks to distinguish them from other peoples.

These, illustrious and pious Lady, are the replies which I have here to make to your questions. In respect of which I have no desire to impose my opinion upon you, but would rather advise you to seek the counsel of others more versed in such questions than I. May you continue long to reign.

PART II

FROM THE PHILOSOPHICAL WORKS

SUMMA CONTRA GENTILES

Liber III, Caput LXXXI

De ordinatione hominum ad invicem et ad alia.

Inter alias vero intellectuales substantias, humanae animae infimum gradum habent; quia, sicut supra dictum est, in sui institutione, cognitionem ordinis providentiae divinae in sola quadam universali cognitione suscipiunt; ad perfectam vero ordinis singularium cognitionem oportet quod ex ipsis rebus, in quibus ordo divinae providentiae iam particulariter institutus est, perducantur; unde oportuit quod haberent organa corporea, per quae a rebus corporalibus cognitionem haurirent, ex quibus tamen, propter debilitatem intellectualis luminis, perfectam notitiam eorum quae ad hominem spectant adipisci non valent, nisi per lumen superioris spiritus adiuventur, hoc exigente divina dispositione ut inferiores per superiores spiritus perfectionem acquirant, ut supra ostensum est. Quia tamen aliquid homo de lumine intellectuali participat, ei, secundum providentiae divinae ordinem, subduntur animalia bruta, quae de intellectu nullo modo participant; unde dicitur: « *Faciamus hominem ad imaginem et similitudinem nostram* », scilicet secundum quod intellectum habet, « *et praesit piscibus maris, et volatilibus coeli, et bestiis, universaeque terrae* ». (*Gen.*, I, 26).

Animalia vero bruta, etsi intellectu careant, quia tamen cognitionem aliquam habent, plantis et aliis quae cognitione carent, secundum divinae providentiae ordinem, praeferuntur; unde dicitur: « *Ecce dedi vobis omnem herbam afferentem semen super terram, et universa ligna quae habent in semetipsis sementem generis sui, ut sint vobis in escam et cunctis animantibus terrae* ». (*Gen.*, I, 29-30).

Inter ea vero quae penitus cognitione carent, unum subiacet alteri, secundum quod unum est altero potentius in agendo; non enim participant aliquid de dispositione providentiae, sed solum de executione. Quia vero homo habet intellectum et sensum et corporalem virtutem, haec in ipso ad invicem ordinantur, secundum divinae pro-

SUMMA CONTRA GENTILES

Book III, Chapter 81

Of the Ordering of Men among Themselves and with respect to Other Creatures

Compared with other intellectual substances the human soul takes the lowest place, because, as has already been stated, it has, when first created, only a general apprehension of the order of divine providence: consequently, it must perfect its knowledge of what pertains to that order in the particular, by reference to things themselves, in which the order of divine providence is already established in detail. So it is that the human soul must rely on bodily organs to acquire knowledge from the sensible world. But, such is the weakness of its intellectual light, that it could never acquire a perfect knowledge of all that concerns man unless it were assisted and enlightened by higher spirits; for it is the disposition of divine providence, as we have seen, that lower spirits shall reach their perfection aided by the higher. Furthermore, because man possesses a certain measure of the light of intelligence, it is disposed by divine providence that brute animals, being altogether without intelligence, shall be subject to him. So it is said, 'Let us make man to our own image and likeness'—that is as far as his intellectual powers are concerned—'and let him have dominion over the fishes of the sea, and the fowls of the air, and the beasts and the whole earth' (*Genesis* I, 26).

Brute animals, though without intelligence, do arrive at a certain knowledge, and, in consequence, are placed by the order of divine providence over plants and all else that is without knowledge. So it is said: 'Behold I have given you every herb bearing seed upon the earth, and all trees that have in themselves seed of their own kind, to be your meat: and to all beasts of the earth' (*Genesis* I, 29–30).

As for those things which are altogether without knowledge one is superior to the other in so far as it has greater power to produce effects; for such things are not determined as to their values by divine providence but only as to their effects. Now since man has both intelligence and sense and also bodily strength, these, by the disposition

videntiae dispositionem, ad similitudinem ordinis qui in universo invenitur; nam virtus corporea subditur sensitivae et intellectivae virtuti, velut exequens earum imperium; ipsa vero sensitiva potentia intellectivae subditur, et sub eius imperio continetur.

Ex eadem ratione, et inter ipsos homines ordo invenitur; nam illi qui intellectu praeeminent naturaliter dominantur, illi vero qui sunt intellectu deficientes, corpore vero robusti, a natura videntur instituti ad serviendum, sicut Aristoteles dicit in sua *Politica*; cui etiam concordat sententia Salomonis, qui dicit: « *Qui stultus est serviet sapienti* » (*Prov.*, XI, 29); et dicitur: « *Provide de omni plebe viros sapientes et timentes Deum . . . qui iudicent populum omni tempore* » (*Exod.*, cap. XVIII, 21-22). Sicut autem, in operibus unius hominis, ex hoc inordinatio provenit quod intellectus sensualem virtutem sequitur, sensualis vero virtus propter corporis indispositionem trahitur ad corporis motum, ut in claudicantibus apparet, ita, et in regimine humano, inordinatio provenit ex eo quod non propter intellectus praeeminentiam aliquis praeest, sed vel robore corporali dominium sibi usurpat vel propter sensualem affectionem aliquis ad regendum praeficitur; quam quidem inordinationem nec Salomon tacet, qui dicit: « *Est malum quod vidi sub sole quasi per errorem egrediens a facie principis, positum stultum in dignitate sublimi* » (*Eccle.*, X, 5-6). Huiusmodi autem inordinatio divinam providentiam non excludit; provenit enim ex permissione divina, propter defectum inferiorum agentium, sicut et de aliis malis superius dictum est. Neque per huiusmodi inordinationem totaliter naturalis ordo pervertitur; nam stultorum dominium infirmum est, nisi sapientum consilio roboretur. Unde dicitur: « *Cogitationes consiliis roborantur, et gubernaculis tractanda sunt bella* » (*Prov.*, XX, 18); et « *Vir sapiens fortis est, et vir doctus robustus et validus, quia cum dispositione initur bellum, et erit salus ubi multa consilia sunt* » (*Prov.*, XXIV, 5-6). Et quia consilians regit eum qui consilium accipit, et quodammodo ei dominatur, dicitur quod « *servus sapiens dominabitur filiis stultis* » (*Prov.*, XVII, 2).

Patet ergo quod divina providentia omnibus rebus ordinem imponit, ut sic verum sit quod dicit Apostolus: « *Quae autem sunt, a Deo ordinata sunt* » (*Rom.* XIII, 1).

of divine providence, are subordinated to one another on the pattern of that order which is found throughout the universe. Bodily strength being subordinate to the sensitive and intellectual powers and ready to obey their commands, while the senses are subject to the intelligence and follow its dictates.

For the same reason there is an order to be found among men themselves; for men of outstanding intelligence naturally take command, while those who are less intelligent but of more robust physique, seem intended by nature to act as servants; as Aristotle points out in the *Politics*. Solomon also was of like opinion, for he said: 'Let the foolish serve the wise' (*Proverbs*, XI, 29); and again: 'Seek out from the people wise and God-fearing men who shall be judges over the people at all times' (*Exodus*, XVIII, 21–22). So, just as in the case of a man there is a lack of balance if his reason follows the dictates of his senses, or his sensible powers are affected by some bodily infirmity, as happens for instance in lameness, so also in human government. Lack of order arises from the fact that somebody is in control, not because of his superior intelligence, but because he has seized power by physical violence or has been set up to rule through ties of sensible affection. Nor does Solomon fail to remark upon such injustice, but says: 'There is an evil I have seen under the sun, as it were by an error proceeding from the face of the prince: a fool set in high dignity' (*Ecclesiastes*, X, 5, 6). Such lack of order is, however, not incompatible with divine providence. It comes about by divine permission, and because of defects in subordinate agents, as we have already pointed out in the case of other sorts of evil. Nor is the natural order wholly perverted in such cases: for the rule of the foolish must needs be weak if it be not aided by counsel from the wise. So it is said: 'Designs are strengthened by counsels; and wars are to be managed by governments' (*Proverbs*, XX, 18). And again: 'A wise man is strong: and a knowing man stout and valiant. Because war is managed by due ordering: and there shall be safety where there are many counsels' (*Proverbs*, XXIV, 5–6). And, because a counsellor rules whoever accepts his counsel, and, in a sense, commands him, it is said: 'The wise servant shall rule over foolish children' (*Proverbs*, XVII, 2).

So it is clear that divine providence imposes an order on all things and manifests the truth of the Apostle's saying: 'All things that are, are set in order by God' (*Romans*, XIII, 1).

SUMMA THEOLOGICA

Quaestio XCII.—DE PRODUCTIONE MULIERIS.

ART. 1.—*Utrum mulier debuerit produci in prima rerum productione.*

Ad secundum dicendum quod duplex est subiectio. Una servilis, secundum quam praesidens utitur subiecto ad sui ipsius utilitatem; et talis subiectio introducta est post peccatum. Est autem alia subiectio oeconomica vel civilis, secundum quam praesidens utitur subiectis ad eorum utilitatem et bonum. Et ista subiectio fuisset etiam ante peccatum: defuisset enim bonum ordinis in humana multitudine, si quidam per alios sapientiores gubernati non fuissent. Et sic, ex tali subiectione naturaliter foemina subiecta est viro: quia naturaliter in homine magis abundat discretio rationis. Nec inaequalitas hominum excluditur per innocentiae statum, ut infra dicetur.

Quaestio XCVI.—DE DOMINIO, QUOD HOMINI IN STATU INNOCENTIAE COMPETEBAT.

ART. 3.—*Utrum homines in statu innocentiae fuissent aequales.*

Respondeo dicendum quod necesse est dicere aliquam disparitatem in primo statu fuisse, ad minus quantum ad sexum: quia sine diversitate sexus, generatio non fuisset. Similiter etiam quantum ad aetatem: sic enim quidam ex aliis nascebantur; nec illi qui miscebantur, steriles erant. Sed et secundum animam diversitas fuisset, et quantum ad iustitiam et quantum ad scientiam. Non enim ex necessitate homo operabatur, sed per liberum arbitrium; ex quo homo habet quod possit magis et minus animum applicare ad aliquid faciendum vel volendum vel cognoscendum. Unde quidam magis profecissent in iustitia et scientia quam alii. Ex parte etiam corporis, poterat esse disparitas. Non enim erat exemptum corpus humanum totaliter a legibus naturae, quin ex exterioribus agentibus aliquod commodum aut auxilium reciperet magis et minus: cum etiam et cibis eorum vita sustentaretur. Et sic nihil prohibet dicere quin secundum diversam dispositionem aeris et diversum situm stellarum, aliqui robustiores

SUMMA THEOLOGICA

First Part

1. *POLITICAL LIFE NATURAL TO MAN*

Contrast between the relationship of slavery and the political relationship. (Qu. 92, Art. 1, ad 2um.)

There are two forms of subjection. The first is servile; in which case the master makes use of his servant for his own convenience: and such subjection began as a consequence of sin. Then there is another form of subjection in virtue of which the master rules those who are subject to him for their own good and benefit. Such subjection already existed before sin: for it would argue a lack of reasonable order in human society if it were not regulated by those who are more wise. It is according to this type of subjection that woman is naturally subject to man: for man is more gifted by nature with powers of reasonable discretion than woman. Nor did the state of innocence exclude a certain inequality, even among men, as we shall later see.

Natural inequalities among men. (Qu. 96, Art. 3, concl.)

We must admit that there had to be some disparity among men, even before the fall, at least with respect to the sexes. For without the sexes there could have been no procreation. Similarly with regard to age; as children were born of one generation, and they, marrying, produced further children. There would have been a difference of spiritual capacities also, with respect both to justice and to knowledge. For man would not have acted from blind necessity, but from free choice, being thus able to apply his powers to a greater or less degree in acting, willing and knowing. Thus some would have made greater progress in righteousness and in knowledge than others. Equally, there would have been a certain difference of bodily powers; for the human body was not altogether exempt from the laws of nature, but was capable of receiving greater or less assistance from natural agencies. Even in the state of innocence food was necessary for the sustenance of the human frame. So we may well say that according to the different states of the ether, and of different portions of the stars,

103

corpore generarentur, quam alii, et maiores et pulchriores et melius complexionati. Ita tamen quod in illis qui excederentur, nullus esset defectus, sive peccatum; sive circa animam sive circa corpus.

ART. 4.—*Utrum homo in statu innocentiae homini dominabatur.*

Respondeo dicendum, quod dominium accipitur dupliciter. Uno modo secundum quod opponitur servituti: Et sic dominus dicitur, cui aliquis subditur ut servus. Alio modo accipitur dominium secundum quod communiter refertur ad subiectum qualitercumque: Et sic etiam ille qui habet officium gubernandi et dirigendi liberos, dominus dici potest. Primo ergo modo accepto dominio, in statu innocentiae homo homini non dominaretur. Sed secundo modo accepto dominio, in statu innocentiae, homo homini dominari potuisset. Cuius ratio est, quia servus in hoc differt a libero, quod « *liber est causa sui* », ut dicitur in princ. *Metaphysic.* Servus autem ordinatur ad alium. Tunc ergo aliquis dominatur alicui ut servo, quando eum cui dominatur, ad propriam utilitatem sui, scilicet dominantis, refert. Et quia unicuique est appetibile proprium bonum, et per consequens contristabile est unicuique quod illud bonum, quod deberet esse suum, cedat alteri tantum; ideo tale dominium non potest esse sine poena subiectorum, propter quod in statu innocentiae non fuisset tale dominium hominis ad hominem. Tunc vero dominatur aliquis alteri ut libero, quando dirigit ipsum ad proprium bonum eius qui dirigitur, vel ad bonum commune. Et tale dominium hominis ad hominem, in statu innocentiae fuisset propter duo. Primo quidem, quia homo naturaliter est animal sociale; unde homines in statu innocentiae socialiter vixissent. Socialis autem vita multorum esse non posset, nisi aliquis praesideret, qui ad bonum commune intenderet. Multi enim per se intendunt ad multa, unus vero ad unum. Et ideo Philosophus dicit in princ. *Politic.*: quod « *Quandocumque multa ordinantur ad unum, semper invenitur unum ut principale et dirigens* ». Secundo, quia si unus homo habuisset super alium supereminentiam scientiae et iustitiae, inconveniens fuisset, nisi hoc exequeretur in utilitatem aliorum, secundum quod dicitur I *Petr.* 4: « *Unusquisque gratiam, quam accepit, in alterutrum illam administrantes* ». Unde Augustinus dicit XIX *De Civit. Dei*, cap. 14, quod

some would have been born with more powerful bodies, some taller, or more beautiful and better favoured. This, however, would not constitute any defect or shortcoming in those less favoured, either in body or in soul.

Political life is natural to man.   (Qu. 96, Art 4.)

Dominion is to be understood in two senses. In the first it is contrasted with servitude. So a master is one to whom another is subject as a slave. In the second sense it is to be understood in opposition to any form of subjection. In this sense one whose office it is to govern and control free men may also be called a lord. The first sort of dominion which is servitude did not exist between man and man in the state of innocence. Understood in the second way, however, even in the state of innocence, some men would have exercised control over others. The reason for this is that a slave differs from a free man in that the latter is 'a free agent of his own actions' as is said in the *Metaphysics*. A slave, however, is completely under the control of another. Thus a person rules another as a slave when the latter is ordered about solely for the benefit of the ruler. But since it is natural for every one to find pleasure in their own satisfaction, such satisfaction cannot be surrendered to another without suffering loss. Such dominion, then, cannot occur without the accompanying penalties of subjection; and for this reason could not have existed between man and man in the state of innocence.

The control of one over another who remains free, can take place when the former directs the latter to his own good or to the common good. And such dominion would have been found between man and man in the state of innocence for two reasons. First, because man is naturally a social animal; and in consequence men would have lived in society, even in the state of innocence. Now there could be no social life for many persons living together unless one of their number were set in authority to care for the common good. Many individuals are, as individuals, interested in a variety of ends. One person is interested in one end. So the Philosopher says (in the beginning of the *Politics*): 'Whenever a plurality is directed to one object there is always to be found one in authority, giving direction.' Secondly, if there were one man more wise and righteous than the rest, it would have been wrong if such gifts were not exercised on behalf of the rest; as is said in I *Peter*, 4: 'Every one using the grace he has received for the benefit of his fellows.' So Augustine says (XIX *De Civit. Dei*, 14): 'The just

« *iusti non dominandi cupiditate imperant, sed officio consulendi* ». Et cap. 15:
« *Hoc naturalis ordo praescribit: ita Deus hominem condidit* ». Et per hoc
patet responsio ad omnia obiecta, quae procedunt de primo modo
dominii.

Quaestio CIII.—DE GUBERNATIONE RERUM IN COMMUNI.

ART. 3.—*Utrum mundus gubernetur ab uno.*

Respondeo dicendum quod necesse est dicere quod mundus ab uno
gubernetur. Cum enim finis gubernationis mundi sit quod est essen-
tialiter bonum, quod est optimum, necesse est, quod mundi gubernatio
sit optima. Optima autem gubernatio est quae fit per unum. Cuius
ratio est, quia gubernatio nihil aliud est quam directio gubernatorum
ad finem, qui est aliquod bonum: unitas autem pertinet ad rationem
bonitatis, ut Boëtius probat in III *de Consol.* (Prosa XI) per hoc quod
sicut omnia desiderant bonum, ita desiderant unitatem, sine qua esse
non possunt; nam « *unumquodque intantum est, inquantum unum est* ».
Unde videmus quod res repugnant suae divisioni quantum possunt,
et quod dissolutio uniuscuiusque rei provenit ex defectu illius rei. Et
ideo id, ad quod tendit intentio multitudinem gubernantis, est unitas
sive pax: unitatis autem causa per se est unum. Manifestum est enim
quod plures multa unire et concordare non possunt, nisi ipsi aliquo
modo uniantur. Illud autem quod est per se unum, potest convenien-
tius et melius esse causa unitatis quam multi uniti. Unde multitudo
melius gubernatur per unum quam per plures. Relinquitur ergo,
quod gubernatio mundi, quae est optima, sit ab uno gubernante. Et
hoc est quod Philosophus dicit in XII *Metaphys.*: « *Entia nolunt disponi
male, nec bonum pluralitas principatuum; unus ergo Princeps* ».

rule not through desire of domination, but because it is their duty to give counsel'; and (Chapter 15) 'This is ordained by the natural order, for thus did God create man.' And from these considerations follow the reply to all objections concerning the first form of dominion.

2. MONARCHY AND THE DIVINE GOVERNMENT OF THE WORLD. (Qu. 103, Art. 3.)

It must be admitted that the universe is governed by one person. For the object of the government of the universe is what is essentially good, or the best result, so that the government also must be the best. But the best form of government is that which is carried out by one person. The reason for this is that government is the same thing as the direction of the governed to some end, that is to some good: but unity enters into the nature of goodness, as Boethius proves (III, *De Consol.* XI), showing that whatever desires the good does so in so far as it seeks unity, without which it could not even exist; for 'whatever is, exists in so far as it is a unity.' So also we see that things avoid disintegration as far as possible, and that the dissolution of a thing comes about because of some defect in it. So the first object of whoever rules a multitude is unity, or peace: but the cause of unity must be that which is in itself one. It is in fact evident that a number of individuals could not unite and bring others to harmony unless they were themselves in some way united. But what is a natural unity can be more easily a cause of unity than that which is artificially united. So a multitude can be better ruled by one than by several. It follows, then, that the government of the universe, which is the best, is the work of one ruler. This is what the Philosopher said (XII, *Metaphysics*): 'Nature abhors disorder and there is no goodness in a multiplicity of rulers. So there is one Sovereign.'

PRIMA SECUNDAE PARTIS

Quaestio XXI.—DE CONSEQUENTIBUS ACTUS HUMANOS RATIONE BONI-
TATIS VEL MALITIAE.

ART. 4.—*Utrum actus humanus, in quantum est bonus vel malus, habeat
rationem meriti vel demeriti apud Deum.*

Ad tertium dicendum, quod homo non ordinatur ad communitatem
politicam secundum se totum, et secundum omnia sua: et ideo non
oportet quod quilibet actus eius sit meritorius vel demeritorius per
ordinem ad communitatem politicam: sed totum quod homo est,
et quod potest et habet, ordinandum est ad Deum: et ideo omnis actus
hominis bonus, vel malus, habet rationem meriti vel demeriti apud
Deum, quantum est ex ipsa ratione actus.

Quaestio LXXII.—DE PECCATORUM DISTINCTIONE.

ART. 4.—*Utrum peccatum convenienter distinguatur in peccatum in Deum,
in seipsum, et in proximum.*

Respondeo dicendum quod . . . triplex autem ordo in homine debet
esse. Unus quidem secundum comparationem ad regulam rationis,
prout scilicet omnes actiones et passiones nostrae debent secundum
regulam rationis commensurari. Alius autem ordo est per comparationem ad regulam divinae legis, per quam homo in omnibus dirigi
debet. Et siquidem homo naturaliter esset animal solitarium, hic duplex
ordo sufficeret; sed quia homo est naturaliter animal politicum et
sociale, ut probatur in I *Polit.* (cap. 2), ideo necesse est, quod sit tertius
ordo, quo homo ordinetur ad alios homines quibus convivere debet.

Quaestio XC.—DE ESSENTIA LEGIS.

ART. 1.—*Utrum lex sit aliquid rationis.*

Respondeo dicendum quod lex quaedam regula est et mensura
actuum, secundum quam inducitur aliquis ad agendum, vel ab agendo
retrahitur: dicitur enim lex a « ligando », quia obligat ad agendum.
Regula autem et mensura humanorum actuum est ratio, quae est
primum principium actuum humanorum, ut ex praedictis patet:

PRIMA SECUNDAE

3. VALUE AND SIGNIFICANCE OF THE POLITICAL ORDER.

The sense in which the State has the value of an end. (Qu. 21, Art. 4.)

Not all that a man has or is, is subject to political obligation: hence it is not necessary that all of his actions be considered worthy of praise or blame with respect to the political community. But all that a man is, and all that he has or can be, must bear a certain relationship to God. Hence every human act, be it good or bad, so far as it proceeds from reason is meritorious or demeritorious before God.

The Political Order compared with the Divine and Natural Order. (Qu. 72, Art. 4.)

There is a threefold order to be found in man. The first is that which derives from the rule of reason: in so far as all our actions and experiences should be commensurate with the guidance of reason. The second arises from comparison with the rule of divine law, which should be our guide in all things. And if man were actually a solitary animal, this double order would suffice: but because man is naturally a social and political animal, as is proved in I. *Politics,* chap. 2, it is necessary that there should be a third order, regulating the conduct of man to his fellows with whom he has to live.

4. LAW IN GENERAL. (Qu. 90.)

The Nature of Law. (Art. 1, concl.)

Law is a rule or measure of action in virtue of which one is led to perform certain actions and restrained from the performance of others. The term 'law' derives [etymologically] from 'binding,' because by it one is bound to a certain course of action. But the rule and measure of human action is reason, which is the first principle of human action: this is clear from what we have said elsewhere. It is

rationis enim est ordinare ad finem, qui est principium primum in
agendis, secundum Philosophum.

Ad tertium dicendum quod ratio habet vim movendi a voluntate,
ut supra dictum est: ex hoc enim quod aliquis vult finem, ratio imperat de his quae sunt ad finem. Sed voluntas de his quae imperantur,
ad hoc quod legis rationem habeat, oportet quod sit aliqua ratione
regulata. Et hoc modo intelligitur quod voluntas principis habet vigorem legis: alioquin voluntas principis magis esset iniquitas quam lex.

ART. 2.—*Utrum lex ordinetur semper ad bonum commune.*

(*Concl.*) Rursus, cum omnis pars ordinetur ad totum sicut imperfec-
tum ad perfectum; unus autem homo est pars communitatis perfectae:
necesse est quod lex proprie respiciat ordinem ad felicitatem communem. Unde et Philosophus, in praemissa definitione legalium,
mentionem facit et de felicitate et communione politica. Dicit enim, in
V *Ethic.* (cap. 1), quod « *legalia iusta dicimus factiva et conservativa
felicitatis et particularum ipsius, politica communicatione* »: perfecta enim
communitas civitas est, ut dicitur in I *Polit.* (cap. 1).

ART. 3.—*Utrum ratio cuiuslibet sit factiva legis.*

Respondeo dicendum quod lex proprie, primo et principaliter
respicit ordinem ad bonum commune. Ordinare autem aliquid in
bonum commune est vel totius multitudinis, vel alicuius gerentis vicem
totius multitudinis. Et ideo condere legem vel pertinet ad totam multitudinem, vel pertinet ad personam publicam quae totius multitudinis
curam habet. Quia et in omnibus aliis ordinare in finem est eius cuius
est proprius ille finis.

Ad secundum dicendum quod persona privata non potest inducere
efficaciter ad virtutem. Potest enim solum monere, sed si sua monitio
non recipiatur, non habet vim coactivam; quam debet habere lex, ad

reason which directs action to its appropriate end; and this, according to the philosopher, is the first principle of all activity.

Reason and Will in Law. (Ibid. ad 3um.)

Reason has power to move to action from the will, as we have shown already: for reason enjoins all that is necessary to some end, in virtue of the fact that that end is desired. But will, if it is to have the authority of law, must be regulated by reason when it commands. It is in this sense that we should understand the saying that the will of the prince has the power of law.[1] In any other sense the will of the prince becomes an evil rather than law.

The Object of the Law is the Common Good. (Ibid. Art. 2, concl.)

Since every part bears the same relation to its whole as the imperfect to the perfect, and since one man is a part of that perfect whole which is the community, it follows that the law must have as its proper object the well-being of the whole community. So the Philosopher, in his definition of what pertains to law, makes mention both of happiness and of political union. He says (*Ethics* V, chap. 1): 'We call that legal and just which makes for and preserves the well-being of the community through common political action': and the perfect community is the city, as is shown in the first book of the *Politics* (chap. 1).

Who has the right to promulgate Law. (Ibid. Art. 3, concl.)

Law, strictly understood, has as its first and principal object the ordering of the common good. But to order affairs to the common good is the task either of the whole community or of some one person who represents it. Thus the promulgation of law is the business either of the whole community or of that political person whose duty is the care of the common good. Here as in every other case it is the one who decrees the end who also decrees the means thereto.

(Ibid. ad 2um.)

A private person has no authority to compel right living. He may only advise; but if his advice is not accepted he has no power of compulsion. But law, to be effective in promoting right living must

---

[1] The reference is to the text in the Roman law: '*Quod principi placuit legis habet vigorem.*' (*Dig.*, I, iv, 1, Ulpianus.)

hoc quod efficaciter inducat ad virtutem, ut Philosophus dicit, in X
Ethic. (cap. 9). Hanc autem virtutem coactivam habet multitudo vel
persona publica, ad quam pertinet poenas infligere, ut infra dicetur.
Ed ideo solius eius est leges facere.

Ad tertium dicendum quod, sicut homo est pars domus, ita domus
est pars civitatis: civitas autem est communitas perfecta, ut dicitur in
I. *Polit.* Et ideo sicut bonum unius hominis non est ultimus finis, sed
ordinatur ad commune bonum, ita etiam et bonum unius domus
ordinatur ad bonum unius civitatis, quae est communitas perfecta.
Unde ille qui gubernat aliquam familiam, potest quidem facere aliqua
praecepta vel statuta; non tamen quae proprie habeant rationem legis.

Art. 4.—*Utrum promulgatio sit de ratione legis.*

(*Concl.*) Ex . . . praedictis potest colligi definitio legis, quae nihil
est aliud quam quaedam rationis ordinatio ad bonum commune, ab
eo qui curam communitatis habet, promulgata.

Quaestio XCI.—De diversitate legum.

Art. 1.—*Utrum sit aliqua lex aeterna.*

Respondeo dicendum quod, sicut supra dictum est, nihil est aliud
lex quam quoddam dictamen practicae rationis « in principe » qui
gubernat aliquam communitatem perfectam. Manifestum est autem,
supposito quod mundus divina providentia regatur, ut in Primo
habitum est, quod tota communitas universi gubernatur ratione
divina. Et ideo ipsa ratio gubernationis rerum in Deo sicut in principe
universitatis existens, legis habet rationem . . . Huiusmodi legem
oportet dicere aeternam.

Art. 2.—*Utrum sit in nobis aliqua lex naturalis.*

(*Concl.*) Cum omnia, quae divinae providentiae subduntur, a lege
aeterna regulentur et mensurentur, ut ex dictis patet; manifestum est

have such compelling force; as the Philosopher says (X *Ethics*, chap.9). But the power of compulsion belongs either to the community as a whole, or to its official representative whose duty it is to inflict penalties, as we shall see later. He alone, therefore, has the right to make laws.

(Ibid., ad 3um.)

Just as one man is a member of a family, so a household forms part of a city: but a city is a perfect community, as is shown in the first book of the *Politics*. Similarly, as the well-being of one man is not a final end, but is subordinate to the common good, so also the well-being of any household must be subordinate to the interests of the city, which is a perfect community. So the head of a family may make certain rules and regulations, but not such as have, properly speaking, the force of law.

Definition of Law. (Ibid. Art. 4, concl.)

From the foregoing we may gather the correct definition of law. It is nothing else than a rational ordering of things which concern the common good; promulgated by whoever is charged with the care of the community.

5. *THE VARIOUS TYPES OF LAW*. (Qu. 91.)

The Eternal Law. (Art. 1, concl.)

As we have said above, law is nothing else but a certain dictate of the practical reason 'in the prince' who rules a perfect community. It is clear, however, supposing the world to be governed by divine providence as we demonstrated in the First Part,[1] that the whole community of the Universe is governed by the divine reason. Thus the rational guidance of created things on the part of God, as the Prince of the universe, has the quality of law. . . . This we can call the eternal law.

The Natural Law. (Art. 2, concl.)

Since all things which are subject to divine providence are measured and regulated by the eternal law—as we have already shown—it is

[1] Ia: q. XXII, Art. 1, 2.

H

quod omnia participant aliqualiter legem aeternam, inquantum scilicet
ex impressione eius habent inclinationes in proprios actus et fines. Inter
cetera autem rationalis creatura excellentiori quodam modo divinae
providentiae subiacet, inquantum et ipsa fit providentiae particeps,
sibi ipsi et aliis providens. Unde et in ipsa participatur ratio aeterna,
per quam habet naturalem inclinationem ad debitum actum et finem.
Et talis participatio legis aeternae in rationali creatura lex naturalis
dicitur. Unde cum Psalmista dixisset (*Psalm.* IV, 6) : « *Sacrificate sacrificium iustitiae* », quasi quibusdam quaerentibus quae sunt iustitiae
opera, subiungit : « *Multi dicunt, Quis ostendit nobis bona?* », cui quaestioni respondens, dicit : « *Signatum est super nos lumen vultus tui, Domine* » :
quasi lumen naturalis rationis, quo discernimus quid sit bonum et
malum, quod pertinet ad naturalem legem, nihil aliud sit quam im-
pressio divini luminis in nobis. Unde patet quod lex naturalis nihil
aliud est quam participatio legis aeternae in rationali creatura.

ART. 3.—*Utrum sit aliqua lex humana.*

(*Concl.*) Dicendum est quod, sicut in ratione speculativa ex principiis indemonstrabilibus naturaliter cognitis producuntur conclusiones
diversarum scientiarum, quarum cognitio non est nobis naturaliter
indita, sed per industriam rationis inventa ; ita etiam ex praeceptis legis
naturalis, quasi ex quibusdam principiis communibus et indemonstrabilibus, necesse est quod ratio humana procedat ad aliqua magis
particulariter disponenda. Et istae particulares dispositiones adinventae
secundum rationem humanam, dicuntur leges humanae, servatis aliis
conditionibus quae pertinent ad rationem legis, ut supra dictum est.
Unde et Tullius dicit, in sua *De Invent. Rhetor.* (II, c. 53), quod « *initium
iuris est a natura profectum; deinde quaedam in consuetudinem ex utilitate
rationis venerunt; postea res et a natura profectas et a consuetudine probatas
legum metus et religio sanxit* ».

ART. 4.—*Utrum fuerit necessarium esse aliquam legem divinam*

(*Concl.*) Dicendum quod praeter legem naturalem et legem humanam necessarium fuit ad directionem humanae vitae habere legem
divinam. Et hoc propter quatuor rationes. Primo quidem quia per

clear that all things participate to some degree in the eternal law; in so far as they derive from it certain inclinations to those actions and aims which are proper to them. But, of all others, rational creatures are subject to divine providence in a very special way; being themselves made participators in providence itself, in that they control their own actions and the actions of others. So they have a certain share in the divine reason itself, deriving therefrom a natural inclination to such actions and ends as are fitting. This participation in the eternal law by rational creatures is called the natural law. Thus when the Psalmist said (*Psalm* IV, 6): 'Offer up the sacrifice of justice,' he added, as though being asked the question, what is the sacrifice of justice, 'Many say, who sheweth us good things?', and then replied, saying: 'The light of Thy countenance, O Lord, is signed upon us.' As though the light of natural reason, by which we discern good from evil, and which is the natural law, were nothing else than the impression of the divine light in us. So it is clear that the natural law is nothing else than the participation of the eternal law in rational creatures.

Human Law. (Art. 3, concl.)

Just as in speculative reason we proceed from indemonstrable principles, naturally known, to the conclusions of the various sciences, such conclusions not being innate but arrived at by the use of reason; so also the human reason has to proceed from the precepts of the natural law, as though from certain common and indemonstrable principles, to other more particular dispositions. And such particular dispositions, arrived at by an effort of reason, are called human laws: provided that the other conditions necessary to all law, which we have already noted, are observed. So Cicero says (*De Invent. Rhetor.* II, 53): 'Law springs in its first beginnings from nature: then such standards as are judged to be useful become established by custom: finally reverence and holiness add their sanction to what springs from nature and is established by custom.'

The Necessity for a Divine Law. (Art. 4, concl.)

In addition to natural law and to human law there had of necessity to be also a divine law to direct human life: and this for four reasons. In the first place because it is by law that man is directed in his actions

legem dirigitur homo ad actus proprios in ordine ad ultimum finem. Et si quidem homo ordinaretur tantum ad finem qui non excederet proportionem naturalis facultatis hominis, non oporteret quod homo haberet aliquid directivum ex parte rationis supra legem naturalem et legem humanitus positam, quae ab ea derivatur. Sed quia homo ordinatur ad finem beatitudinis aeternae quae excedit proportionem naturalis facultatis humanae, ut supra habitum est, ideo necessarium fuit ut supra legem naturalem et humanam, dirigeretur etiam ad suum finem lege divinitus data. — Secundo, quia propter incertitudinem humani iudicii, praecipue de rebus contingentibus et particularibus, contingit de actibus humanis diversorum esse diversa iudicia, ex quibus etiam diversae et contrariae leges procedunt. Ut ergo homo absque omni dubitatione scire possit quid ei sit agendum et quid vitandum, necessarium fuit ut in actibus propriis dirigeretur per legem divinitus datam, de qua constat quod non potest errare. — Tertio, quia de his potest homo legem facere, de quibus potest iudicare. Iudicium autem hominis esse non potest de interioribus motibus, qui latent, sed solum de exterioribus actibus, qui apparent. Et tamen ad perfectionem virtutis requiritur quod in utrisque actibus homo rectus existat. Et ideo lex humana non potuit cohibere et ordinare sufficienter interiores actus, sed necessarium fuit quod ad hoc superveniret lex divina. — Quarto quia, sicut Augustinus dicit in I *De Lib. Arb.* lex humana non potest omnia quae male fiunt, punire vel prohibere, quia dum auferre vellet omnia mala, sequeretur quod etiam multa bona tollerentur, et impediretur utilitas boni communis, quod est necessarium ad conversationem humanam. Ut ergo nullum malum improhibitum et impunitum remaneat, necessarium fuit supervenire legem divinam, per quam omnia peccata prohibentur.

Quaestio XCII. De effectibus legis.

Art. 1.—*Utrum effectus legis sit facere homines bonos.*

(*Concl.*) Manifestum est quod hoc sit proprium legis, inducere subiectos ad propriam ipsorum virtutem. Cum igitur virtus sit « *quae bonum facit habentem* », sequitur quod proprius effectus legis sit bonos facere eos quibus datur, vel simpliciter vel secundum quid. Si enim intentio ferentis legem tendat in verum bonum, quod est bonum commune secundum iustitiam divinam regulatum, sequitur quod per

with respect to his final end. If, therefore, man were destined to an end which was no more than proportionate to his natural faculties, there would be no need for him to have any directive on the side of reason above the natural law and humanly enacted law which is derived from it. But because man is destined to an end of eternal blessedness, and this exceeds what is proportionate to natural human faculties as we have already shown, it was necessary that he should be directed to this end not merely by natural and human law, but also by a divinely given law.—Secondly: because of the uncertainty of human judgement, particularly in matters that are contingent and specific, it is often the case that very differing judgements are passed by various people on human activities; and from these there proceed different, and even contrary, laws. In order, therefore, that man should know without any doubt what he is to do and what to avoid, it was necessary that his actions should be directed by a divinely given law, which is known to be incapable of error.—Thirdly: because laws are enacted in respect of what is capable of being judged. But the judgement of man cannot reach to the hidden interior actions of the soul, it can only be about external activities which are apparent. Nevertheless, the perfection of virtue requires that a man should be upright in both classes of actions. Human law being thus insufficient to order and regulate interior actions, it was necessary that for this purpose there should also be a divine law.—Fourthly: because, as Augustine says (I De Lib. Arb.), human law can neither punish nor even prohibit all that is evilly done. For in trying to prevent all that is evil it would render impossible also much that is good; and thus would impede much that is useful to the common welfare and therefore necessary to human intercourse. In order, therefore, that no evil should go unforbidden and unpunished it was necessary that there should be a divine law which would prohibit all manner of sin.

6. THE EFFECTS OF LAW. (Qu. 92.)

The Moral Object of Law. (Art. 1, concl.)

It is clear that the true object of law is to induce those subject to it to seek their own virtue. And since virtue is 'that which makes its possessor good,' it follows that the proper effect of law is the welfare of those for whom it is promulgated: either absolutely or in some certain respect. If the intention of the law-giver is directed to that which is truly good, that is to the common good regulated by divine

legem homines fiant simpliciter boni. Si vero intentio legislatoris
feratur ad id quod non est bonum simpliciter, sed utile vel delectabile
sibi vel repugnans iustitiae divinae; tunc lex non facit homines bonos
simpliciter, sed secundum quid, scilicet in ordine ad tale regimen.
Sic autem bonum invenitur etiam in per se malis: sicut aliquis dicitur
bonus latro, quia operatur accomode ad finem.

Ad tertium dicendum quod bonitas cuiuslibet partis consideratur
in proportione ad suum totum: unde et Augustinus dicit, in III *Confess.*
(cap. 8), quod, « *turpis est omnis pars quae suo toto non congruit* ». Cum
igitur quilibet homo sit pars civitatis, impossibile est quod aliquis
homo sit bonus, nisi sit bene proportionatus bono communi: nec totum
potest bene consistere nisi ex partibus sibi proportionatis. Unde impossibile est quod bonum commune civitatis bene se habeat, nisi cives
sint virtuosi, ad minus illi quibus convenit principari. Sufficit autem,
quantum ad bonum communitatis, quod alii intantum sint virtuosi
quod principum mandatis obediant. Et ideo Philosophus dicit, in III
Polit. (cap. 2), quod « *eadem est virtus principis et boni viri; non autem
eadem est virtus cuiuscumque civis et boni viri* ».

Ad quartum dicendum quod lex tyrannica, cum non sit secundum
rationem, non est simpliciter lex, sed magis est quaedam perversitas
legis. Et tamen inquantum habet aliquid de ratione legis, intendit ad
hoc quod cives sint boni. Non enim habet de ratione legis nisi secundum hoc quod est dictamen alicuius praesidentis in subditis et ad hoc
tendit ut subditi legi sint bene obedientes; quod est eos esse bonos,
non simpliciter, sed in ordine ad tale regimen.

Quaestio XCIII.—DE LEGE AETERNA.

ART. 1.—*Utrum lex aeterna sit summa ratio in Deo existens.*

(*Concl.*) Dicendum quod sicut in quolibet artifice praeexistit ratio
eorum quae constituuntur per artem, ita etiam in quolibet gubernante

justice, it will follow that man will, by such a law, be made unconditionally good. If on the other hand the intention of the law-giver is
directed, not to that which is absolutely good, but merely to what is
useful—in that it is pleasurable to himself or contrary to divine justice—
then such a law does not make men good unconditionally, but only
in a certain respect; namely, in so far as it has reference to some particular political regime. In this sense good is to be found even in those
things which are intrinsically evil: as when a man is termed a good thief,
because he is expert in attaining the object he sets before himself.

(Ibid. ad 3um.)

The goodness of any part is to be considered with reference to the
whole of which it forms a part: so Augustine says (III *Confess.*, 8):
'All parts are base which are not fittingly adapted to their whole.'
So, all men being a part of the city, they cannot be truly good
unless they adapt themselves to the common good. Nor can the whole
be well constituted if its parts be not properly adapted to it. So it is
impossible for the welfare of the community to be in a healthy state
unless the citizens are virtuous: or at least such of them as are called
to take up the direction of affairs. It would be sufficient for the common
well-being if the rest were virtuous to the extent of obeying the
commands of the ruler. So the Philosopher says (III *Polit.*, 2): 'A
ruler must have the virtue of a truly upright man: but not every
citizen is bound to reach a similar degree of uprightness.'

(Ibid. ad 4um.)

Tyrannical law, not being according to reason, is not law at all
in the true and strict sense, but is rather a perversion of law. It does,
however, assume the nature of law to the extent that it provides for
the well-being of the citizens. Thus it bears relationship to law in so
far as it is the dictate to his subjects of some one in authority; and to
the extent that its object is the full obedience of those subjects to the
law. For them such obedience is good, not unconditionally, but with
respect to the particular regime under which they live.

7. *THE ETERNAL LAW.* (Qu. 93.)

Its Derivation from the Divine Wisdom. (Art. 1, concl.)

Just as in the mind of every artist there already exists the idea of
what he will create by his art, so in the mind of every ruler there

oportet quod praeexistat ratio ordinis eorum quae agenda sunt per eos qui gubernationi subduntur. Et sicut ratio rerum fiendarum per artem vocatur ars vel exemplar rerum artificiatarum, ita etiam ratio gubernantis actus subditorum, rationem legis obtinet, servatis aliis quae supra esse diximus de legis ratione. Deus autem per suam sapientiam conditor est universarum rerum, ad quas comparatur sicut artifex ad artificiata ut in Primo habitum est. Est etiam gubernator omnium actuum et motionum quae inveniuntur in singulis creaturis, ut etiam in Primo habitum est. Unde sicut ratio divinae sapientiae inquantum per eam cuncta sunt creata, rationem habet artis vel exemplaris vel ideae; ita ratio divinae sapientiae moventis omnia ad debitum finem, obtinet rationem legis. Et secundum hoc, lex aeterna nihil aliud est quam ratio divinae sapientiae, secundum quod est directiva omnium actuum et motionum.

ART. 3.—*Utrum omnis lex a lege aeterna derivetur.*

(*Concl.*) . . . In omnibus gubernantibus idem videmus, quod ratio gubernationis a primo gubernante ad secundos derivatur; sicut ratio eorum quae sunt agenda in civitate, derivatur a rege per praeceptum in inferiores administratores . . . Cum ergo lex aeterna sit ratio gubernationis in supremo gubernante, necesse est quod omnes rationes gubernationis quae sunt in inferioribus gubernantibus, a lege aeterna deriventur. Huiusmodi autem rationes inferiorum gubernantium sunt quaecumque aliae leges praeter aeternam. Unde omnes leges, inquantum participant de ratione recta, intantum derivantur a lege aeterna. Et propter hoc Augustinus dicit in I *De Lib. Arb.*, quod « *in temporali lege nihil est iustum ac legitimum, quod non ex lege aeterna homines sibi derivaverunt* ».

Ad secundum dicendum quod lex humana intantum habet rationem legis, inquantum est secundum rationem rectam; et secundum hoc manifestum est quod a lege aeterna derivatur. Inquantum vero a ratione recedit, sic dicitur lex iniqua; et sic non habet rationem legis, sed magis violentiae cuiusdam. Et tamen in ipsa lege iniqua inquantum servatur aliquid de similitudine legis propter ordinem potestatis eius qui legem facit, secundum hoc etiam derivatur a lege aeterna; « *omnis enim potestas a Domino Deo est* », ut dicitur *Rom.* XIII.

must already exist an ideal of order with respect to what shall be done by those subject to his rule. And just as the ideal of those things that have yet to be produced by any art is known as the exemplar, or actual art of the things so to be produced, the ideal in the mind of the ruler who governs the actions of those subject to him has the quality of law—provided that the conditions we have already mentioned above are also present. Now God, in His wisdom, is the creator of all things, and may be compared to them as the artist is compared to the product of his art; as we have shown in Part I. Moreover he governs all actions and movements of each individual creature, as we also pointed out. So, as the ideal of divine wisdom, in so far as all things are created by it, has the quality of an exemplar or art or idea, so also the ideal of divine wisdom considered as moving all things to their appropriate end has the quality of law. Accordingly, the eternal law is nothing other than the ideal of divine wisdom considered as directing all actions and movements.

All Law derives ultimately from the Eternal Law. (Ibid. Art. 3, concl.)

In every case of ruling we see that the design of government is passed from the head of the government to his subordinate governors; just as the scheme of what shall be done in a city derives from the king to his subordinate ministers by statute; or again, in artistic construction, the plan of what is to be made is passed from the architect to the subordinate operators. Since, then, the eternal law is the plan of government in the supreme governor, all schemes of government in those who direct as subordinates must derive from the eternal law. Consequently, all laws, so far as they accord with right reason, derive from the eternal law. For this reason Augustine says (I *De Lib. Arb.*): 'In human law nothing is just or legitimate if it has not been derived by men from the eternal law.'

(Ibid. ad 2um.)

Human law has the quality of law only in so far as it proceeds according to right reason: and in this respect it is clear that it derives from the eternal law. In so far as it deviates from reason it is called an unjust law, and has the quality not of law but of violence. Nevertheless, even an unjust law, to the extent that it retains the appearance of law through its relationship to the authority of the lawgiver, derives in this respect from the eternal law. 'For all power is from the Lord God' (*Rom.* XIII, 1).

Quaestio XCIV.—DE LEGE NATURALI.

ART. 2.—*Utrum lex naturalis contineat plura praecepta vel unum tantum.*

(*Concl.*) Secundum . . . ordinem inclinationum naturalium, est ordo praeceptorum legis naturae. Inest enim primo inclinatio homini ad bonum secundum naturam in qua communicat cum omnibus substantiis: prout scilicet quaelibet substantia appetit conservationem sui esse secundum suam naturam. Et secundum hanc inclinationem, pertinent ad legem naturalem ea per quae vita hominis conservatur, et contrarium impeditur. Secundo inest homini inclinatio ad aliqua magis specialia, secundum naturam in qua communicat cum ceteris animalibus. Et secundum hoc, dicuntur ea esse de lege naturali « *quae natura omnia animalia docuit* », ut est coniunctio maris et feminae, et educatio liberorum, et similia. Tertio modo inest homini inclinatio ad bonum secundum naturam rationis, quae est sibi propria: sicut homo habet naturalem inclinationem ad hoc quod veritatem cognoscat de Deo, et ad hoc quod in societate vivat. Et secundum hoc, ad legem naturalem pertinent ea quae ad huiusmodi inclinationem spectant: utpote quod homo ignorantiam vitet, quod alios non offendat cum quibus debet conversari, et cetera huiusmodi quae ad hoc spectant.

ART. 4.—*Utrum lex naturae sit una apud omnes.*

Respondeo dicendum quod, sicut supra dictum est, ad legem naturae pertinent ea ad quae homo naturaliter inclinatur; inter quae homini proprium est ut inclinetur ad agendum secundum rationem. Ad rationem autem pertinet ex communibus ad propria procedere, ut patet ex I *Physic.* (cap. 1). Aliter tamen circa hoc se habet ratio speculativa, et aliter ratio practica. Quia enim ratio speculativa praecipue negotiatur circa necessaria, quae impossibile est aliter se habere, absque aliquo defectu invenitur veritas in conclusionibus propriis, sicut et in principiis communibus. Sed ratio practica negotiatur circa contingentia, in quibus sunt operationes humanae: et ideo, etsi in communibus sit aliqua necessitas, quanto magis ad propria descenditur, tanto magis invenitur defectus. . . .

Sic igitur patet quod, quantum ad communia principia rationis sive speculativae sive practicae, est eadem veritas sive rectitudo apud

8. *THE NATURAL LAW*. (Qu. 94.)

Precepts of the Natural Law. (Art. 2, concl.)

The order of the precepts of the natural law corresponds to the order of our natural inclinations. For there is in man a natural and initial inclination to good which he has in common with all substances; in so far as every substance seeks its own preservation according to its own nature. Corresponding to this inclination, the natural law contains all that makes for the preservation of human life, and all that is opposed to its dissolution. Secondly, there is to be found in man a further inclination to certain more specific ends, according to the nature which man shares with other animals. In virtue of this inclination there pertains to the natural law all those instincts 'which nature has taught all animals,'[1] such as sexual relationship, the rearing of off-spring, and the like. Thirdly, there is in man a certain inclination to good, corresponding to his rational nature: and this inclination is proper to man alone. So man has a natural inclination to know the truth about God and to live in society. In this respect there come under the natural law, all actions connected with such inclinations: namely, that a man should avoid ignorance, that he must not give offence to others with whom he must associate and all actions of like nature.

The Universality of the Natural Law. (Art. 4, concl.)

As we have just said, all those actions pertain to the natural law to which man has a natural inclination: and among such it is proper to man to seek to act according to reason. Reason, however, proceeds from general principles to matters of detail, as is proved in the *Physics* (Book I, 1). The practical and the speculative reason, however, go about this process in different ways. For the speculative reason is principally employed about necessary truths, which cannot be otherwise than they are; so that truth is to be found as surely in its particular conclusions as in general principles themselves. But practical reason is employed about contingent matters, into which human actions enter: thus, though there is a certain necessity in its general principles, the further one departs from generality the more is the conclusion open to exception.

So it is clear that as far as the general principles of reason are concerned, whether speculative or practical, there is one standard of truth

---

[1] This is the definition of Ulpian in the *Digest*, I, i, 1.

omnes, et aequaliter nota. Quantum vero ad proprias conclusiones rationis speculativae, est eadem veritas apud omnes, non tamen aequaliter omnibus nota: apud omnes enim verum est quod triangulus habet tres angulos aequales duobus rectis, quamvis hoc non sit omnibus notum. Sed quantum ad proprias conclusiones rationis practicae, nec est eadem veritas seu rectitudo apud omnes; nec etiam apud quos est eadem, est aequaliter nota. Apud omnes enim hoc rectum est et verum, ut secundum rationem agatur. Ex hoc autem principio sequitur quasi conclusio propria, quod deposita sint reddenda. Et hoc quidem ut in pluribus verum est: sed potest in aliquo casu contingere quod sit damnosum, et per consequens irrationabile, si deposita reddantur; puta si aliquis petat ad impugnandam patriam. Et hoc tanto magis invenitur deficere, quanto magis ad particularia descenditur, puta si dicatur quod deposita sunt reddenda cum tali cautione, vel tali modo: quanto enim plures conditiones particulares apponuntur, tanto pluribus modis poterit deficere, ut non sit rectum vel in reddendo vel in non reddendo.

Sic igitur dicendum est quod lex naturae, quantum ad prima principia communia, est eadem apud omnes et secundum rectitudinem, et secundum notitiam. Sed quantum ad quaedam propria, quae sunt quasi conclusiones principiorum communium, est eadem apud omnes ut in pluribus et secundum rectitudinem et secundum notitiam: sed ut in paucioribus potest deficere et quantum ad rectitudinem, propter aliqua particularia impedimenta (sicut etiam naturae generabiles et corruptibiles deficiunt ut in paucioribus, propter impedimenta), et etiam quantum ad notitiam; et hoc propter hoc quod aliqui habent depravatam rationem ex passione, seu ex mala consuetudine, seu ex mala habitudine naturae; sicut apud Germanos olim latrocinium non reputabatur iniquum, cum tamen sit expresse contra legem naturae, ut refert Julius Caesar, in libro *de Bello Gallico* (lib. VI, cap. 23).

Art. 5.—*Utrum lex naturae mutari possit.*

Respondeo dicendum quod lex naturalis potest intelligi mutari dupliciter. Uno modo, per hoc quod aliquid ei addatur. Et sic nihil prohibet legem naturalem mutari: multa enim supra legem naturalem superaddita sunt, ad humanam vitam utilia, tam per legem divinam, quam etiam per leges humanas.

or rightness for everybody, and that this is equally known by every one. With regard to the particular conclusions of speculative reason, again there is one standard of truth for all; but in this case it is not equally known to all: it is universally true, for instance, that the three interior angles of a triangle equal two right angles; but this conclusion is not known by everybody. When we come to the particular conclusions of the practical reason, however, there is neither the same standard of truth or rightness for every one, nor are these conclusions equally known to all. All people, indeed, realize that it is right and true to act according to reason. And from this principle we may deduce as an immediate conclusion that debts must be repaid. This conclusion holds in the majority of cases. But it could happen in some particular case that it would be injurious, and therefore irrational, to repay a debt; if for instance, the money repaid were used to make war against one's own country. Such exceptions are all the more likely to occur the more we get down to particular cases: take, for instance, the question of repaying a debt together with a certain security, or in some specific way. The more specialized the conditions applied, the greater is the possibility of an exception arising which will make it right to make restitution or not.

So we must conclude that the law of nature, as far as general first principles are concerned, is the same for all as a norm of right conduct and is equally well known to all. But as to more particular cases which are conclusions from such general principles it remains the same for all only in the majority of cases, both as a norm and as to the extent to which it is known. Thus in particular instances it can admit of exceptions: both with regard to rightness, because of certain impediments, (just as in nature the generation and change of bodies is subject to accidents caused by some impediment), and with regard to its knowability. This can happen because reason is, in some persons, depraved by passion or by some evil habit of nature; as Caesar relates in *De Bello Gallico* (VI, 23), of the Germans, that at one time they did not consider robbery to be wrong; though it is obviously against natural law.

The Immutability of Natural Law. (Art. 5.)

There are two ways in which natural law may be understood to change. One, in that certain additions are made to it. And in this sense there is no reason why it should not change. Both the divine law and human laws do, in fact, add much to the natural law which is useful to human activity.

Alio modo intelligitur mutatio legis naturalis per modum substractionis, ut scilicet aliquid desinat esse de lege naturali, quod prius fuit secundum legem naturalem. Et sic quantum ad prima principia legis naturae, lex naturae est omnino immutabilis. Quantum autem ad secunda praecepta, quae diximus esse quasi quasdam proprias conclusiones propinquas primis principiis, sic lex naturalis non immutatur quin ut in pluribus rectum sit semper quod lex naturalis habet. Potest tamen immutari in aliquo particulari, et in paucioribus, propter aliquas speciales causas impedientes observantiam talium praeceptorum, ut supra dictum est.

Ad tertium dicendum quod aliquid dicitur esse de iure naturali dupliciter. Uno modo, quia ad hoc natura inclinat: sicut non esse iniuriam alteri faciendam. Alio modo, quia natura non induxit contrarium: sicut possemus dicere quod hominem esse nudum est de iure naturali, quia non dedit ei vestitum, sed ars adinvenit. Et hoc modo « *communis omnium possessio, et omnium una libertas* », dicitur esse de iure naturali: quia scilicet distinctio possessionum et servitus non sunt inductae a natura, sed per hominum rationem, ad utilitatem humanae vitae. Et sic in hoc lex naturae non est mutata nisi per additionem.

Quaestio XCV.—De lege humana, secundum se.

Art. 1.—*Utrum fuerit utile aliquas leges poni ab hominibus.*

Respondeo dicendum quod, sicut ex supradictis patet, homini naturaliter inest quaedam aptitudo ad virtutem; sed ipsa virtutis perfectio necesse est quod homini adveniat per « *aliquam disciplinam* » . . . Ad hanc autem disciplinam non de facili invenitur homo sibi sufficiens . . . Et ideo oportet quod huiusmodi disciplinam, per quam ad virtutem perveniatur, homines ab alio sortiantur. Et quidem quantum ad illos iuvenes qui sunt proni ad actus virtutum, ex bona dispositione naturae, vel consuetudine, vel magis divino munere, sufficit disciplina paterna, quae est per monitiones. Sed quia inveniuntur quidam protervi et ad vitia proni, qui verbis de facili moveri non possunt; neces-

Or again the natural law would be understood to change by having something subtracted from it. If, for instance, something ceased to pertain to the natural law which was formerly part of it. In this respect, and as far as first principles are concerned, it is wholly unchangeable. As to secondary precepts, which, as we have said, follow as immediate conclusions from first principles, the natural law again does not change; in the sense that it remains a general rule for the majority of cases that what the natural law prescribes is correct. It may, however, be said to change in some particular case, or in a limited number of examples; because of some special causes which make its observation impossible; as we have already pointed out.

(Ibid., ad 3um.)

Things may be said to pertain to the natural law for two reasons. First, if there is a natural inclination to them: as, for example, that it is wrong to do injury to one's neighbour. Secondly, if nature does not lead us to do what is contrary. So we might say that man has a natural right to go naked because, nature not having provided him with clothing he has had to fashion it for himself. In this sense the 'common possession of all things and the equal liberty of all'[1] can be said to pertain to the natural law. For neither private possession nor servitude were imposed by nature: they are the adoptions of human reason in the interests of human life. And in these cases the natural law is not altered but is added to.

9. HUMAN LAW. (Qu. 95.)

The Necessity for Human Laws. (Art. 1, concl.)

From the foregoing it is clear that there is in man a natural aptitude to virtuous action. But men can achieve the perfection of such virtue only by the practice of a 'certain discipline.'—And men who are capable of such discipline without the aid of others are rare indeed.— So we must help one another to achieve that discipline which leads to a virtuous life. There are, indeed, some young men, readily inclined to a life of virtue through a good natural disposition or upbringing, or particularly because of divine help; and for such, paternal guidance and advice are sufficient. But there are others, of evil disposition and prone to vice, who are not easily moved by words. These it is neces-

---

[1] The definition is from St. Isidore of Seville, *Etymologiae*, V, 4.

sarium fuit ut per vim et metum cohiberentur a malo, ut saltem sic male
facere desistentes, et aliis quietam vitam redderent, et ipsi tandem per
huiusmodi assuetudinem ad hoc perducerentur quod voluntarie
facerent quae prius metu implebant, et sic fierent virtuosi. Huiusmodi
autem disciplina cogens metu poenae, est disciplina legum. Unde
necessarium fuit ad pacem hominum et virtutem, ut leges ponerentur:
quia sicut Philosophus dicit, in I *Polit.* (cap. 2), « *sicut homo, si sit
perfectus virtute, est optimum animalium; sic, si sit separatus a lege et
iustitia, est pessimum omnium* »; quia homo habet arma rationis ad
explendas concupiscentias et saevitias, quae non habent alia animalia.

ART. 2.—*Utrum omnis lex humanitus posita a lege naturali derivetur.*

Respondeo dicendum quod, sicut Augustinus dicit, in I *de Lib. Arb.*
(cap. 5), « *non videtur esse lex, quae iusta non fuerit* ». Unde inquantum
habet de iustitia, intantum habet de virtute legis. In rebus autem
humanis dicitur esse aliquid iustum ex eo quod est rectum secundum
regulam rationis. Rationis autem prima regula est lex naturae, ut ex
supradictis patet. Unde omnis lex humanitus posita intantum habet de
ratione legis, inquantum a lege naturae derivatur. Si vero in aliquo a
lege naturali discordet, iam non erit lex, sed legis corruptio.

Sed sciendum est quod a lege naturali potest aliquid dupliciter
derivari: uno modo, sicut conclusiones ex principiis; alio modo, sicut
determinationes quaedam aliquorum communium. Primus quidem
modus est simile eis quo in scientiis ex principiis conclusiones demon-
strativae producuntur. Secundo vero modo simile est quod in artibus
formae communes determinantur ad aliquid speciale: sicut artifex
formam communem domus necesse est quod determinet ad hanc vel
illam domus figuram. Derivantur ergo quaedam a principiis communibus legis naturae per modum conclusionum: sicut hoc quod est « *non
esse occidendum* », ut conclusio quaedam derivari potest ab eo quod
est « *nulli esse malum faciendum* ». Quaedam vero per modum
determinationis: sicut lex naturae habet quod ille qui peccat, puniatur;
sed quod tali poena puniatur, hoc est quaedam determinatio legis
naturae.

Utraque igitur inveniuntur in lege humana posita. Sed ea quae sunt
primi modi, continentur lege humana non tamquam sint solum lege
posita, sed habent etiam aliquid vigoris ex lege naturali. Sed ea quae
sunt secundi modi, ex sola lege humana vigorem habent.

sary to restrain from wrongdoing by force and by fear. When they are thus prevented from doing evil, a quiet life is assured to the rest of the community; and they are themselves drawn eventually, by force of habit, to do voluntarily what once they did only out of fear, and so to practice virtue. Such discipline which compels under fear of penalty is the discipline of law. Thus the enactment of laws was necessary to the peaceful and virtuous life of men. And the Philosopher says (I *Politics*, 2): 'Man, when he reaches the perfection of virtue is the best of all animals: but if he goes his way without law and justice he becomes the worst of all brutes.' For man, unlike other animals, has the weapon of reason with which to exploit his base desires and cruelty.

The Subordination of Human Laws to the Natural Law. (Art. 2, concl.)

Saint Augustine says (I *De Lib. Arbitrio*, 5): 'There is no law unless it be just.' So the validity of law depends upon its justice. But in human affairs a thing is said to be just when it accords aright with the rule of reason: and, as we have already seen, the first rule of reason is the natural law. Thus all humanly enacted laws are in accord with reason to the extent that they derive from the natural law. And if a human law is at variance in any particular with the natural law, it is no longer legal, but rather a corruption of law.

But it should be noted that there are two ways in which anything may derive from natural law. First, as a conclusion from more general principles. Secondly, as a determination of certain general features. The former is similar to the method of the sciences in which demonstrative conclusions are drawn from first principles. The second way is like to that of the arts in which some common form is determined to a particular instance: as, for example, when an architect, starting from the general idea of a house, then goes on to design the particular plan of this or that house. So, therefore, some derivations are made from the natural law by way of formal conclusion: as the conclusion, 'Do no murder,' derives from the precept, 'Do harm to no man.' Other conclusions are arrived at as determinations of particular cases. So the natural law establishes that whoever transgresses shall be punished. But that a man should be punished by a specific penalty is a particular determination of the natural law.

Both types of derivation are to be found in human law. But those which are arrived at in the first way are sanctioned not only by human law, but by the natural law also; while those arrived at by the second method have the validity of human law alone.

I

Art. 4.—*Utrum Isidorus convenienter ponat divisionem humanarum legum.*

(*Concl.*) Sunt autem multa de ratione legis humanae, secundum quorum quodlibet lex humana proprie et per se dividi potest. Est enim primo de ratione legis humanae quod sit derivata a lege naturae, ut ex dictis patet. Et secundum hoc dividitur ius positivum in ius gentium et ius civile, secundum duos modos quibus aliquid derivatur a lege naturae, ut supra dictum est. Nam ad ius gentium pertinent ea quae derivantur ex lege naturae sicut conclusiones ex principiis: ut iustae emptiones, venditiones, et alia huiusmodi, sine quibus homines ad invicem convivere non possent; quod est de lege naturae, quia homo est naturaliter animal sociale, ut probatur in I *Polit.* (cap. 1). Quae vero derivantur a lege naturae per modum particularis determinationis, pertinent ad ius civile, secundum quod quaelibet civitas aliquid sibi accomodum determinat.

Secundo est de ratione legis humanae quod ordinetur ad bonum commune civitatis. Et secundum hoc lex humana dividi potest secundum diversitatem eorum qui specialiter dant operam ad bonum commune: sicut sacerdotes, pro populo Deum orantes; principes, populum gubernantes; et milites, pro salute populi pugnantes. Et ideo istis hominibus specialia quaedam iura aptantur.

Tertio est de ratione legis humanae ut instituatur a gubernante communitatem civitatis, sicut supra dictum est. Et secundum hoc distinguuntur leges humanae secundum diversa regimina civitatum. Quorum unum, secundum Philosophum, in III *Polit.* (cap. 5), est *regnum,* quando scilicet civitas gubernatur ab uno: et secundum hoc accipiuntur « *constitutiones principum* ». Aliud vero regimen est *aristocratia,* idest principatus optimorum, et optimatum: et secundum hoc sumuntur « *responsa prudentum* », et etiam « *senatusconsulta* ». Aliud regimen est *oligarchia,* idest principatus paucorum divitum et potentum: et secundum hoc sumitur « *ius praetorium* », quod etiam « *honorarium* » dicitur. Aliud autem regimen est populi, quod nominatur *democratia*: et secundum hoc sumuntur « *plebiscita* ». Aliud autem est tyrannicum, quod est omnino corruptum: unde ex hoc non sumitur aliqua lex. Est etiam aliquod regimen ex istis commixtum,

The Divisions of Human Law. (Art. 4, concl.)

Many elements enter into the notion of human law which may be taken as grounds for its classification. In the first place it is clear from what we have said above that the essential characteristic of human law is that it derived from natural law. From this point of view positive law may be divided into the law of nations (*ius gentium*) and civil law (*ius civile*): and this corresponds to the twofold derivation from natural law which we have already examined. To the law of nations pertain all those conclusions which are directly derived from natural law as immediate conclusions. Such are the norms governing buying and selling and other similar activities which are necessary to social intercourse: these derive from natural law because man is naturally a social animal as the Philosopher proves in the First Book of *Politics* (chapter 1). Those norms which derive from the natural law as particular applications, on the other hand, make up the civil law which any city determines according to its particular requirements.

The second essential characteristic of human law is that it is directed to the common welfare of the city. From this point of view human laws may be divided according to the different offices of those who are specially charged with the common welfare: there are the priests who pray to God for the people; the rulers who govern the community; and the soldiers who fight for its safety. To each of these categories there corresponds a particular code.

The third essential characteristic of human law is that it should be promulgated by the ruler of the civil community, as we have already said. From this point of view human laws may be distinguished according to the different political regimes. One of these, as the Philosopher says in the *Politics* (III, 5), is monarchy, which occurs when the city is governed by one man: to this correspond the 'constitutions of princes'. Another form of government is aristocracy, that is government by the best and the nobility: to this corresponds the 'opinions of the wise' and the 'counsels of the senate'. Another is oligarchy, or government by the rich and powerful: and to this corresponds the 'praetorian law' which is also known as the 'ius honorarium'. Then there is government by the entire people or democracy: and to this corresponds the 'plebiscite'. Lastly there is the tyrannical regime which is entirely corrupt, and which in consequence has no corresponding law. There is, in addition, another form of mixed government, constituted from all the elements just mentioned, and

SUMMA THEOLOGICA

quod est optimum: et secundum hoc sumitur « *lex* » « *quam maiores natu simul cum plebibus sanxerunt* », ut Isidorus dicit (*Etym.*, lib. V, cap. 10).

Quarto vero de ratione legis humanae est quod sit directiva humanorum actuum. Et secundum hoc, secundum diversa de quibus leges ferunter, distinguuntur leges, quae interdum ab auctoribus nominantur: sicut distinguitur « *Lex Julia de Adulteriis* », « *Lex Cornelia de Sicariis* » et sic de aliis, non propter auctores, sed propter res de quibus sunt.

Quaestio XCVI.—DE POTESTATE LEGIS HUMANAE.

ART. 1.—*Utrum lex humana debeat poni in communi magis quam in particulari.*

Respondeo dicendum quod unumquodque quod est propter finem, necesse est quod sit fini proportionatum. Finis autem legis est bonum commune: quia ut Isidorus dicit, in libro *Etymol.* (lib. II, cap. 10), « *nullo privato commodo, sed pro communi utilitate civium lex debet esse conscripta* ». Unde oportet leges humanas esse proportionatas ad bonum commune. Bonum autem commune constat ex multis. Et ideo oportet quod lex ad multa respiciat, et secundum personas, et secundum negotia, et secundum tempora. Constituitur enim communitas civitatis ex multis personis; et eius bonum per multiplices actiones procuratur; nec ad hoc solum instituitur quod aliquo modico tempore duret, sed quod omni tempore perseveret per civium successionem, ut Augustinus dicit, in XXII *de Civ. Dei* (cap. 6).

ART. 2.—*Utrum ad legem humanam pertineat omnia vitia cohibere.*

(*Concl.*) Oportet quod etiam leges imponantur hominibus secundum eorum conditionem: quia, ut Isidorus dicit (*Etymol.*, lib. II, cap. 10), lex debet esse « *possibilis et secundum naturam, et secundum consuetudinem patriae* ». Potestas autem sive facultas operandi ex interiori habitu seu dispositione procedit; non enim idem est possibile ei qui non habet habitum virtutis, et virtuoso; sicut etiam non est idem possibile puero et viro perfecto. Et propter hoc non ponitur eadem lex pueris quae ponitur adultis: multa enim pueris permittuntur quae in adultis lege puniuntur, vel etiam vituperantur. Et similiter multa sunt permit-

this is the best form of government. In this, law is enacted according to the definition of Isidore (*Etym*. V, 10): 'by the common sanction of nobles and people.'

A fourth essential characteristic of law is that it is directive of human actions. From this point of view laws may be distinguished according to their different objects, and are sometimes named according to their authors: so we speak of the 'Julian law concerning adultery' and the 'Cornelian Law concerning assassination,' etc. The reference being not to the author but the matter with which they deal.

10. *THE POWERS OF HUMAN LAW*. (Qu. 96.)

Its Generality. (Art. 1, concl.)

Whatever exists in virtue of some end must be proportionate to that end. But the end of law is the common welfare: for, as Isidore says (*Etym*. II, 10): 'Laws must be formulated, not in view of some particular interest, but for the general benefit of the citizens.' So human laws must be related to the common welfare. But the common well-being is made up of many different elements. It is, therefore, necessary that the law should take account of these diverse elements, both with respect to persons and to affairs, and with reference to different times. For the political community is composed of many persons; its welfare entails much varied provision; and such provision is not confined to any one period of time, but should continue through successive generations of citizens: as St. Augustine says in *De Civitate Dei* (XXII, 6).

Its Limits. (Art. 2, concl.)

Laws when they are passed should take account of the condition of the men who will be subject to them; for, as Isidore says (*Etym*. II, 10): the law should be 'possible both with regard to nature and with regard to the custom of the country.' But capacity to act derives from habit, or interior disposition: not everything that is possible to a virtuous man is equally possible to one who lacks the habit of virtue; just as a child is incapable of doing all that a grown man can do. For this reason there is not the same law for children and for adults: there are many things permitted to children which are punished by the law, and even abhorred, in adults. Equally, it is possible to permit

tenda hominibus non perfectis virtute, quae non essent toleranda in hominibus virtuosis.

Lex autem humana ponitur multitudini hominum, in qua maior pars est hominum non perfectorum virtute. Et ideo lege humana non prohibentur omnia vitia, a quibus virtuosi abstinent; sed solum graviora, a quibus possibile est maiorem partem multitudinis abstinere; et praecipue quae sunt in nocumentum aliorum, sine quorum prohibitione societas humana conservari non posset, sicut prohibentur lege humana homicidia et furta et huiusmodi.

ART. 3.—*Utrum lex humana praecipiat actus omnium virtutum.*

(*Concl.*) Omnia autem obiecta virtutum referri possunt vel ad bonum privatum alicuius personae, vel ad bonum commune multitudinis: sicut ea quae sunt fortitudinis potest aliquis exsequi vel propter conservationem civitatis, vel ad conservandum ius amici sui; et simile est in aliis. Lex autem, ut dictum est, ordinatur ad bonum commune. Et ideo nulla virtus est de cuius actibus lex praecipere non possit. Non tamen de omnibus actibus omnium virtutum lex humana praecipit: sed solum de illis qui sunt ordinabiles ad bonum commune, vel immediate, sicut cum aliqua directe propter bonum commune fiunt; vel mediate, sicut cum aliqua ordinantur a legislatore pertinentia ad bonam disciplinam, per quam cives informantur ut commune bonum iustitiae et pacis conservent.

ART. 4.—*Utrum lex humana imponat homini necessitatem in foro conscientiae.*

Respondeo dicendum quod leges positae humanitus vel sunt iustae, vel iniustae. Si quidem iustae sint, habent vim obligandi in foro conscientiae a lege aeterna, a qua derivantur; secundum illud *Prov.* VIII: « *Per me reges regnant, et legum conditores iusta decernunt* ». Dicuntur autem leges iustae et ex fine, quando scilicet ordinantur ad bonum commune; et ex auctore, quando scilicet lex lata non excedit potestatem ferentis; et ex forma, quando scilicet secundum aequalitatem proportionis imponuntur subditis onera in ordine ad bonum commune. Cum enim unus homo sit pars multitudinis, quilibet homo hoc

many things to those not far advanced in virtue which would not be tolerated in a virtuous man.

Now human law is enacted on behalf of the mass of men, the majority of whom are far from perfect in virtue. For this reason human law does not prohibit every vice from which virtuous men abstain; but only the graver vices from which the majority can abstain; and particularly those vices which are damaging of others, and which, if they were not prohibited, would make it impossible for human society to endure: as murder, theft, and suchlike, which are prohibited by human law.

(Ibid. Art. 3, concl.)

The object of the different virtues may be considered either with respect to the private benefit of the individual person, or with respect to the general welfare of the community. So, for example, the virtue of fortitude may be exercised by a person either for the protection of the city or in defence of the rights of his friends: and similarly with respect to the other virtues. Law, however, as we have said, regards the common welfare. So there is no virtue whose practice may not be prescribed by law. At the same time not every act of all virtues is ordered by the law, but only those which may be directed towards the common welfare; either directly, when something is done explicitly for the common benefit; or indirectly, as when, for example, the legislator enacts certain provisions relative to good discipline, which accustom the citizens to respect the common need for justice and peace.

The Obligation of Human Law. (Art. 4, concl.)

Laws enacted by men are either just or unjust. If just, they draw from the eternal law, from which they derive, the power to oblige in conscience; as is said in the book of *Proverbs* (VIII, 15): 'By me kings reign, and lawgivers decree just things.' Now laws can be considered just, either with respect to their object, that is when they are directed to the common welfare; or with respect to their author, that is when the law which is enacted does not exceed the powers of him who enacts it; or again with reference to their form, when the burdens they impose upon the citizens are distributed in such proportion as to promote the common welfare. For since every man is part of the

ipsum quod est et quod habet, est multitudinis: sicut et quaelibet pars
id quod est, est totius. Unde et natura aliquod detrimentum infert
parti, ut salvet totum. Et secundum hoc, leges huiusmodi, onera
proportionabiliter inferentes, iustae sunt, et obligant in foro conscientiae, et sunt leges legales.

Iniustae autem sunt leges dupliciter. Uno modo, per contrarietatem
ad bonum humanum, e contrario praedictis: vel ex fine, sicut cum aliquis praesidens leges imponit onerosas subditis non pertinentes ad
utilitatem communem, sed magis ad propriam cupiditatem vel gloriam;
vel etiam ex auctore, sicut cum aliquis legem fert ultra sibi commissam
potestatem; vel etiam ex forma, puta cum inaequaliter onera multitudini dispensantur, etiam si ordinentur ad bonum commune. Et
huiusmodi magis sunt violentiae quam leges: quia, sicut Augustinus
dicit, in libro *de Lib. Arb.* (lib. I, cap. 5), « *Lex esse non videtur, quae
iusta non fuerit* ». Unde tales leges non obligant in foro conscientiae:
nisi forte propter vitandum scandalum vel turbationem, propter quod
etiam homo iuri suo debet cedere, secundum illud *Matth.* V (v 40-41),
« *Qui angariaverit te mille passus, vade cum eo alia duo; et qui abstulerit
tibi tunicam, da ei pallium* ».

Alio modo leges possunt esse iniustae per contrarietatem ad bonum
divinum: sicut leges tyrannorum inducentes ad idololatriam, vel ad
quodcumque aliud quod sit contra legem divinam. Et tales leges
nullo modo licet observare: quia sicut dicitur *Act.* V (v. 29), « *obedire
oportet Deo magis quam hominibus* ».

ART. 5.—*Utrum omnes subiiciantur legi.*

Respondeo dicendum quod, sicut ex supradictis patet, lex de sui
ratione duo habet: primo quidem, quod est regula humanorum actuum; secundo, quod habet vim coactivam. Dupliciter ergo aliquis
homo potest esse legi subiectus. Uno modo, sicut regulatum regulae.
Et hoc modo omnes illi qui subduntur potestati, subduntur legi quam
fert potestas. Quod autem aliquis potestati non subdatur, potest contingere dupliciter. Uno modo, quia est simpliciter absolutus ab eius
subiectione. Unde illi qui sunt de una civitate vel regno, non subduntur
legibus principis alterius civitatis vel regni, sicut nec eius dominio.

community, all that any man is or has, has reference to the community: just as any part belongs, in that which it is, to the whole. For this reason nature is seen to sacrifice a part for the preservation of the whole. In the light of this principle, laws which observe due proportion in the distribution of burdens are just, and oblige in conscience; they are legitimate laws.

Contrariwise, laws may be unjust for two reasons. Firstly, when they are detrimental to human welfare, being contrary to the norms we have just established. Either with respect to their object, as when a ruler enacts laws which are burdensome to his subjects and which do not make for common prosperity, but are designed better to serve his own cupidity and vainglory. Or with respect to their author; if a legislator should enact laws which exceed the powers vested in him. Or, finally with respect to their form; if the burdens, even though they are concerned with the common welfare, are distributed in an inequitable manner throughout the community. Laws of this sort have more in common with violence than with legality: for, as St. Augustine says, in the *De Libro Arbitrio* (I, 5): 'A law which is not just cannot be called a law.' Such laws do not, in consequence, oblige in conscience, except, on occasion, to avoid scandal or disorder. For in this case a man may be bound even to give up his rights, as St. Matthew teaches (V, 40–41): 'Whosoever will force thee one mile, go with him other two: and if a man take away thy coat, let go thy cloak also unto him.'

Secondly, laws may be unjust through being contrary to divine goodness: such as tyrannical laws enforcing idolatry, or any other action against the divine law. Such laws may under no circumstances be obeyed: for, as it is said (*Acts* V, 29): 'We must obey God rather than man.'

Its Powers of Compulsion. (Art. 5, concl.)

Law, as we see from what has been said, has two essential characteristics: the first, that of a rule directive of human action: the second, that of power to compel. So there are two ways in which a man may be subject to the law. Either as that which is ruled is subject to the rule. And, in this respect, all who are subject to a certain power are subject also to the laws which emanate from that power. There are two cases in which such subjection does not obtain. First, when a person is wholly absolved from such subjection. So the citizens of one city or realm are not bound by the laws of the ruler of another city or realm,

Alio modo, secundum quod regitur superiori lege. Puta si aliquis subiectus sit proconsuli, regulari debet eius mandato, non tamen in his quae dispensantur ei ab imperatore: quantum enim ad illa, non adstringitur mandato inferioris, cum superiori mandato dirigatur. Et secundum hoc contingit quod aliquis simpliciter subiectus legi, secundum aliqua legi non adstringitur, secundum quae regitur superiori lege.

Alio vero modo dicitur aliquis subdi legi sicut coactum cogenti. Et hoc modo homines virtuosi et iusti non subduntur legi sed soli mali. Quod enim est coactum et violentum, est contrarium voluntati. Voluntas autem bonorum consonat legi, a qua malorum voluntas discordat. Et ideo secundum hoc boni non sunt sub lege, sed solum mali.

Ad tertium dicendum quod princeps dicitur esse solutus a lege, quantum ad vim coactivam legis: nullus enim proprie cogitur a seipso; lex autem non habet vim coactivam nisi ex principis potestate. Sic igitur princeps dicitur esse solutus a lege, quia nullus in ipsum potest iudicium condemnationis ferre, si contra legem agat. Unde super illud *Psalmi* L (v. 6), « *Tibi soli peccavi* », etc., dicit *Glossa* quod « *rex non habet hominem qui sua facta diiudicet* ». — Sed quantum ad vim directivam legis, princeps subditur legi propria voluntate; secundum quod dicitur (*Extra, de Constitutionibus*, cap. *Cum Omnes*): « *Quod quisque iuris in alterum statuit, ipse eodem iure uti debet. Et Sapientis dicit auctoritas: Patere legem quam ipse tuleris* ». Et in *Codice*, Theodosius et Valentinianus Imperatores Volusiano Praefecto scribunt: « *Digna vox est maiestate regnantis, legibus alligatum se principem profiteri: adeo de autoritate iuris nostra pendet autoritas. Et re vera maius imperio est subiicere legibus principatum* ». Improperatur etiam his a Domino qui « *dicunt et non faciunt* »; et qui « *aliis onera gravia imponunt, et ipsi nec digito volunt ea movere* », ut habetur *Matth*. XXIII (v. 3, 4). Unde

just as they do not come under his dominion. Secondly, when persons are subject to a higher law. So, for instance, one who is subject to a proconsul must obey his command, but not in those matters in which he is dispensed by the emperor: for in these matters, being subject to higher commands, he is not bound by the orders of a subordinate. In such a case it happens that one who is subject to a certain law in principle, is in certain matters exempt from it, being subject in such matters to a higher law.

The second way in which a man may be said to be subject to the law is as one who is constrained to what constrains him. In this sense virtuous and just men are not subject to the law, but only the wicked. For whatever pertains to constraint and to violence is against the will. But the will of the good is at one with the law, whereas in the bad the will is opposed to the law. So, in this sense, the good are not under the law, but only the bad.

(Ibid. ad 3um.)

A ruler is said to be above the law[1] with respect to its constraining force: for nobody can be constrained by himself; and law derives its power of constraint only from the power of the ruler. So it is said that the prince is above the law, because if he should act against the law nobody can bring a condemnatory judgement against him. So, commenting on the text of *Psalm* L (verse 6) 'To thee only have I sinned' etc., the Gloss explains that 'there is no man who can judge the actions of a king.'—But with respect to the directive power of law, a ruler is voluntarily subject to it, in conformity with what is laid down [in the *Decretals*, I, II, 6]: 'Whoever enacts a law for another should apply the same law to himself. And we have it on the authority of the wise man that you should subject yourself to the same law which you promulgate.' And in the *Codex*, the Emperors, Theodosius and Valentinian, write to the Prefect Volusianus: 'It is a saying worthy of the majesty of a ruler, if the prince professes himself bound by the laws: for even our authority depends upon that of the law. And, in fact, the most important thing in government is that power should be subject to laws.'[2] The Lord also reproves those who 'say and do not do'; and who 'bind heavy and insupportable burdens for others, but with a finger of their own they will not move them' (*Matthew*,

---

[1] This principle also derives from Roman law: '*Princeps legibus solutus est*' (*Dig.*, I, iii, 31, Ulpianus).   [2] *Codex*, I, xiv, 4.

quantum ad Dei iudicium, princeps non est solutus a lege, quantum
ad vim directivam eius; sed debet voluntarius, non coactus, legem
implere. — Est etiam princeps supra legem, inquantum, si expediens
fuerit, potest legem mutare, et in ea dispensare, pro loco et tempore.

Art. 6.—*Utrum ei qui subditur legi, liceat praeter verba legis agere.*

Respondeo dicendum quod, sicut supra dictum est, omnis lex
ordinatur ad communem hominum salutem, et intanto obtinet vim
et rationem legis; secundum vero quod ab hoc deficit, virtutem
obligandi non habet. Unde Iurisperitus dicit quod « *nulla iuris ratio
aut aequitatis benignitas patitur ut quae salubriter pro utilitate hominum
introducuntur, ea nos duriori interpretatione, contra ipsorum commodum,
perducamus ad severitatem* ». Contingit autem multoties quod aliquid
observari communi saluti est utile ut in pluribus, quod tamen in aliquibus casibus est maxime nocivum. Quia igitur legislator non potest
omnes singulares casus intueri, proponit legem secundum ea quae
in pluribus accidunt, ferens intentionem suam ad communem utilitatem. Unde si emergat casus in quo observatio talis legis sit damnosa
communi saluti, non est observanda. Sicut si in civitate obsessa
statuatur lex quod portae civitatis maneant clausae, hoc est utile
communi saluti ut in pluribus: si tamen contingat casus quod hostes
insequantur aliquos cives, per quos civitas conservatur, damnosissimum
esset civitati nisi eis portae aperientur: et ideo in tali casu essent portae
aperiendae, contra verba legis, ut servaretur utilitas communis, quam
legislator intendit.

Sed tamen hoc est considerandum, quod si observatio legis secundum
verba non habeat subitum periculum, cui oporteat statim occurri,
non pertinet ad quemlibet ut interpretetur quid sit utile civitati et
quid inutile: sed hoc solum pertinet ad principes, qui propter huiusmodi
casus habent auctoritatem in legibus dispensandi. Si vero sit subitum
periculum, non patiens tantam moram ut ad superiorem recurri
possit, ipsa necessitas dispensationem habet annexam: quia necessitas
non subditur legi.

XXIII, 3, 4). So, in the judgement of God, a ruler is not free from the directive power of the law; but should voluntarily and without constraint fulfil it.—A ruler is above the law also in the sense that he may, if it be expedient, change the law, or dispense from it according to time and to place.

The Interpretation of Human Laws. Exceptional Cases. (Art. 6, concl.)

As we have said above, all law is directed to the common well-being of men, and for this reason alone does it obtain the power and validity of law: so to the extent that it falls short of this object it has no power of obligation. So the Jurisconsult[1] says that 'neither justice nor equity permit that what has been usefully established in the interests of men should be made harsh and damaging to the community through too rigid an interpretation.' Now it frequently happens that the observance of a certain rule, though generally useful to the community, is, in certain other cases, extremely damaging. For the legislator, not being able to foresee all particular cases, frames the law to meet what is commonly the case, and with a view to its general usefulness. Consequently, if it should happen that the observance of such a law would be damaging to the general well-being, it should not be observed. So, for example, in a city during a state of siege there might be a law ordering that all gates should be kept closed, and such a regulation would, in general, be useful to the common welfare. But if it should happen that the enemy were pursuing some of the citizens on whom the safety of the city depended, it would be a disaster for the city if the gates were not opened to them. In such a case the gates should obviously be opened, against the letter of the law, but for the sake of the common welfare which the legislator intended.

It must, however, be borne in mind, that if the decision on the letter of the law is not a matter of immediate danger which requires prompt action, it is not open to anybody to act as interpreter of what is and what is not in the public interest: such decision belongs rightly to rulers, and it is to meet such cases that they have authority to dispense from the law. When, however, danger is so imminent that there is no time to refer the matter to the authorities, necessity itself carries its own dispensation: for necessity knows no law.

[1] *Dig.*, I, iii, 25 (Modestinus).

Quaestio XCVII.—De mutatione legum humanarum.

Art. 1.—*Utrum lex humana debeat aliquo modo mutari.*

Respondeo dicendum quod, sicut supra dictum est, lex humana est quoddam dictamen rationis quo diriguntur humani actus. Et secundum hoc, duplex causa esse potest quod lex humana iuste mutetur: una quidem ex parte rationis; alia vero ex parte hominum, quorum actus lege regulantur. Ex parte quidem rationis, quia humanae rationi naturale esse videtur ut gradatim ab imperfecto ad perfectum perveniat. Unde videmus in scientiis speculativis quod qui primo philosophati sunt, quaedam imperfecta tradiderunt, quae postmodum per posteriores sunt magis perfecta. Ita etiam est et in operabilibus. Nam primi qui intenderunt invenire aliquid utile communitati hominum, non valentes omnia ex seipsis considerare, instituerunt quaedam imperfecta in multis deficientia; quae posteriores mutaverunt, instituentes aliqua quae in paucioribus deficere possent a communi utilitate.

Ex parte vero hominum, quorum actus lege regulantur, lex recte mutari potest propter mutationem conditionum hominum, quibus secundum diversas eorum conditiones diversa expediunt. Sicut Augustinus ponit exemplum, in I *de Lib. Arb.* (cap. 6), quod « *si populus sit bene moderatus et gravis, communisque utilitatis diligentissimus custos, recte lex fertur qua tali populo liceat sibi creare magistratus, per quos respublica administretur. Porro si paulatim idem populus depravatus habeat venale suffragium, et regimen flagitiosis sceleratisque committat; recte adimitur tali populo potestas dandi honores, et ad paucorum redit arbitrium* ».

Art. 2.—*Utrum lex humana semper sit mutanda, quando occurrit aliquid melius.*

Respondeo dicendum quod, sicut dictum est, lex humana intantum recte mutatur, inquantum per eius mutationem communi utilitati providetur. Habet autem ipsa legis mutatio, quantum in se est, detrimentum quoddam communis salutis. Quia ad observantiam legum plurimum valet consuetudo: intantum quod ea quae contra communem

11. *THE MUTABILITY OF HUMAN LAW*. (Qu. 97.)

Reasons for Such Mutability. (Art. 1, concl.)

As we have said above, human law is a certain dictate of reason by which human actions are regulated. From this point of view there can be two causes which justify a changing of human law. The first is on the part of reason: the second on the part of men whose actions are regulated by the law. On the part of reason because it would seem natural for human reason to proceed by stages from the imperfect to the more perfect. So we see in speculative science that those who first began to philosophize arrived at an incomplete system which their successors later elaborated into something more perfect. It is the same also in practical affairs. For those who first set themselves to consider what was useful to the common well-being of man, not being able to solve the entire problem themselves, established certain regulations which were imperfect and deficient in many respects; and these regulations were later modified by their successors to retain those which were the least defective from the point of view of the public interest.

On the part of men, whose actions are regulated by law, changes in law may be justified on account of altered circumstances: for according to the different circumstances in which men are found, different standards obtain. St. Augustine gives an example of this in (I *De Lib. Arbitrio*, 6): 'If a people is orderly, serious-minded and jealously observes the public interest, there is justification for a law which confers upon them the faculty of electing their own magistrates for the administration of public affairs. But if that people should gradually become dishonest, and the elections become corrupt, so that the government falls into the hands of dishonourable and vicious men, then it is right that the power of electing to office should be taken from them and that a return should be made to limited suffrage for the few and honest.'

The Limits of Such Mutability. (Art. 2.)

As has been said, change in human law is justified only to the extent that it benefits the general welfare. Now the very fact of change in the law is, in a certain sense, detrimental to the public welfare. This is because, in the observance of law, custom is of great importance: so much so, that any action which is opposed to general custom, even

consuetudinem fiunt, etiam si sint leviora de se, graviora videantur. Unde quando mutatur lex, diminuitur vis constrictiva legis, inquantum tollitur consuetudo. Et ideo numquam debet lex humana mutari nisi ex aliqua parte tantum recompensetur communi saluti, quantum ex ista parte derogatur. Quod quidem contingit vel ex hoc quod aliqua maxima et evidentissima utilitas ex novo statuto provenit: vel ex eo quod est maxima necessitas, ex eo quod lex consueta aut manifestam iniquitatem continet, aut eius observatio est plurium nociva. Unde dicitur a Iurisperito quod « *in rebus novis constituendis, evidens debet esse utilitas, ut recedatur ab eo iure quod diu aequum visum est* ».

Art. 3.—*Utrum consuetudo possit obtinere vim legis.*

Respondeo dicendum quod omnis lex proficiscitur a ratione et voluntate legislatoris: lex quidem divina et naturalis a rationabili Dei voluntate; lex autem humana a voluntate hominis ratione regulata. Sicut autem ratio et voluntas hominis manifestantur verbo in rebus agendis, ita etiam manifestantur facto: hoc enim unusquisque eligere videtur ut bonum, quod opere implet. Manifestum est autem quod verbo humano potest et mutari lex, et etiam exponi, inquantum manifestat interiorem motum et conceptum rationis humanae. Unde etiam et per actus, maxime multiplicatos, qui consuetudinem efficiunt, mutari potest lex, et exponi, et etiam aliquid causari quod legis virtutem obtineat: inquantum scilicet per exteriores actus multiplicatos interior voluntatis motus, et rationis conceptus, efficacissime declaratur; cum enim aliquid multoties fit, videtur ex deliberato rationis iudicio provenire. Et secundum hoc, consuetudo et habet vim legis, et legem abolet, et est legum interpretatrix.

Ad tertium dicendum quod multitudo in qua consuetudo introducitur, duplicis conditionis esse potest. Si enim sit libera multitudo, quae possit sibi legem facere, plus est consensus totius multitudinis ad aliquid observandum quem consuetudo manifestat, quam auctoritas principis, qui non habet potestatem condendi legem, nisi inquantum gerit personam multitudinis. Unde licet singulae personae non possint condere legem, tamen totus populus legem condere potest. — Si vero multitudo non habeat liberam potestatem condendi sibi legem, vel

if itself of little importance, always seems more serious. So when law is changed its coercive power is diminished, to the extent that custom is set aside. Thus human law should never be changed unless the benefits which result to the public interest are such as to compensate for the harm done. This may be the case if the new statutes contain great and manifest advantages; or if there is urgent necessity due to the fact that the old law contains evident injustice, or its observance is excessively harmful. So the Jurisconsult[1] says that 'in passing new constitutions their utility must be very evident before renouncing those laws which have long been regarded as equitable.'

The Value of Custom. (Art. 3, concl.)

All law proceeds from the reason and will of a legislator: divine and natural law from the rational will of God; human law from man's will, regulated by reason. Now reason and will in man are manifested in action both by word and by deed: for the test of what one considers good is to be found in the way one acts. Now it is clear that by words, which are the expression of the interior motions and concepts of the human reason, law can be changed and also explained. In the same way law can be changed and explained by means of actions, many times repeated, such as result in custom: and it can thus happen that new customs arise, which have the validity of law; in the sense that such exterior actions, frequently verified, clearly manifest the interior movement of the will and the concept of reason. For whatever is done frequently would seem to result from a deliberate judgement of reason. In this sense custom has the power of law, it may annul law and it may act as the interpreter of law.

The Relationship between Custom and Law. (Ibid. ad 3um.)

The community within which a custom becomes established may be of two conditions. If it is a case of a free community possessing the right to enact its own laws, the consent of the whole community in the observance of a certain custom has more value than the authority of the ruler, whose power to enact laws derives from the fact that he represents the community. In this case it is open to the entire community, though not to single individuals, to establish a law.—If, on the other hand, it is a community which does not enjoy the right to establish its own laws or to abrogate a law emanating from some

---

[1] *Dig.*, I, iv, 2 (Ulpianus).

K

legem a superiori potestate positam removendi; tamen ipsa consuetudo in tali multitudine praevalens obtinet vim legis, inquantum per eos toleratur ad quos pertinet multitudini legem imponere: ex hoc enim ipso videntur approbare quod consuetudo induxit.

Quaestio C.—DE PRAECEPTIS MORALIBUS VETERIS LEGIS.

ART. 9.—*Utrum modus virtutis cadat sub praecepto legis.*

Respondeo dicendum quod sicut supra dictum est, praeceptum legis habet vim coactivam. Illud ergo directe cadit sub praecepto legis, ad quod lex cogit. Coactio autem legis est per metum poenae, ut dicitur X *Ethic.*; nam illud proprie cadit sub praecepto legis, pro quo poena legis infligitur. Ad instituendam autem poenam aliter se habet lex divina, et aliter lex humana. Non enim poena legis infligitur nisi pro illis de quibus legislator habet iudicare; quia ex iudicio lex punit. Homo autem qui est legislator humanae, non habet iudicare nisi de exterioribus actibus, quia « *homines vident ea quae patent* », ut dicitur I *Regum*, XVI. Sed solius Dei qui est lator legis divinae, est iudicare de interioribus motibus voluntatum secundum illud *Psalmi* VII: « *Scrutans corda et renes Deus* ».

Secundum hoc igitur dicendum est quod modus virtutis quantum ad aliquid respicitur a lege humana et divina, quantum ad aliquid autem a lege divina, sed non a lege humana; quantum ad aliquid vero nec a lege humana nec a lege divina. Modus autem virtutis in tribus consistit, secundum Philosophum in II *Ethic*, cap. 4. Quorum primum est, si aliquis operetur sciens. Hoc autem diiudicatur et a lege divina, et a lege humana: quod enim aliquis facit ignorans, per accidens facit. Unde secundum ignorantiam aliqua diiudicantur ad poenam vel ad veniam, tam secundum legem humanam, quam secundum legem divinam.

Secundum autem est ut aliquis operetur volens, vel eligens et propter hoc eligens; in quo importatur duplex motus interior, scilicet voluntatis et intentionis, de quibus supra dictum est. Et ista duo non diiudicat lex humana, sed solum divina; lex enim humana non punit eum qui

superior authority, a custom which becomes established in such a community may, nevertheless, attain the status of law if it continues to be tolerated by those whose duty it is to legislate for the community. For, from the fact that it is so tolerated, it follows that the legislator approves what is established by the custom.

12. THE DIFFERENCE BETWEEN LEGAL AND MORAL OBLIGATION

Law and the Practice of Virtue. (Qu. 100, Art. 9.)

As we have shown above, a precept of law has power to compel: thus whatever is obliged by law may be said to fall directly under the precept of law. But the compulsion of law obtains through fear of penalty, as is shown in the tenth book of the *Ethics*; for those matters may be said to come strictly under the precept of law for which a legal penalty is inflicted. Hence divine law differs from human law in the imposition of its penalties. For a legal penalty is inflicted only for those matters about which the law-giver is competent to judge, since the law punishes in view of a judgement passed. Now man, the maker of human law, can pass judgement only upon external actions, because 'man seeth those things that appear,' as we are told in the first book of *Kings*. God alone, the divine Law-giver, is able to judge the inner movements of the will, as the Psalmist says, 'The searcher of hearts and reins is God.'

In view of this we must conclude that the practice of virtue is in one respect subject both to human and to divine law, while in another respect it is subject to divine but not to human law. Again there is a third sense in which it is affected neither by divine nor by human law. Now the mode of the practice of virtue consists, according to Aristotle (II *Ethics*, 4), in three things. The first of these is that a person should act knowingly. And this is subject to judgement both by divine and by human law. For whatever a man does in ignorance he does accidentally, and in consequence both human and divine law must consider the question of ignorance in judging whether certain matters are punishable or pardonable.

The second point is that a man should act voluntarily, deliberately chosing a particular action for its own sake. This involves a two-fold interior action of the will and of intention, and of these we have already spoken above. Divine law alone is competent to judge of these, but not human law. For human law does not punish the man

vult occidere, et non occidit; punit autem autem eum lex divina, secundum illud *Matth*. V, 22: « *Qui irascitur fratri suo, reus erit iudicio* ».

Tertium autem ut firmiter et immobiliter habeat et operetur; et ista firmitas proprie pertinet ad habitum, ut scilicet aliquis ex habitu radicato operetur. Et quantum ad hoc modus virtutis non cadit sub praecepto neque legis divinae, neque legis humanae: neque enim ab homine neque a Deo punitur tanquam praecepti transgressor, qui debitum honorem impendit parentibus, quamvis non habeat habitum pietatis.

Quaestio CV.—DE IUDICIALIUM PRAECEPTORUM RATIONE.

ART. 1.—*Utrum convenienter lex vetus de principibus ordinaverit.*

Respondeo dicendum quod circa bonam ordinationem principum in aliqua civitate vel gente, duo sunt attendenda. Quorum unum est ut omnes aliquam partem habeant in principatu: per hoc enim conservatur pax populi, et omnes talem ordinationem amant et custodiunt, ut dicitur in II *Polit*. (cap. 1, vel 2). Aliud est, quod attenditur secundum speciem regiminis, vel ordinationis principatuum. Cuius cum sint diversae species, ut Philosophus tradit, in III *Polit*. (cap. 5, 6, 7 et deinceps) praecipuae tamen sunt *regnum*, in quo unus principatur secundum virtutem; et *aristocratia*, id est *potestas optimorum*, in qua aliqui pauci principantur secundum virtutem. Unde optima ordinatio principum est in aliqua civitate vel regno, in quo unus praeficitur secundum virtutem qui omnibus praesit; et sub ipso sunt aliqui principantes secundum virtutem; et tamen talis principatus ad omnes pertinet, tum quia ex omnibus eligi possunt, tum quia etiam ab omnibus eliguntur. Talis enim est optima politia bene commixta ex *regno*, in quantum unus praeest; ex *aristocratia*, in quantum multi principantur secundum virtutem; et ex *democratia*, id est *potestate populi*, in quantum ex popularibus possunt eligi principes, et ad populum pertinet electio principum. Et hoc fuit institutum secundum legem divinam. Nam Moyses et eius successores gubernabant populum quasi singulariter omnibus principantes, quod est quaedam species regni. Eligebantur autem Septuaginta duo Seniores secundum virtutem: dicitur enim *Deuteron*. I, 15: « *Tuli de vestris tribubus viros sapientes et nobiles et con-*

who meditates murder but does not commit it, though divine law does punish him, as we are told by *St. Matthew* (V, 22): 'Whosoever is angry with his brother shall be in danger of the judgement.'

The third point is that a man should act upon a firm and unchanging principle; and such firmness proceeds strictly from habit, and obtains when a man acts from a rooted habit. In this sense the practice of virtue does not fall under the precept either of divine or of human law for no man is punished for breaking the law, either by God or by man, if he duly honours his parents, though lacking the habit of filial piety.

13. *A MIXED CONSTITUTION.* (Qu. 105.)

The Various Forms of Government, and Their Fusion in the Government Given by God to the Jews. (Art. 1.)

With respect to the right ordering of power in a city or nation, two points must be considered: the first is that all should in some respect participate in the government. It is this, in fact, that ensures peace within the community, and, as we are told in the *Politics* (II, chaps. 1 and 2), all peoples prize and guard such a state of affairs. The other consideration refers to the form of government or of regulating affairs. Among the various forms of government which the Philosopher enumerates in the third book of the *Politics* (chaps. 5, 6, and 7) the more important are the *kingdom*, in which one alone governs according to virtue; and *aristocracy*, that is government by the best elements, in which a few hold office according to virtue. So the best ordering of power within a city or a kingdom is obtained when there is one virtuous head who commands over all; and who has under him others who govern virtuously; and when, furthermore, all participate in such government, both because all are eligible, and because all participate in the election of those who rule. This is the best form of constitution which results from a judicious admixture of the *kingdom*, in that there is one person at the head of it; of *aristocracy* in that many participate in the government according to virtue; and of *democracy* or popular rule, in that rulers may be elected from the people and the whole population has the right of electing its rulers. It was such a form of government which was established by the divine law. For Moses and his successors governed their people as sole heads over all: but they elected to their assistance seventy-two Elders according to virtue: as it is said (*Deuteronomy*, I, 15): 'And I took out

stitui eos principes »: et hoc erat aristocraticum. Sed democraticum erat
quod isti de omni populo eligebantur; dicitur enim *Exod.* XVIII, 21:
« *Provide de omni plebe viros sapientes* », etc., et etiam quod populus eos
eligebat; unde dicitur *Deuteron.* I, 13: « *Date ex vobis viros sapientes* »,
etc. Unde patet quod optima fuit ordinatio principum quam lex
instituit.

Ad secundum dicendum, quod regnum est optimum regimen populi,
si non corrumpatur. Sed propter magnam potestatem quae regi
conceditur, de facili regnum degenerat in tyrannidem, nisi sit perfecta
virtus eius cui talis potestas conceditur: quia « *non est nisi virtuosi bene
ferre bonas fortunas* », ut Philosophus dicit, in IV *Ethic.* Perfecta autem
virtus in paucis invenitur: et praecipue Iudaei crudeles erant et ad
avaritiam proni, per quae vitia maxime homines in tyrannidem
decidunt. Et ideo Dominus a principio eis regem non instituit cum
plena potestate, sed iudicem et gubernatorem in eorum custodiam.
Sed postea regem ad petitionem populi, quasi indignatus, concessit: ut
patet per hoc quod dixit ad Samuelem, 1 *Reg.* VIII: « *Non te abiecerunt,
sed me, ne regnem super eos* ». Instituit tamen a principio circa regem
instituendum, primo quidem, modum eligendi, in quo duo deter-
minavit: ut scilicet in eius electione « *expectarent iudicium Domini, et
ut non facerent regem alterius gentis* », quia tales reges solent parum
affici ad gentem cui praeficiuntur, et per consequens non curare de
eis. Secundo, ordinavit circa reges institutos qualiter deberent se
habere quantum ad seipsos: ut scilicet non « *multiplicarent currus et
equos, neque uxores, neque etiam immensas divitias* »; quia ex cupiditate
horum principes ad tyrannidem declinant, et iustitiam derelinquunt.
Instituit etiam qualiter se deberent habere ad Deum: ut scilicet « *semper
legerent et cogitarent de lege Dei, et semper essent in Dei timore et obedientia* ». Instituit etiam qualiter se haberent ad subditos suos: ut
scilicet « *non superbe eos contemnerent, aut opprimerent, neque etiam a
iustitia declinarent* ».

of your tribes men, wise and honourable, and appointed them rulers.'
And this was aristocracy. But it was democratic in the sense that they
were elected from the whole people, for it is said in *Exodus* (XVIII, 21):
'Seek out from the whole people wise men,' etc.; and also in the sense
that the people elected them, for it is said in *Deuteronomy* (I, 13):
'Let me have from among you wise and understanding men,' etc.
So it is clear that there was an excellent ordering of authority in the
Law [of the Old Testament].

Limited Monarchy. Its Advantages and Characteristics. (Ibid. ad 2um.)

A monarchy is the best form of government for a people, provided
it does not become corrupt. But because of the wide powers conferred upon a king, it is easy for a monarchy to degenerate into a
tyranny, unless there is perfect virtue in the one into whose hands
such power is given: for 'only the virtuous can remain upright in good
fortune,' as the Philosopher says (IV, *Ethics*). But perfect virtue is
found in few persons: and the Jews, particularly, were greatly prone to
cruelty and to avarice, which are the chief vices inclining men to
tyranny. So the Lord did not from the beginning set over them kings
having supreme power, but a judge and governor to control them:
only later, at the request of the people, and as though in anger, did
He give them a king, as we see from what He said to Samuel (1 *Kings*,
VIII, 7), 'They have not rejected thee, but me, that I should not reign
over them.' But with regard to the institution of monarchy, He laid
it down from the beginning how the king should be elected: and here
He prescribed two things; that in making election they should 'consider the judgement of the Lord and not seek a king from another
nation'; for such kings do not, in general, become well adapted to the
people over whom they are set; and, in consequence, have little love
for them. In the second place He laid it down with regard to the
institution of kings, how they [the kings] should bear themselves:
that they should not 'multiply the numbers of their chariots or of their
horses or of their wives, nor should they store up immense riches,'
because from desire of such, princes soon become tyrants, and depart
from justice. He also laid down how they should bear themselves
towards God: that they should 'always read and think upon the law
of God, and remain always in obedience and fear of God.' Lastly, He
laid down how they should bear themselves towards their subjects:
that they should not 'look down upon them with pride, nor oppress
them nor ever fail in justice to them.'

SECUNDA SECUNDAE PARTIS

Quaestio X.—DE INFIDELITATE.

ART. 8.—*Utrum infideles compellendi sint ad fidem.*

Respondeo dicendum, quod infidelium quidam sunt, qui numquam susceperunt fidem, sicut Gentiles et Iudaei: et tales nullo modo sunt ad fidem compellendi, ut ipsi credant: quia credere voluntatis est. Sunt tamen compellendi a fidelibus si facultas adsit ut fidem non impediant, vel blasphemiis, vel malis persuasionibus, vel etiam apertis persecutionibus. Et propter hoc fideles Christi frequenter contra infideles bellum movent: non quidem, ut eos ad credendum cogant (quia si etiam eos vicissent, et captivos haberent, in eorum libertate relinquerent an credere vellent), sed propter hoc, ut eos compellant, ne fidem Christi impediant. Alii vero sunt infideles, qui quandoque fidem susceperunt, et eam profitentur, sicut haeretici vel quicumque apostatae: et tales sunt etiam corporaliter compellendi, ut impleant quod promiserunt, et teneant quod semel susceperunt.

ART. 10.—*Utrum infideles possint habere praelationem, seu dominium supra fideles.*

Respondeo dicendum quod circa hoc [*sc.* utrum infideles possint habere praelationem seu dominium super fideles] dupliciter loqui possumus. Uno modo de dominio, vel praelatione infidelium super fideles de novo instituenda: et hoc nullo modo permitti debet. Cedit enim hoc in scandalum et in periculum fidei. Defacili enim illi qui subiiciuntur aliorum iurisdictioni, immutari possunt ab eis quibus subsunt, ut sequantur eorum imperium, nisi illi qui subsunt fuerint magnae virtutis. Et similiter, infideles contemnunt fidem, si fidelium defectus cognoscant. Et ideo Apost. prohibuit, quod fideles non contendant iudicio coram iudice infideli. Et ideo nullo modo permittit Ecclesia, quod infideles acquirant dominium super fideles, vel qualitercumque eis praeficiantur in aliquo officio. Alio modo possumus loqui de dominio vel praelatione iam praeexistenti. Ubi considerandum est, quod dominium et praelatio introducta sunt ex

SECUNDA SECUNDAE

14. *POLITICAL AND RELIGIOUS DUTY*

The Free Acceptance of the Christian Faith. (Qu. 10, Art. 8.)

Among infidels there are some who have never accepted the Christian faith, such as Gentiles and Jews: and these should in no way be constrained to embrace the faith and profess belief. For belief depends upon the will. The faithful may, however, if they wish, use force to prevent them from impeding the faith by blasphemy or by evil persuasion or even by open persecution. For this reason Christians have often gone to war against the infidel: not to force them into belief (for even if they were to conquer them and bring them captive the latter would still be at liberty to believe or not); but to prevent them from putting obstacles in the way of the Christian faith. Then there are infidels who at one time accepted the faith and professed it, such as heretics and all apostates: such should be constrained, even physically, to fulfil what they have promised and to observe what once they accepted for ever.

The Validity of Political Duty in the Case of Difference of Faith. (Ibid. Art. 10.)

We can consider the question [whether infidels may exercise government or dominion over the faithful] from two points of view. Firstly, when the government or dominion of infidels over the faithful has yet to be constituted: and this is not, under any circumstances, permissible. For this gives rise to scandal and puts the faith in peril. For it can easily come about that those who are under the jurisdiction of others, can be induced to change, out of obedience to their superiors and to follow their directions, unless they happen to be of very high virtue. And at the same time the infidel are led to despise the faith, when they learn of the defection of the faithful. So the Apostle forbade the faithful to seek judgement of an infidel judge. Similarly the Church under no circumstances permits infidels to acquire dominion over the faithful, or in any way to be set in office over them. Secondly, we must consider the case when government or dominion is already established. Here we must note that government and

iure humano; distinctio autem fidelium et infidelium est ex iure divino. Ius autem divinum, quod est ex gratia, non tollit ius humanum, quod est ex naturali ratione. Ideo distinctio fidelium et infidelium, secundum se considerata, non tollit dominium et praelationem infidelium supra fideles. Potest tamen iuste per sententiam vel ordinationem Ecclesiae auctoritatem Dei habentis, tale ius dominii vel praelationis tolli: quia infideles merito suae infidelitatis merentur potestatem amittere super fideles, qui transferuntur in filios Dei. Sed hoc quidem Ecclesia quandoque facit, quandoque autem non facit.

ART. 11.—*Utrum infidelium ritus sint tolerandi.*

Respondeo dicendum, quod humanum regimen derivatur a divino regimine, et ipsum debet imitari. Deus autem quamvis sit omnipotens et summe bonus, permittit tamen aliqua mala fieri in universo, quae prohibere posset, ne eis sublatis maiora bona tollerentur, vel etiam peiora mala sequerentur. Sic igitur et in regimine humano, illi qui praesunt recte aliqua mala tolerant, ne aliqua bona impediantur, vel etiam ne aliqua mala peiora incurrantur. Sicut Augustinus dicit in lib. *de Ord.* (II, cap. 4): « *Aufer meretrices de rebus humanis, turbaveris omnia libidinibus* ». Sic igitur, quamvis infideles in suis ritibus peccent, tolerari possunt, vel propter aliquod bonum quod ex eis provenit, vel propter aliquod malum quod vitatur. Ex hoc autem quod Iudaei ritus suos observant, in quibus olim praefigurabatur veritas fidei, quam tenemus, hoc bonum provenit, quod testimonium fidei nostrae habemus ab hostibus, et quasi in figura nobis repraesentatur quod credimus: et ideo in suis ritibus tolerantur. Aliorum infidelium ritus, qui nihil veritatis aut utilitatis afferunt, non sunt aliqualiter tolerandi, nisi forte ad aliquod malum vitandum, scilicet ad vitandum scandalum vel dissidium, quod ex hoc posset provenire, vel impedimentum salutis eorum, qui paulatim sic tolerati convertuntur ad fidem. Propter hoc enim etiam haereticorum et paganorum ritus aliquando Ecclesia toleravit, quando erat magna infidelium multitudo.

dominion depend from human law; but the distinction between the faithful and infidels is from divine law. The divine law, however, which is a law of grace, does not abolish human law which is founded upon natural reason. So the distinction between the faithful and the infidel, considered in itself, does not invalidate the government and dominion of infidels over the faithful. Such right to dominion or government may, however, with justice be abrogated by order of the Church in virtue of her divine authority; for the infidel, on account or their unbelief, deserve to lose their power over the faithful who are become the sons of God. But the Church sometimes does and sometimes does not take such steps.

Tolerance of non-Christian Cults. (Ibid. Art. 11.)

Human government derives from divine government and should imitate it. Now God, in His omnipotence and sovereign goodness, sometimes permits evil to be done in the world, though He could prevent it; lest, by so doing, a greater good be destroyed or even greater evils might follow. So also in human government those who are in power, rightly permit certain evils lest some good be brought to nothing or perhaps even greater evils take their place. As St. Augustine says in the *De Ordinatione* (II, 4): 'If prostitution be suppressed, licence will rage unchecked.' So, therefore, though infidels may sin by their rites, they are to be tolerated either because of some good they may draw from them or because of some evil which is thus avoided. Thus, from the fact that the Jews observe their rites, in which the true faith, which we hold, was foreshadowed of old, there derives this benefit that we obtain testimony to our faith from our enemies, and a symbolic representation of our beliefs: so they are tolerated in their rites. But the rites of other infidels, which have nothing of truth or usefulness in them, are to be in no-wise tolerated; unless perhaps to avoid some evil, such as the avoidance of scandal or the discord which might arise from their suppression; or the obstacle which would thus be put in the way of the salvation of those who might, on account of such tolerance, end by being converted to the faith. For this reason the Church has sometimes tolerated the rites even of heretics and pagans, when the infidels were very great in number.

Quaestio XI.—DE HAERESI.

ART. 3.—*Utrum haeretici sint tolerandi.*

Respondeo dicendum, quod circa haereticos duo sunt consideranda: unum quidem ex parte ipsorum; aliud ex parte Ecclesiae. Ex parte quidem ipsorum est peccatum, per quod meruerunt non solum ab Ecclesia per excommunicationem separari, sed etiam per mortem a mundo excludi. Multo enim gravius est corrumpere fidem per quam est animae vita, quam falsare pecuniam, per quam temporali vitae subvenitur. Unde si falsarii pecuniae vel alii malefactores statim per saeculares principes iuste morti traduntur; multo magis haeretici statim, cum de haeresi convincuntur, possunt non solum excommunicari, sed et iuste occidi. Ex parte autem Ecclesiae, est misericordia ad errantium conversionem: et ideo non statim condemnat, « *sed post primam et secundam correptionem* », ut Apostolus docet: postmodum vero, si adhuc pertinax inveniatur, Ecclesia de eius conversione non sperans, aliorum saluti providet, eum ab Ecclesia separando per excommunicationis sententiam; et ulterius relinquit eum iudicio saeculari, a mundo exterminandum per mortem. Dicit enim Hieronimus et habetur quaest. 3: « *Resecandae sunt putridae carnes, et scabiosa ovis a caulis repellenda, ne tota domus, massa, corpus et pecora, ardeat, corrumpatur, putrescat, intereat. Arius in Alexandria una scintilla fuit: sed quoniam non statim oppressus est, totum orbem eius flamma populata est* ».

Quaestio XII.—DE APOSTASIA.

ART. 2.—*Utrum Princeps propter apostasiam a fide, amittat dominium in subditos, ita quod ei obedire non teneantur.*

Respondeo dicendum, quod sicut supra dictum est, infidelitas secundum seipsam non repugnat dominio, eo quod dominium introductum est de iure gentium, quod est ius humanum. Distinctio autem fidelium et infidelium est secundum ius divinum, per quod non tollitur ius humanum. Sed aliquis per infidelitatem peccans potest sententialiter ius dominii amittere, sicut et quandoque propter alias culpas. Ad Ecclesiam autem non pertinet punire infidelitatem in illis, qui numquam fidem susceperunt, secundum illud Apostoli I *ad Corint.* 5: « *Quid mihi de his, qui foris sunt, iudicare?* ». Sed infidelitatem illorum,

Heresy may not be Tolerated. (Qu. 11, Art. 3.)

In regard to heretics two points must be kept in mind. The first with regard to heretics themselves. The second with regard to the Church. From the point of view of heretics themselves there is their sin, by which they have deserved not only to be separated from the Church, but to be eliminated from the world by death. For it is a far graver matter to corrupt the faith which is the life of the soul than to falsify money which sustains temporal life. So, if it be just that forgers and other malefactors are put to death without mercy by the secular authority, with how much greater reason may heretics be not only excommunicated, but also put to death, when once they are convicted of heresy. On the part of the Church there is merciful hope of the conversion of those in error. For this reason She does not immediately condemn, 'but only after a first and second admonition,' as the Apostle teaches. Only then, if the heretic remains pertinacious, the Church, despairing of his conversion, makes provision for the safety of others; and separating him, by the sentence of excommunication, from the Church, passes him to secular judgement to be exterminated from the world by death. St. Jerome says, and we read[1]: 'The tainted flesh must be cut away, and the infected sheep cast out from the fold: lest the whole house burn, the mass be corrupted, the body become infected and the flock perish. Arius was but a spark in Alexandria, but for want of being immediately quenched, a conflagration has devastated the whole world.'

The Cessation of Civil Obligation for Religious Reasons. (Qu. 12, Art. 2.)

As we have said above, unbelief is not in itself incompatible with dominion since dominion derives from the law of nations which is human law. Whereas the distinction between believers and unbelievers follows from divine law, which does not abrogate human law. But he who sins through unbelief may, by judicial sentence, be deprived of his right to rule, as also for other faults. But it is not the province of the Church to punish infidelity in those who have never embraced the faith, according to what the Apostle says, (I *Corinthians*, V, 12): 'What have I to do to judge them that are without?' But the infidelity of those who have once embraced the faith, She may punish

---

[1] In the *Decretum Gratiani*, Secunda Pars, xxix, iii, 16.

qui fidem susceperunt, potest sententialiter punire, et convenienter in hoc puniuntur, quod subditis fidelibus dominari non possint. Hoc enim vertere posset in magnam fidei corruptionem: quia, ut dictum est, « *homo apostata suo corde machinatur malum, et iurgia seminat* », intendens homines separare a fide. Et ideo quam cito aliquis per sententiam denuntiatur excommunicatus propter apostasiam a fide, ipso facto eius subditi sunt absoluti a dominio eius, et iuramento fidelitatis, quo ei tenebantur.

Quaestio XL.—De Bello.

Art. 1.—*Utrum bellare sit semper peccatum.*

Respondeo dicendum, quod ad hoc quod aliquod bellum sit iustum tria requiruntur. Primo quidem auctoritas principis, cuius mandato bellum est gerendum. Non enim pertinet ad personam privatam bellum movere: quia potest ius suum in iudicio superioris prosequi. Similiter etiam quia convocare multitudinem, quod in bellis oportet fieri, non pertinet ad privatam personam. Cum autem cura reipublicae commissa sit principibus, ad eos pertinet rempublicam civitatis, vel regni, seu provinciae sibi subditae tueri. Et sicut licite defendunt eam materiali gladio contra interiores quidem perturbatores, dum malefactores puniunt, secundum illud Apostoli *ad Rom.* XIII: « *Non sine causa gladium portat: minister enim Dei est, vindex in iram ei qui male agit* »: ita etiam gladio bellico ad eos pertinet rempublicam tueri ab exterioribus hostibus. Unde et principibus dicitur in *Psalm.* LXXXI: « *Eripite pauperem, et egenum de manu peccatoris liberate* ». Unde Aug. dicit *contra Faustum* (lib. XXIII, cap. 73): « *Ordo naturalis mortalium paci accomodatus hoc poscit, ut suscipiendi belli auctoritas atque consilium penes principes sit* ». Secundo requiritur causa iusta, ut scilicet illi, qui impugnantur propter aliquam culpam, impugnationem mereantur. Unde Augustinus dicit in lib. LXXXIII q. (*super Iosue* qu. X): « *Iusta bella solent diffiniri, quae ulciscuntur iniurias, si gens vel civitas plectenda est, quae vel vindicare neglexerit, quod a suis improbe factum est: vel reddere quod per iniuriam ablatum est* ». Tertio requiritur ut sit intentio bellantium recta, qua scilicet intenditur, vel ut bonum promoveatur, vel ut malum vitetur. Unde Augustinus in lib. *de Verbis Domini:* « *Apud veros Dei cultores etiam illa bella pacata sunt, quae non cupiditate aut crudelitate, sed pacis studio geruntur, ut mali coerceantur, et boni subleventur* ».

by judicial sentence; and it is just that they be punished by loss of the right to rule believers. For this could lead to widespread corruption of the faith: as it is said, 'the apostate breeds evil in his heart, and sows discord,' seeking to detach men from the faith. And therefore, as soon as a ruler falls under sentence of excommunication for apostasy from the faith, his subjects are *ipso facto* absolved from his rule, and from the oath of fealty which bound them to him.

15. *WAR*. (Qu. 40.)

The Conditions of a Just War. (Art. 1.)

For a war to be just three conditions are necessary. First, the authority of the ruler within whose competence it lies to declare war. A private individual may not declare war; for he can have recourse to the judgement of a superior to safeguard his rights. Nor has he the right to mobilize the people, which is necessary in war. But since responsibility for public affairs is entrusted to the rulers, it is they who are charged with the defence of the city, realm, or province, subject to them. And just as in the punishment of criminals they rightly defend the state against all internal disturbance with the civil arm; as the Apostle says (*Romans*, XIII, 4): 'He beareth not the sword in vain. For he is God's minister: an avenger to execute wrath upon him that doth evil.' So also they have the duty of defending the state, with the weapons of war, against external enemies. For this reason rulers are told in *Psalm* LXXXI to 'Rescue the poor; and deliver the needy out of the hand of the sinner.' And St. Augustine says in his book, *Contra Faustum* (XXIII, 73): 'The natural order of men, to be peacefully disposed, requires that the power and decision to declare war should lie with the rulers.'

Secondly, there is required a just cause: that is that those who are attacked for some offence merit such treatment. St. Augustine says (Book LXXXIII q.; *Super Josue*, qu. X): 'Those wars are generally defined as just which avenge some wrong, when a nation or a state is to be punished for having failed to make amends for the wrong done, or to restore what has been taken unjustly.'

Thirdly, there is required a right intention on the part of the belligerents: either of achieving some good object or of avoiding some evil. So St. Augustine says in the book *De Verbis Domini*: 'For the true followers of God even wars are peaceful, not being made for greed or out of cruelty, but from desire of peace, to restrain the evil

Potest autem contingere, quod etiam si sit legitima auctoritas indicentis bellum, et causa iusta, nihilominus propter pravam intentionem bellum reddatur illicitum. Dicit enim Augustinus in lib. *contra Faustum* (cap. LXXIV): « *Nocendi cupiditas, ulciscendi crudelitas, implacatus et implacabilis animus, feritas debellandi, libido dominandi, et si quae sunt similia, haec sunt quae in bellis iure culpantur* ».

Quaestio XLII.—DE SEDITIONE.

ART. 2.—*Utrum seditio sit semper peccatum mortale.*

Ad tertium dicendum, quod regimen tyrannicum non est iustum; quia non ordinatur ad bonum commune, sed ad bonum privatum regentis: ut patet per Philos. in III *Polit.* et in VIII *Ethic.* Et ideo perturbatio huius regiminis non habet rationem seditionis; nisi forte quando sic inordinate perturbatur tyranni regimen quod multitudo subiecta maius detrimentum patitur ex perturbatione consequenti, quam ex tyranni regimine. Magis autem tyrannus seditiosus est, qui in populo sibi subiecto discordias et seditiones nutrit, ut tutius dominari possit. Hoc enim tyrannicum est, cum sit ordinatum ad bonum proprium praesidentis, cum multitudinis nocumento.

Quaestio XLVII.—DE PRUDENTIA.

ART. 10.—*Utrum prudentia se extendat ad regimen multitudinis.*

Ad secundum dicendum, quod ille qui quaerit bonum commune multitudinis, ex consequenti etiam quaerit bonum suum propter duo. Primo quidem, quia bonum proprium non potest esse sine bono communi vel familiae, vel civitatis aut regni. Unde et Valerius Maximus dicit de antiquis Romanis, quod « *malebant esse pauperes in divite imperio, quam divites in paupere imperio* ». Secundo, quia cum homo sit pars domus et civitatis oportet quod homo consideret quid sit sibi bonum ex hoc, quod est prudens circa bonum multitudinis. Bona enim dispositio partis accipitur secundum habitudinem ad totum: quia, ut Aug. dicit in libro *Confessionum:* « *Turpis est omnis pars suo toti non congruens* ».

and assist the good.' So it can happen that even when war is declared by legitimate authority and there is just cause, it is, nevertheless, made unjust through evil intention. St. Augustine says in *Contra Faustum* (LXXIV): 'The desire to hurt, the cruelty of vendetta, the stern and implacable spirit, arrogance in victory, the thirst for power, and all that is similar, all these are justly condemned in war.'

16. *THE RIGHT TO RESIST TYRANNICAL GOVERNMENT*. (Qu. 42, Art. 2.)

Tyrannical government is unjust government because it is directed not to the common welfare but to the private benefit of the ruler. This is clear from what the Philosopher says in the *Politics*, Book III, and in the *Ethics*, Book VIII. Consequently the overthrowing of such government is not strictly sedition; except perhaps in the case that it is accompanied by such disorder that the community suffers greater harm from the consequent disturbances than it would from a continuance of the former rule. A tyrant himself is, in fact, far more guilty of sedition when he spreads discord and strife among the people subject to him, so hoping to control them more easily. For it is a characteristic of tyranny to order everything to the personal satisfaction of the ruler at the expense of the community.

17. *POLITICAL PRUDENCE*

Its Nature. (Qu. 47, Art. 10.)

Whoever promotes the common welfare of the community promotes his own welfare at the same time: and this for two reasons. First, because individual well-being cannot exist without the welfare of the family, or city, or realm. Valerius Maximus says of the Romans of old that, 'They preferred rather to be poor men in a rich empire, than rich men in a poor empire.' Secondly, because man, being part of the family, or of the city, it is right that he should consider his personal well-being in the light of what prudence advises with regard to the common welfare. For the good disposition of any part must be determined by its relationship to the whole. For, as St. Augustine says in the *Confessions*: 'All parts are base which do not fit or harmonise with their whole.'

L

Quaestio L.—DE PARTIBUS PRUDENTIAE POLIARCHICAE SUBIECTIVIS.

ART. 1.—*Utrum regnativa debeat poni species prudentiae.*

Respondeo dicendum quod ad prudentiam pertinet regere et praecipere; et ideo ubi invenitur specialis ratio regiminis et praecepti in humanis actibus, ibi etiam invenitur specialis ratio prudentiae. Manifestum est autem quod in eo qui non solum seipsum habet regere, sed etiam communitatem perfectam civitatis vel regni, invenitur specialis et perfecta ratio regiminis. Tanto enim regimen perfectius est, quanto universalius ad plura se extendens, et ulteriorem finem attingens; et ideo regi ad quem pertinet regere civitatem vel regnum, prudentia competit secundum specialem et perfectissimam sui rationem. Et propter hoc *regnativa* ponitur species prudentiae.

Quaestio LVII.—DE IUSTITIA ET PRIMO DE IURE QUOD EST UT OBIECTUM.

ART. 2.—*Utrum ius convenienter dividatur in ius naturale et ius positivum.*

Respondeo dicendum quod, sicut dictum est, ius, sive iustum, est aliquod opus adaequatum alteri secundum aliquem aequalitatis modum. Dupliciter autem potest alicui homini aliquid esse adaequatum. Uno quidem modo, ex ipsa natura rei: puta cum aliquis tantum dat ut tantumdem recipiat. Et hoc vocatur ius naturale. — Alio modo aliquid est adaequatum vel commensuratum alteri ex condicto, sive ex communi placito: quando scilicet aliquis reputat se contentum si tantum accipiat. Quod quidem potest fieri dupliciter. Uno modo, per aliquod privatum condictum: sicut quod firmatur aliquo pacto inter privatas personas. Alio modo, ex condicto publico: puta cum totus populus consentit quod aliquid habeatur quasi adaequatum et commensuratum alteri; vel cum hoc ordinat princeps, qui curam populi habet et eius personam gerit. Et hoc dicitur ius positivum.

Ad secundum dicendum quod voluntas humana ex communi condicto potest aliquid facere iustum in his quae secundum se non habent aliquam repugnantiam ad naturalem iustitiam. Et in his habet locum ius positivum. Unde Philosophus dicit, in V *Ethic.*, quod legale iustum est « *quod ex principio quidem nihil differt sic vel aliter:*

Its Object. (Qu. 50, Art. 1.)

The object of prudence is government and command. So wherever there is to be found a special form of government and command in human actions, there is to be found also a special form of prudence. But it is clear that in a man whose duty it is to govern, not only himself, but also a perfect community such as a city or realm, there is to be found a special and perfect form of governing. For government is the more perfect the more universal it is, and the further it extends and the higher its aims. Therefore a king, whose duty it is to rule a city or kingdom, must possess prudence of a special and most perfect quality. For this reason we distinguish a species of 'political' prudence.

18. *NATURAL AND POSITIVE JUSTICE.* (Qu. 57.)

The Origin of Positive Justice. (Art. 2, concl.)

Right, or what is just, lies in the due proportion between some exterior action and another according to a certain relationship of equality. Now there are two ways in which such a proportion may be established for man. First, from the nature of the thing itself: as for example when some one gives so much that he may receive equal in return. And this is called natural justice (*ius naturale*).—Secondly, something may be comparable or commensurate with another by agreement or common consent: as when, for example, some one declares himself content to receive such an amount. This again can happen in two ways. Either by private agreement, as when a pact is reached among a number of private individuals: or by public agreement, when such a proportion or standard of measurement is agreed by the consent of the whole community, or by decree of the ruler who administers and represents the community. And this is called positive justice (*ius positivum*).

The Subordination of Positive to Natural Justice. (Ibid. ad 2um.)

The human will can, by common consent, attribute juridical value to anything which is not in itself contrary to natural justice. And this is precisely the field of positive law. So the Philosopher (V, *Ethics*) defines the legally just as 'that which does not in itself present any difference of values, but which acquires them on being laid down.'

quando autem ponitur, differt ». Sed si aliquid de se repugnantiam habeat ad ius naturale, non potest voluntate humana fieri iustum: puta si statuatur quod liceat furari vel adulterium committere. Unde dicitur *Isaiae* X (vers. I): « *Vae qui condunt leges iniquas* ».

Quaestio LVIII.—DE IPSA IUSTITIA.

ART. 1.—*Utrum convenienter diffiniatur iustitia, quod est « perpetua et constans voluntas, ius suum unicuique tribuendi* ».[1]

Ad quintum dicendum quod iudex reddit quod suum est per modum imperantis et dirigentis: quia « *iudex est iustum animatum* » et « *princeps est custos iusti* », ut dicitur in V *Ethic.* (cap. 4). Sed subditi reddunt quod suum est unicuique per modum executionis. (*Cp.* art. 6, *concl.*: iustitia . . . est in principe principaliter, et quasi architectonice; in subditis autem secundario et quasi ministrative).

ART. 5.—*Utrum iustitia sit virtus generalis.*

Respondeo dicendum quod iustitia, sicut dictum est, ordinat hominem in comparatione ad alium. Quod quidem potest esse dupliciter. Uno modo, ad alium singulariter consideratum. Alio modo, ad alium in communi: secundum scilicet quod ille qui servit alicui communitati servit omnibus hominibus qui sub communitate illa continentur. Ad utrumque igitur se potest habere iustitia secundum propriam rationem. Manifestum est autem quod omnes qui sub communitate aliqua continentur comparantur ad communitatem sicut partes ad totum. Pars autem id quod est totius est: unde et quodlibet bonum partis est ordinabile in bonum totius. Secundum hoc igitur bonum cuiuslibet virtutis, sive ordinantis aliquem hominem ad seipsum sive ordinantis ipsum ad aliquas alias personas singulares, est referibile ad bonum commune, ad quod ordinat iustitia. Et secundum hoc actus omnium virtutum possunt ad iustitiam pertinere, secundum quod ordinat hominem ad bonum commune.

ART. 7.—*Utrum sit aliqua iustitia particularis praeter iustitiam generalem.*

Ad secundum dicendum quod bonum commune civitatis et bonum singulare unius personae non differunt solum secundum multum et paucum, sed secundum formalem differentiam: alia enim est ratio boni communis et boni singularis, sicut alia est ratio totius et partis. Et ideo Philosophus, in I *Polit.* (cap. 1), dicit quod: « *non bene dicunt*

[1] *Dig.*, I, i, 10 (Ulpianus).

But if a thing is in itself contrary to natural justice, it cannot be made just by human volition: if, for example, it were laid down that it is permissible to steal or commit adultery, so it is said in *Isaias* (X, 1): 'Woe to those who make evil laws.'

19. JUSTICE AND THE STATE. (Qu. 58.)

The various ways in which Justice is achieved in the State. (Art. 1, ad 5um.)

The judge renders to each his due in that he commands and directs: because, as is said in the *Ethics* (V, 4), 'the judge is the embodiment of justice' and 'the ruler is the custodian of justice.' Subjects, on the other hand, render to each his due in the capacity of executors. (Cp. Art. 6, concl.: Justice . . . is in the ruler as in principle and constructively; in subjects, however, it is derivative and executive).

Justice and the Common Welfare. (Art. 5, concl.)

The scope of justice, as we have said, is to regulate men in their relations with others. Here there are two cases to be considered. Either when the reference is to others considered individually. Or when the reference is to others considered as a community: to the extent, that is, to which one who is a subject of a certain community is subject also to all the persons who go to form it. Justice, as such, enters into both cases. For it is evident that all those who make up the community, have to it the same relationship as that of parts to a whole. Now the part, as such, belongs to the whole: consequently any partial interest is subordinate to the good of the whole. From this point of view, whatever is good and virtuous, whether in respect of a man to himself or with respect to the relationships between men, can have reference to the common well-being which is the object of justice. In this sense all virtues may come within the province of justice, in so far as it orders men to the common welfare.

The Common Welfare and Individual Interest. (Art. 7, ad 2um.)

The common welfare of the city and the individual welfare of one person are distinguished not only by a quantative but also by a formal difference: for the common welfare is different in nature from that of the individual, just as the nature of the part is different from that of the whole. So the Philosopher (I, *Politics*, 1), says: 'they are in

qui dicunt civitatem et domum et alia huiusmodi differre solum multitudine et paucitate, et non specie ».

Quaestio LX.—DE IUDICIO.

ART. 6.—*Utrum iudicium per usurpationem reddatur perversum.*

Ad tertium dicendum quod potestas saecularis subditur spirituali, sicut corpus animae (ut Gregorius Nazianz. dicit *Orat.* XVII). Et ideo non est usurpatum iudicium, si spiritualis Praelatus se intromittat de temporalibus, quantum ad ea in quibus subditur ei saecularis potestas, vel quae ei a saeculari potestate relinquuntur.

Quaestio LXVII.—DE INIUSTITIA IUDICIS.

ART. 1.—*Utrum aliquis possit iuste iudicare eum, qui non est sibi subiectus.*

Ad secundum dicendum, quod in rebus humanis aliqui propria sponte possunt se subiicere aliorum iudicio, quamvis non sint eis superiores: sicut patet in his qui compromittunt in aliquos arbitros. Et inde est quod necesse est arbitrium poena vallari: quia arbitri qui non sunt superiores, non habent de se plenam potestatem coercendi. Sic igitur et Christus propria sponte humano iudicio se subdidit; sicut etiam et Papa Leo iudicio Imperatoris se subdidit.

Quaestio CXLVII.—DE IEIUNIO.

ART. 3.—*Utrum ieiunium sit in praecepto.*

Respondeo dicendum quod, sicut ad saeculares principes pertinet praecepta legalia, iuris naturalis determinativa, tradere, de his quae pertinent ad utilitatem communem in temporalibus rebus; ita etiam ad praelatos ecclesiasticos pertinet ea statutis praecipere, quae ad utilitatem communem fidelium pertinent in spiritualibus bonis.

Quaestio LXVI.—DE PECCATIS IUSTITIAE OPPOSITIS.

ART. 1.—*Utrum naturalis sit homini possessio exteriorum rerum.*

Respondeo dicendum quod res exterior potest dupliciter considerari. Uno modo, quantum ad eius naturam: quae non subiacet humanae

error who say that the city, and the family and other similar groups, differ only in size and not specifically.'

20. THE RELATIONSHIP BETWEEN THE TEMPORAL AND THE SPIRITUAL POWER.

The Right of the Spiritual Power to interpose in temporal affairs. (Qu. 60, Art. 6, ad 3um.)

The temporal power is subject to the spiritual as the body to the soul, as St. Gregory Nazianzenus says (*Orat.* XVII). Therefore there is no usurpation of power if a spiritual Prelate should interest himself in temporal affairs with respect to those things in which the temporal power is subject to him or in matters which have been left to him by the secular power.

Possibility of the Submission of the Spiritual to the Temporal Authority. (Qu. 67, Art. 1, ad 2um.)

. In human affairs it can happen that persons submit themselves spontaneously to the judgement of others, even though these may not be their superiors; as for instance when people have recourse to arbitration. But arbiters, not being superiors, have not in themselves the full power of enforcing their decision and therefore it is necessary for such decision to be accompanied by some sanction. In this sense, Christ freely subjected Himself to human judgement, and Pope Leo also submitted himself to the judgement of the Emperor.

Distinction between the Temporal and the Spiritual Sphere. (Qu. 147, Art. 3, concl.)

Just as it falls to temporal princes to enact legal statutes which are particular determinations of the natural law, in all those matters which concern the common welfare in mundane affairs; so also it is the province of ecclesiastical prelates to regulate by precept those matters which affect the common interest of the faithful to their spiritual well-being.

21. THE RIGHT TO PROPERTY. (Qu. 66.)

Man's Control over Nature. (Art. 1, concl.)

Material things may be considered under two aspects. First, as to their nature: and this in no way lies within human power, but only

potestati, sed solum divinae, cui omnia ad nutum obediunt. Alio modo quantum ad usum ipsius rei. Et sic habet homo naturale dominium exteriorum rerum: quia per rationem et voluntatem potest uti rebus exterioribus ad suam utilitatem, quasi propter se factis: semper enim imperfectiora sunt propter perfectiora, ut supra habitum est. Et ex hac ratione Philosophus probat, in I *Polit.*, quod possessio rerum exteriorum est homini naturalis. Hoc autem naturale dominium super ceteras creaturas quod competit homini secundum rationem in qua imago Dei consistit, manifestatur in ipsa hominis creatione, *Gen. I.*, ubi dicitur: « *Faciamus hominem ad similitudinem et imaginem nostram, et praesit piscibus maris* », etc.

ART. 2.—*Utrum liceat alicui rem aliquam quasi propriam possidere.*

Respondeo dicendum quod circa rem exteriorem duo competunt homini. Quorum unum est potestas procurandi et dispensandi. Et quantum ad hoc licitum est quod homo propria possideat. Et est etiam necessarium ad humanam vitam, propter tria. Primo quidem quia magis sollicitus est unusquisque ad procurandum aliquid quod sibi soli competit quam aliquid quod est commune omnium vel multorum: quia unusquisque, laborem fugiens, relinquit alteri id quod pertinet ad commune: sicut accidit in multitudine ministrorum. — Alio modo, quia ordinatius res humanae tractantur si singulis immineat propria cura alicuius rei procurandae: esset autem confusio si quilibet indistincte quaelibet procuraret. — Tertio quia per hoc magis pacificus status hominum conservatur, dum unusquisque re sua contentus est. Unde videmus quod inter eos qui communiter et ex indiviso aliquid possident, frequentius iurgia oriuntur.

Aliud vero quod competit homini circa res exteriores est usus ipsarum. Et quantum ad hoc non debet homo habere res exteriores ut proprias, sed ut communes: ut scilicet de facili aliquis eas communicet in necessitates aliorum. Unde Apostolus dicit, I ad *Tim.*, ult. « *Divitibus huius saeculi praecipe facile tribuere, communicare* ».

Ad primum ergo dicendum quod communitas rerum attribuitur iuri naturali, non quia ius naturale dictet omnia esse possidenda communiter et nihil esse quasi proprium possidendum: sed quia secundum ius naturale non est distinctio possessionum, sed magis secundum

within the divine power whose wish all things obey. Secondly, as to the use of such things. And in this respect, man has a natural control over material things; for he can, in virtue of his reason and will, make use of material things for his own benefit, as though they were created for this purpose: for imperfect things exist to serve the advantage of the more perfect as we have already seen. On this principle the Philosopher proves (I, *Politics*), that the possession of material things is natural to man. And this natural dominion which man has over other creatures, in virtue of reason which makes him the image of God, is clearly shown in the creation of man (*Genesis* I) where it is said: 'Let us make man to our own image and likeness, and he shall rule over the fish of the sea,' etc.

The Limits of Private Property. (Art. 2, concl.)

With respect to material things there are two points which man must consider. First, concerning the power of acquisition and disposal: and in this respect private possession is permissible. It is also necessary to human life for three reasons. First, because every one is more concerned with the obtaining of what concerns himself alone than with the common affairs of all or of many others: for each one, avoiding extra labour, leaves the common task to the next man; as we see when there are too many officials. Secondly, because human affairs are dealt with in a more orderly manner when each has his own business to go about: there would be complete confusion if every one tried to do everything. Thirdly, because this leads to a more peaceful condition of man; provided each is content with his own. So we see that it is among those who possess something jointly and in common that disputes most frequently arise.

The other point which concerns man with regard to material things is their use. As to this, men should not hold material things as their own but to the common benefit: each readily sharing them with others in their necessity. So the Apostle says (I *Tim.*, ult.): 'Charge the rich of this world to give easily, to communicate to others.'

The Right to Private Property Derives from Human Law. (Ibid. ad 1um.)

The common possession of things is to be attributed to natural law, not in the sense that natural law decrees that all things are to be held in common and that there is to be no private possession: but in the sense that there is no distinction of property on grounds of natural

humanum condictum, quod pertinet ad ius positivum, ut supra dictum est. Unde proprietas possessionum non est contra ius naturale, sed iuri naturali superadditur per adinventionem rationis humanae.

Art. 7.—*Utrum liceat alicui furari propter necessitatem.*

Respondeo dicendum quod ea quae sunt iuris humani non possunt derogare iuri naturali vel iuri divino. Secundum autem naturalem ordinem ex divina providentia institutum, res inferiores sunt ordinatae ad hoc quod ex his subveniatur hominum necessitati. Et ideo per rerum divisionem et appropriationem, de iure humano procedentem, non impeditur quin hominis necessitati sit subveniendum ex huiusmodi rebus. Et ideo res quas aliqui superabundanter habent, ex naturali iure debentur pauperum sustentationi. Unde Ambrosius dicit, et habetur in Decretis, dist. XLVII., « *Esurientium panis est quem tu detines; nudorum indumentum est quod tu recludis; miserorum redemptio et absolutio est pecunia quam tu in terram defodis* ». Sed quia multi sunt necessitatem patientes, et non potest ex eadem re omnibus subveniri, committitur arbitrio uniuscuiusque dispensatio propriarum rerum, ut ex eis subveniat necessitatem patientibus. Si tamen adeo sit urgens et evidens necessitas ut manifestum sit instanti necessitati de rebus occurentibus esse subveniendum, puta cum imminet personae periculum et aliter subveniri non potest; tunc licite potest aliquis ex rebus alienis suae necessitati subvenire, sive manifeste sive occulte sublatis. Nec hoc proprie habet rationem furti vel rapinae.

Quaestio LXXVII.—De Fraudulentia.

Art. 4.—*Utrum liceat negotiando aliquid carius vendere quam emere.*

Respondeo dicendum quod ad negotiatores pertinet commutationibus rerum insistere. Ut autem Philosophus dicit, in I *Polit.*, duplex est rerum commutatio. Una quidem quasi naturalis et necessaria: per quam scilicet fit commutatio rei ad rem, vel rerum et denariorum, propter necessitatem vitae. Et talis commutatio non proprie pertinet ad negotiatores, sed magis ad oeconomicos vel politicos, qui habent providere vel domui vel civitati de rebus necessariis ad vitam. Alia vero commutationis species est vel denariorum ad denarios, vel quarumcumque rerum ad denarios, non propter res necessarias vitae, sed

law, but only by human agreement; and this pertains to positive law, as we have already shown. Thus private property is not opposed to natural law, but is an addition to it, devised by the human reason.

The Duty of Charity. (Art. 7, concl.)

What pertains to human law can in no way detract from what pertains to natural law or to divine law. Now according to the natural order, instituted by divine providence, material goods are provided for the satisfaction of human needs. Therefore the division and appropriation of property, which proceeds from human law, must not hinder the satisfaction of man's necessity from such goods. Equally, whatever a man has in superabundance is owed, of natural right, to the poor for their sustenance. So Ambrosius says, and it is also to be found in the *Decretum Gratiani* (Dist. XLVII): 'The bread which you withhold belongs to the hungry; the clothing you shut away, to the naked; and the money you bury in the earth is the redemption and freedom of the penniless.' But because there are many in necessity, and they cannot all be helped from the same source, it is left to the initiative of individuals to make provision from their own wealth, for the assistance of those who are in need. If, however, there is such urgent and evident necessity that there is clearly an immediate need of necessary sustenance,—if, for example, a person is in immediate danger of physical privation, and there is no other way of satisfying his need,— then he may take what is necessary from another person's goods, either openly or by stealth. Nor is this, strictly speaking, fraud or robbery.

22. USURY

The Profit Motive. (Qu. 77, Art. 4, concl.)

Traders are those who apply themselves to the exchange of goods. But as the Philosopher says (I *Politics*, ch. 3) there are two reasons for the exchange of things. The first may be called natural and necessary; and obtains when exchange is made either of goods against goods, or of goods against money, to meet the necessities of life. Such exchange is not, strictly speaking, the business of traders; but is rather the province of the steward or politician whose duty it is to see that the household or the state obtain the necessities of life. The other form of exchange, either of money against money or of any sort of goods against money, is carried on not for the necessary business of life,

propter lucrum quaerendum. Et haec quidem negotiatio proprie videtur ad negotiatores pertinere. Secundum Philosophum autem, prima commutatio laudabilis est; quia deservit naturali necessitati. Secunda autem iuste vituperatur; quia quantum est de se, deservit cupiditati lucri, quae terminum nescit sed in infinitum tendit. Et ideo negotiatio secundum se considerata, quandam turpitudinem habet: inquantum non importat de sui ratione finem honestum vel necessarium.

Lucrum tamen, quod est negotiationis finis, etsi in sui ratione non importet aliquid honestum vel necessarium, nihil tamen importat in sui ratione vitiosum vel virtuti contrarium. Unde nihil prohibet lucrum ordinari ad aliquem finem necessarium vel etiam honestum. Et sic negotiatio licita reddetur. Sicut cum aliquis lucrum moderatum, quod negotiando quaerit, ordinat ad domus suae sustentationem, vel etiam ad subveniendum indigentibus: vel etiam cum aliquis negotiationi intendit propter publicam utilitatem ne scilicet res necessariae ad vitam patriae desint, et lucrum expetit non quasi finem, sed quasi stipendium laboris.

Quaestio LXXVIII.—De Peccato Usurae.

Art. 1.—*Utrum accipere usuram pro pecunia mutuata sit peccatum.*

Respondeo dicendum quod accipere usuram pro pecunia mutuata est secundum se iniustum: quia venditur id quod non est, per quod manifeste inaequalitas constituitur; quae iustitiae contrariatur. Ad cuius evidentiam, sciendum est quod quaedam res sunt quarum usus est ipsarum rerum consumptio: sicut vinum consumimus eo utendo ad potum, et triticum consumimus eo utendo ad cibum. Unde in talibus non debet seorsum computari usus rei a re ipsa, sed cuicumque conceditur usus, ex hoc ipso conceditur res. Et propter hoc in talibus per mutuum transfertur dominium. Si quis ergo seorsum vellet vendere vinum et seorsum vellet vendere usum vini venderet eandem rem bis, vel venderet id quod non est. Unde manifeste per iniustitiam peccaret. Et simili ratione, iniustitiam committit qui mutuat vinum aut triticum petens sibi duas recompensiones, unam quidem restitutionem aequalis rei, aliam vero pretium usus, quod usura dicitur.

Quaedam vero sunt quorum usus non est ipsa rei consumptio: sicut usus domus est inhabitatio, non autem dissipatio. Et ideo in

but for the sake of profit. And it is this form of exchange which would seem, strictly speaking, to be the business of traders. Now, according to the Philosopher, the first form of exchange, because it serves natural necessity, is praiseworthy. But the second form is rightly condemned; for of itself it serves only the desire for gain, which knows no bounds but spreads always further. Therefore trading, considered in itself, always implies a certain baseness, in that it has not of itself any honest or necessary object.

Though profit, which is the object of trading does not of itself imply any honest or necessary aim, neither does it imply anything vicious or contrary to virtue. So there is nothing to prevent its being turned to some honest or necessary object. In this way trading is made lawful. As, for example, when a person uses a moderate profit, which he seeks from trading, for the upkeep of his household, or for assisting the poor, or again, when a person carries on trade for the public welfare, and to provide the country with the necessities of life; and when he seeks profit, not for its own sake, but as a reward for his labour.

Usury Never Permissible on Moral Grounds. (Qu. 78, Art. 1, concl.)

To accept usury for the loan of money is in itself unjust; because this is selling what does not exist, and must obviously give rise to inequality, which is contrary to justice. For the better understanding of this point it should be noted that there are some things whose use lies in their consumption: as, for example, wine is consumed when it is used as drink, and wheat is consumed when it is used for food. In such cases the use of the thing and the thing itself cannot be separately taken into account, so that whenever the use of the thing is granted to some one the thing itself is given at the same time. For this reason ownership is transferred by a loan in such cases. If a man were to sell separately both the wine and the use of the wine he would be selling the same thing twice over; that is he would be selling what does not exist: and he would clearly be sinning against justice. For the same reason he commits an injustice who requires two things in return for the loan of wine or wheat, namely the return of an equal quantity of the thing itself and the price of its use. This is what is called usury.

There are other things whose use does not lie in the consumption of the thing itself; as for instance the use of a house, which lies in the

talibus seorsum potest utrumque concedi: puta cum aliquis tradit alteri dominium domus, reservato sibi usu ad aliquod tempus; vel, e converso, cum quis concedit alicui usum domus, reservato sibi eius dominio. Et propter hoc licite potest homo accipere pretium pro usu domus, et praeter hoc petere domum commodatam: sicut patet in conductione et locatione domus.

Pecunia autem, secundum Philosophum in V. *Ethic.* et in I *Polit.*, principaliter est inventa ad commutationes faciendas: et ita proprius et principalis pecuniae usus est ipsius consumptio sive distractio, secundum quod in commutationes expeditur. Et propter hoc secundum se est illicitum pro usu pecuniae mutuatae accipere pretium quod dicitur usura. Et sicut alia iniuste acquisita tenetur homo restituere, ita pecuniam quam per usuram accepit.

Ad tertium dicendum quod leges humanae dimittunt aliqua peccata impunita propter conditiones hominum imperfectorum, in quibus multae utilitates impedirentur si omnia peccata distincte prohiberentur poenis adhibitis. Et ideo usuras lex humana concessit, non quasi existimans eas esse secundum iustitiam, sed ne impedirentur utilitates multorum. Unde in ipso iure civili dicitur quod « *res quae usu consummuntur neque ratione naturali neque civili recipiunt usumfructum* »; et quod « *Senatus non fecit earum rerum usumfructum, nec enim poterat: sed quasi usumfructum constituit* », concedens scilicet usuras. Et Philosophus, naturali ratione ductus, dicit in I *Polit.* quod usuraria acquisitio pecuniarum est maxime praeter naturam.

Quaestio CIV.—DE OBEDIENTIA.

ART. 1.—*Utrum unus homo teneatur alii obedire.*

Respondeo dicendum, quod sicut actiones rerum naturalium procedunt ex potentiis naturalibus, ita etiam operationes humanae procedunt ex humana voluntate. Oportuit autem in rebus naturalibus, ut superiora moverent inferiora ad suas actiones per excellentiam

living in it and not in its destruction. In such cases both the use and the thing itself can be separately granted; as when, for instance, some one passes the ownership of a house to another, but reserves to himself the right to live there for a certain time; or on the other hand when some one grants the use of a house to another, reserving to himself its ownership. For this reason it is permissible for a man to accept a price for the use of a house, and in addition to sell the freehold of the house itself, as is clear in the sale and leasing of houses.

Now money, according to the Philosopher in the *Ethics* (V, 5) and *Politics* (I, 3), is devised mainly to facilitate exchange; and therefore the proper and principal use of money lies in its consumption or expenditure in the business of exchange. For this reason, therefore, it is wrong to accept a price, or money, for the use of a sum of money which is lent. And just as a man is bound to make restitution of other things which he has unjustly acquired, so also must he restore the money he has obtained from usury.

(Ibid. ad 3um.)

Human laws allow certain sins to go unpunished because of the imperfection of man's condition which brings it about that much which is useful would be prevented if all sins were separately punished by explicit penalties. Therefore human law permits usury, not as though considering it to be just, but to avoid interference with the useful activities of many persons. So in Roman law itself[1] we read that, 'things consumed in use do not bear usufruct either upon natural or upon civil grounds': and that the Senate did not grant usufruct upon such things, nor indeed had it power to do so: but that it did institute a quasi-usufruct, by permitting usury. And the Philosopher, arguing from natural reason, says in the first book of the *Politics* (ch. 3) that the acquisition of money by usury is wholly contrary to nature.

23. *OBEDIENCE.* (Qu. 104.)

Obedience is a Precept of both the Divine and the Natural Law. (Art. 1, concl.)

Just as the operations of natural agents derive from the forces of nature so do human actions derive from the human will. Now in the operations of nature it is necessary that higher things move the lower

---

[1] *Inst.* II, 4, de Usufructu.

naturalis virtutis collatae divinitus. Unde etiam oportet in rebus humanis, quod superiores moveant inferiores per suam voluntatem, ex vi auctoritatis divinitus ordinatae. Movere autem per rationem et voluntatem, est praecipere. Et ideo sicut ex ipso ordine naturali divinitus instituto, inferiora in rebus naturalibus necesse habent subdi motioni superiorum, ita etiam in rebus humanis ex ordine iuris naturalis et divini, tenentur inferiores suis superioribus obedire.

ART. 5.—*Utrum subditi teneantur suis superioribus in omnibus obedire.*

Respondeo dicendum, quod sicut dictum est obediens movetur ad imperium praecipientis, quadam necessitate iustitiae; sicut res naturalis movetur ex virtute sui motoris necessitate naturae . . . Et similiter, ex duobus potest contingere, quod subditus suo superiori non teneatur in omnibus obedire. Uno modo propter praeceptum maioris potestatis. Ut enim dicitur *ad Roman.* XIII super illud: « *Qui resistunt, ipsi sibi damnationem acquirunt* », dicit Glossa « *Si quid iusserit curator, numquid est tibi faciendum, si contra Proconsulem iubeat? Rursum si quid ipse Proconsul iubeat, et aliud Imperator, numquid dubitatur illo contempto illi esse serviendum? Ergo si aliud Imperator, aliud Deus iubeat, contempto illo, obtemperandum est Deo* ». Alio modo non tenetur inferior suo superiori obedire, si ei aliquid praecipiat in quo ei non subdatur. Dicit enim Seneca in III *de Beneficiis* (cap. 20): « *Errat si quis existimat servitutem in totum hominem descendere: pars eius melior excepta est. Corpora obnoxia sunt et adscripta dominis, mens quidem est sui iuris* ». Et ideo in his quae pertinent ad interiorem motum voluntatis, homo non tenetur homini obedire, sed solum Deo. Tenetur autem homo homini obedire in his quae exterius per corpus sunt agenda; in quibus tamen etiam secundum ea quae ad naturam corporis pertinent, homo homini obedire non tenetur, sed solum Deo, quia omnes homines natura sunt pares; puta, in his quae pertinent ad corporis sustentationem et prolis generationem. Unde non tenentur nec servi dominis, nec filii parentibus obedire de matrimonio contrahendo, vel virginitate servanda, aut aliquo alio huiusmodi. Sed in his quae pertinent ad dispositionem actuum et rerum humanarum, tenetur subditus suo superiori obedire,

in virtue of the pre-eminence of natural powers conferred upon them by God. So also in human affairs it is necessary that superiors impose their will upon inferiors, in virtue of the authority established by God. But to impose the reason and will is the same thing as to command. So therefore, in the same way as in the natural order created by God, the lower must remain beneath the direction of the higher, in human affairs inferiors are bound to obey their superiors according to the order established by natural and divine law.

The Limits of Obedience. (Ibid. Art. 5.)

As we have already said, he who obeys is directed by the will of him who commands in virtue of the obligation of justice, just as things in nature are moved by that which acts upon them according to natural necessity. . . . Similarly, there can be two reasons why a subject is not obliged to obey his superior in everything. First, in virtue of the command of some higher power. The *Gloss* says with reference to the text of St. Paul (*Romans* XIII, 'Those who resist authority, bring upon themselves damnation'): 'If the Curator commands something, should you do it if it is contrary to what the Proconsul commands? And again, if the Proconsul commands one thing and the Emperor another can it be doubted that the latter is to be obeyed and the former not? Therefore, when the Emperor commands one thing and God another, one should ignore the former and obey the latter.' Another case in which the subject is not obliged to obey his superior occurs when the latter commands something in matters in which he has no authority. As Seneca says (III *De Beneficiis*, 20): 'It is a mistake to believe that slavery embraces the whole man: the best part escapes it. The body is a slave and subject to a master but the mind is free.' Therefore in those things which depend upon the interior movements of the will man is not bound by obedience to man, but only to God. Man, it is true, is bound by obedience to man with respect to the external operations of the body: but even here, in what regards the nature of the body, he is not bound to obey man, but only God, for all men are equal in nature. Such is the case with regard to sustaining the body and the procreation of children. Thus in contracting matrimony or making a vow of chastity and other similar matters, a slave is not obliged to obey his master nor children their parents. But in those matters which regard the ordering of human affairs and actions, a subject is bound to obey his superiors in virtue of their

M

secundum rationem superioritatis: sicut miles duci exercitus, in his quae pertinent ad bellum; servus domino, in his quae pertinent ad servilia opera exequenda; filius patri, in his quae pertinent ad disciplinam vitae et curam domesticam, et sic de aliis.

Art. 6.—*Utrum Christiani teneantur saecularibus potestatibus obedire.*

Respondeo dicendum, quod fides Christi est iustitiae principium et causa, secundum illud *Rom.* III: « *Iustitia Dei per fidem Iesu Christi* ». Et ideo per fidem Iesu Christi non tollitur ordo iustitiae, sed magis firmatur. Ordo autem iustitiae requirit ut inferiores suis superioribus obediant: aliter enim non posset humanarum rerum status conservari. Et ideo per fidem Christi non excusantur fideles quin principibus saecularibus obedire teneantur.

Ad primum dicendum, quod sicut supra dictum est, servitus qua homo homini subiicitur, ad corpus pertinet; non ad animam, quae libera manet. Nunc autem in statu huius vitae per gratiam Christi liberamur a defectibus animae, non autem a defectibus corporis, ut patet per Apostolum *ad Romanos* VII, qui dicit de seipso quod « *mente servit legi Deo, carne autem legi peccati* ». Et ideo illi qui fiunt filii Dei per gratiam, liberi sunt a spirituali servitute peccati, non autem a servitute corporali, qua temporalibus dominis tenentur adstricti, ut dicit Gloss. super illud I *ad Tim.*, 6, « *Quicumque sunt sub iugo servi,* etc. ».

Ad tertium dicendum, quod Principibus saecularibus in tantum homo obedire tenetur, in quantum ordo iustitiae requirit. Et ideo si non habeant iustum principatum, sed usurpatum; vel si iniusta praecipiant: non tenentur eis subditi obedire, nisi forte per accidens, propter vitandum scandalum vel periculum.

particular authority: thus the soldier obeys his general in matters of war; the slave his master with respect to the tasks allotted to him; the son his father with regard to the discipline and management of family life, and so forth.

Obedience is a Religious Duty. (Ibid. Art. 6.)

The Christian faith is the principle and cause of justice, according to what St. Paul says (*Romans* III, 22): 'The justice of God through faith in Jesus Christ.' So the order of justice is not destroyed through faith in Jesus Christ, but is rather confirmed. Now the order of justice demands that subjects should obey their superiors: for there would otherwise be no stability in human affairs. So, therefore, the Christian faith does not dispense the faithful from the obligation of obeying temporal princes.

Obedience and Christian Liberty. (Ibid. ad 1um)

As we have said above, slavery, by which one man is subject to another, exists in respect of the body, but not of the soul, which remains free. Now in the state of this life we are freed by the grace of Christ from the defects of the soul, but not from those of the body; as we see from the words of the Apostle (*Romans* VII, 25), where he says of himself, that 'with the mind he obeys the law of God, but with the flesh the law of sin.' So, therefore, those who through grace become the sons of God are free from the spiritual slavery of sin, but not from the slavery of the body through which they are bound to earthly masters; as the *Gloss* says in the commentary upon I *Timothy* VI, 1: 'All are under the yoke of slavery,' etc.

The Justification of Civil Disobedience. (Ibid. ad 3um.)

Man is bound to obey secular Rulers to the extent that the order of justice requires. For this reason if such rulers have no just title to power, but have usurped it, or if they command things to be done which are unjust, their subjects are not obliged to obey them; except, perhaps, in certain special cases when it is a matter of avoiding scandal or some particular danger.

COMMENTUM
IN QUATUOR LIBROS SENTENTIARUM
MAGISTRI PETRI LOMBARDI

Liber Secundus

Dist. XLIV, Quaestio II, Art. 2.

Utrum Christiani teneantur obedire potestatibus saecularibus, et maxime tyrannis.

Ad secundum sic proceditur.

1. Videtur quod Christiani non teneantur saecularibus potestatibus obedire, et praecipue tyrannis. *Matth.* XVII, 25, dicitur: « *Ergo liberi sunt filii* ». Si enim in quolibet regno filii illius Regis qui regno illi praefertur, liberi sunt, tunc filii Regis cui onmia regna subduntur, in quolibet regno liberi esse debent. Sed Christiani effecti sunt filii Dei; *Roman.* VIII, 16: « *Ipse enim Spiritus testimonium redit spiritui nostro quod sumus filii Dei* ». Ergo ubique sunt liberi, et ita saecularibus potestatibus obedire non tenentur.

2. Praeterea, servitus pro peccata inducta est, ut supra, quaest. I, art. 1, dictum est. Sed per baptismum homines a peccato mundantur. Ergo a servitute liberantur: et sic idem quod prius.

3. Praeterea, maius vinculum absolvit a minori, sicut lex nova ab observantia legis veteris. Sed in baptismo homo obligatur Deo, quae obligatio est maius vinculum quam id quo homo obligatur homini per servitutem. Ergo per baptismum a servitute absolvitur.

4. Praeterea, quilibet potest licite resumere, cum facultas adest, quod sibi iniuste ablatum est. Sed multi saeculares principes tyrannice terrarum dominia invaserunt. Ergo cum facultas rebellandi illis conceditur, non tenentur illis obedire.

5. Praeterea, nullus tenetur ei obedire, quem licite, immo laudabiliter potest interficere. Sed Tullius in libro *de Officiis* (I num. 26) salvat eos qui Julium Caesarem interfecerunt, quamvis amicum et familiarem, qui quasi tyrannus iura imperii usurpaverat. Ergo talibus nullus tenetur obedire.

COMMENTARY ON THE SENTENCES OF
PETER LOMBARD

BOOK II

The Obedience owed by Christians to the Secular Power and in particular to Tyrants. (Dist. 44, Quest. 2, Art. 2.)

1. It would seem that Christians are not bound to obey the secular powers, and particularly tyrants. For it is said, *Matthew* XVII, 25: 'Therefore the children are free.' And if in all countries the children of the reigning sovereign are free, so also should the children of that Sovereign be free, to whom all kings are subject. But Christians have become the sons of God as we read in the *Epistle to the Romans* (VIII, 16). 'For the Spirit himself giveth testimony to our spirit, that we are the sons of God.' Christians then are everywhere free, and are thus not bound to obey the secular powers.

2. Furthermore: as we have already shown, servitude began in consequence of sin. But men are cleansed from sin by baptism. Therefore they are freed from servitude. So we have the same conclusion.

3. Furthermore: a greater bond absolves from a lesser, as the new law absolved from observance of the old. But man is by baptism bound to God: and this obligation is a greater bond than that by which one man is bound to another by servitude. Therefore man is freed from servitude by baptism.

4. Furthermore: Any one is permitted, if opportunity offers, to take back what has been unjustly taken from him. But many secular princes have possessed themselves tyrannically of the lands they rule. Therefore when the opportunity of rebelling occurs, their subjects are not bound by obedience to them.

5. Furthermore: there can be no duty of obedience towards a person whom it is permissible or even praiseworthy to kill. But Cicero in the *De Officiis* (I, 26) justifies those who killed Julius Caesar, even though he was their friend and relative, because he usurped the imperial powers like a tyrant. To such, then, no obedience is owed.

Sed contra, I *Petri* II, 18: « *Servi subditi estote dominis vestris* ».

Praeterea, *Rom.* XIII, 2: « *Qui potestati resistit, Dei ordinationi resistit* ». Sed non est licitum Dei ordinationi resistere. Ergo nec saeculari potestati resistere licet.

Solutio. — Respondeo dicendum, quod sicut dictum est, obedientia respicit in praecepto quod servat, debitum observandi. Hoc autem debitum causatur ex ordine praelationis, quae virtutem coactivam habet, non tantum temporaliter sed etiam spiritualiter propter conscientiam, ut Apostolus dicit *Roman.* XIII, secundum quod ordo praelationis a Deo descendit, ut Apostolus, *ibid.*, innuit. Et ideo secundum hoc quod a Deo est, obedire talibus Christianus tenetur, non autem secundum quod a Deo praelatio non est. Dictum est autem quod praelatio potest a Deo non esse dupliciter: vel quantum ad modum acquirendi praelationem, vel quantum ad usum praelationis. Quantum ad primum contingit dupliciter: aut propter defectum personae, quia indignus est; aut propter defectum in ipso modo acquirendi, quia scilicet per violentiam vel per simoniam, vel aliquo illicito modo acquirit. Ex primo defectu non impeditur quin ius praelationis ei acquiratur; et quoniam praelatio secundum suam formam semper a Deo est (quod debitum obedientiae causa); ideo talibus praelatis, quamvis indignis, obedire tenentur subditi. Sed secundus defectus impedit ius praelationis: qui enim per violentiam dominium surripit non efficitur vere praelatus vel dominus; et ideo cum facultas adest, potest aliquis tale dominium repellere: nisi forte postmodum dominus verus effectus sit vel per consensum subditorum, vel per auctoritatem superioris. Abusus autem praelationis potest esse dupliciter: vel ex eo quod est praeceptum a praelato, contrarium eius ad quod praelatio ordinata est, ut si praecipiat actum peccati contrarium virtuti ad quam inducendam et conservandam praelatio ordinatur; et tunc aliquis praelato non solum non tenetur obedire, sed etiam tenetur non obedire, sicut et sancti martyres mortem passi sunt, ne impiis iussis tyrannorum

But against the above arguments there is the text of the first *Epistle of St. Peter* (II, 18): 'Servants, be subject to your masters': and that of the *Epistle to the Romans* (XIII, 2): 'He that resisteth the power, resisteth the ordinance of God.' Now it is not permissible to resist the ordinance of God; neither, therefore, is it permissible to resist the secular power.

Solution. We must observe that, as has been stated already, in the observance of a certain precept, obedience is connected with the obligation to such observance. But such obligation derives from the order of authority which carries with it the power to constrain, not only from the temporal, but also from the spiritual point of view, and in conscience; as the Apostle says (*Romans* XIII): and this because the order of authority derives from God, as the Apostle says in the same passage. For this reason the duty of obedience is, for the Christian, a consequence of this derivation of authority from God, and ceases when that ceases. But, as we have already said, authority may fail to derive from God for two reasons: either because of the way in which authority has been obtained, or in consequence of the use which is made of it. There are two ways in which the first case may occur. Either because of a defect in the person, if he is unworthy; or because of some defect in the way itself by which power was acquired, if, for example, through violence, or simony or some other illegal method. The first defect is not such as to impede the acquisition of legitimate authority; and since authority derives always, from a formal point of view, from God (and it is this which produces the duty of obedience), their subjects are always obliged to obey such superiors, however unworthy they may be. But the second defect prevents the establishment of any just authority: for whoever possesses himself of power by violence does not truly become lord or master. Therefore it is permissible, when occasion offers, for a person to reject such authority; except in the case that it subsequently became legitimate, either through public consent or through the intervention of higher authority. With regard to abuse of authority, this also may come about in two ways. First, when what is ordered by an authority is opposed to the object for which that authority was constituted (if, for example, some sinful action is commanded or one which is contrary to virtue, when it is precisely for the protection and fostering of virtue that authority is instituted). In such a case, not only is there no obligation to obey the authority, but one is obliged to disobey it, as did the holy martyrs who suffered death rather than obey the impious commands of tyrants.

obedirent: vel quia cogunt ad hoc ad quod ordo praelationis non se extendit; ut si dominus exigat tributa quae servus non tenetur dare, vel aliquid huiusmodi; et tunc subditus non tenetur obedire, nec etiam tenetur non obedire.

Ad 1um ergo dicendum, quod illa praelatio quae ad utilitatem subditorum ordinatur, libertatem subditorum non tollit; et ideo non est inconveniens quod tali praelationi subiaceant qui per Spiritum sanctum filii Dei effecti sunt. Vel dicendum, quod Christus loquitur de se et suis discipulis, qui nec servilis conditionis erant, nec res temporales habebant, quibus suis dominis obligarentur ad tributa solvenda; et ideo non sequitur quod omnis Christianus huiusmodi libertatis sit particeps, sed solum illi qui sequuntur apostolicam vitam, nihil in hoc mundo possidentes, et a conditione servili immunes.

Ad 2um dicendum, quod baptismus non delet statim omnes poenalitates ex peccato primi parentis consequentes, sicut necessitatem moriendi et caecitatem, vel aliquid huiusmodi; sed regenerat in spem vivam illius vitae in qua omnia ista tollentur; et sic non oportet ut aliquis statim baptizatus a servili conditione liberetur, quamvis illa sit poena peccati.

Ad 3um dicendum, quod maius vinculum non absolvit a minori, nisi quando non compatitur se cum illo; sicut umbra et veritas simul esse non possunt: propter quod veniente veritate Evangelii, umbra veteris legis cessavit. Sed vinculum quo in baptismo quis ligatur, compatitur vinculum servitutis; et ideo non absolvit ab illo.

Ad 4um dicendum, quod qui per violentiam praelationem accipiunt, non sunt veri praelati; unde nec eis obedire tenentur subditi nisi sicut dictum est.

Ad 5um dicendum, quod Tullius loquitur in casu illo quando aliquis dominium sibi per violentiam surripit, nolentibus subditis, vel etiam ad consensum coactis, et quando non est recursus ad superiorem, per quem iudicium de invasore possit fieri: tunc enim qui ad liberationem patriae tyrannum occidit, laudatur, et praemium accipit.

Secondly, when those who bear authority command things which exceed the competence of such authority; as, for example, when a master demands payment from a servant which the latter is not bound to make, and other similar cases. In this instance the subject is free to obey or to disobey.

So, to the first objection we may reply that authority which is instituted in the interests of those subject to it, is not contrary to their liberty; so there is no objection to those who are transformed into sons of God, by the grace of the Holy Spirit, being subject to it. Or again we can say that Christ speaks of Himself and of His disciples, who were neither of servile condition nor had they any temporal possessions for which to pay tribute to temporal lords. So it does not follow that all Christians should enjoy such liberty, but only those who follow the apostolic way of life, without possessions and free from servile condition.

With regard to the second objection we must note that baptism does not take away all the penalties which derive from the sin of our first parents, as for instance the inevitability of death, blindness, and other such evils. But it regenerates in the living hope of that life in which we shall be free from such penalties. Therefore, from the fact that a man is baptized it does not necessarily follow that he should be freed from servile condition, even though this is a consequence of sin.

To the third objection we reply that the greater bond does not absolve from the lesser, unless the two be incompatible, since error and truth cannot be found together; therefore with the coming of the truth of the Gospel the darkness of the Old Law passed away. But the bond with which one is bound in baptism is compatible with the bond of servitude, and does not in consequence absolve from it.

To the fourth objection we reply that those who attain power by violence are not truly rulers; therefore their subjects are not bound to obey them except in the cases already noted.

With regard to the fifth objection it must be noted that Cicero was speaking of a case where a person had possessed himself of power through violence, either against the will of his subjects or by compelling their consent, and where there was no possibility of appeal to a higher authority who could pass judgement on such action. In such a case, one who liberates his country by killing a tyrant is to be praised and rewarded.

DIST. XLIV, QUAESTIO. III, ART. 4.

Ad quartum dicendum quod potestas spiritualis et saecularis utraque deducitur a potestate divina; et ideo intantum saecularis potestas est sub spirituali, inqantum est ei a Deo supposita, scilicet in his quae ad salutem animae pertinent; et ideo in his magis est obediendum potestati spirituali quam saeculari. In his autem quae ad bonum civile pertinent est magis obediendum potestati saeculari quam spirituali secundum illud *Matth.* XXII, 21, « *Reddite quae sunt Caesaris Caesari* ». Nisi forte potestati spirituali etiam saecularis potestas coniungatur, sicut in Papa, qui utriusque potestatis apicem tenet, scilicet spiritualis et saecularis, hoc illo disponente qui est sacerdos et rex, sacerdos in aeternum secundum ordinem Melchisedech, Rex regum, et Dominus dominantium, cuius potestas non auferetur et regnum non corrumpetur in saecula saeculorum. Amen.

The Relation between the Temporal and the Spiritual Power.   (Ibid. Dist. 44, Quest. 3, Art. 4.)

Both the spiritual and the temporal power derive from the divine power; consequently the temporal power is subject to the spiritual only to the extent that this is so ordered by God; namely, in those matters which affect the salvation of the soul. And in these matters the spiritual power is to be obeyed before the temporal. In those matters, however, which concern the civil welfare, the temporal power should be obeyed rather than the spiritual, according to what we are told in *St. Matthew* (XXII, 21) 'Render to Caesar the things that are Caesar's.' Unless, of course, the spiritual and the temporal power are identified in one person as in the Pope, whose power is supreme in matters both temporal and spiritual, through the dispensation of Him Who is both priest and king; a Priest for ever according to the order of Melchisadech, the King of kings and Lord of lords, Whose power shall not fail and Whose dominion shall not pass away to all eternity. Amen.

COMMENTUM IN X. LIBROS ETHICORUM AD NICOMACHUM

LIBER PRIMUS

LECTIO I.

Sicut dicit Philosophus in principio *Metaphysicae*, sapientis est ordinare. Cuius ratio est, quia sapientia est potissima perfectio rationis, cuius proprium est cognoscere ordinem. Nam et si vires sensitivae cognoscant res aliquas absolute, ordinem tamen unius rei ad aliam cognoscere est solius intellectus aut rationis. Invenitur autem duplex ordo in rebus. Unus quidem partium alicuius totius seu alicuius multitudinis, ad invicem, sicut partes domus ad invicem ordinantur. Alius est ordo rerum in finem. Et hic ordo est principalior, quia primus. Nam, ut Philosophus dicit in undecimo *Metaphysicorum*, ordo partium exercitus ad invicem, est propter ordinem totius exercitus ad ducem. Ordo autem quadrupliciter ad rationem comparatur. Est enim quidam ordo quem ratio non facit, sed solum considerat, sicut est ordo rerum naturalium. Alius autem est ordo, quem ratio considerando facit in proprio actu, puta cum ordinat conceptus suos ad invicem, et signa conceptuum, quia sunt voces significativae. Tertius autem est ordo quem ratio considerando facit in operationibus voluntatis. Quartus autem est ordo quem ratio considerando facit in exterioribus rebus, quarum ipsa est causa, sicut in arca et domo. Et quia consideratio rationis per habitum perficitur, secundum hos diversos ordines, quos proprie ratio considerat, sunt diversae scientiae. Nam ad philosophiam naturalem pertinet considerare ordinem rerum quem ratio humana considerat sed non facit; ita quod sub naturali philosophia comprehendamus et metaphysicam. Ordo autem quem ratio considerando facit in proprio actu, pertinet ad rationalem philosophiam, cuius est considerare ordinem partium orationis ad invicem, et ordinem principiorum ad invicem et ad conclusiones.

COMMENTARY ON THE NICOMACHEAN ETHICS

BOOK ONE

INTRODUCTION.

The Philosopher teaches at the beginning of the *Metaphysics* that the proper task of the wise is to bring order into affairs. The explanation for this is to be sought in the fact that wisdom is the highest perfection of reason, and it is reason which brings things to order. In fact, although it is possible to know some things directly by experience, only the intellect or reason can know the order which relates one thing to another. Now there are two sorts of order to be found in things. One is the order which unites together the parts of a whole or of an aggregate; as, for instance, the order which exists between the parts of a house. Another and different sort of order exists between things which are united by some common end. And this latter is more important because it is primary. As the Philosopher points out in Book XI of the *Metaphysics*, the reciprocal order of the different parts of an army exists in virtue of the order which binds the entire army to its commander. Furthermore, order may be considered in four different ways. There is first of all that order which is not a product of reason, but which is merely considered by reason; such as the natural order of the universe. There is furthermore the order which reason produces in the very act of reflection; for example when reason arranges its own concepts to one another and the words corresponding with them. Thirdly, there is the order which reason, in the act of reflection, produces in voluntary action. Lastly, there is a fourth sort of order which reason, by reflection, creates in those external things which it causes. As in the making of a chest or a house. And since reflective reason perfects itself by habit, the various sciences grow out of these different orders which it is the proper object of reason to consider. Natural philosophy is concerned with that order of things which reason considers, but does not create: and in this respect we must include metaphysics under natural philosophy. The order produced by reason itself in the act of reflection pertains to rational philosophy, which is concerned with the inter-relationship of the parts of discourse, and the order of principles among themselves, or with respect to conclusions.

189

Ordo autem actionum voluntariarum pertinet ad considerationem moralis philosophiae. Ordo autem quem ratio considerando facit in rebus exterioribus constitutis per rationem humanam, pertinet ad artes mechanicas. Sic ergo moralis philosophiae, circa quam versatur praesens intentio, proprium est considerare operationes humanas secundum quod sunt ordinatae ad invicem et ad finem. Dico autem operationes humanas, quae procedunt a voluntate hominis secundum ordinem rationis. Nam si quae operationes in homine inveniuntur, quae non subiacent voluntati et rationi, non dicuntur proprie humanae, sed naturales, sicut patet de operationibus animae vegetativae. Quae nullo modo cadunt sub consideratione moralis philosophiae. Sicut autem subiectum philosophiae naturalis est motus, vel res mobilis, ita subiectum moralis philosophiae est operatio humana ordinata in finem, vel etiam homo prout est voluntarie agens propter finem. Sciendum est autem, quod quia homo naturaliter est animal sociale, utpote qui indiget ad vitam suam multis, quae sibi ipse solus praeparare non potest; consequens est, quod homo naturaliter sit pars alicuius multitudinis, per quam praestetur sibi auxilium ad bene vivendum. Quo quidem auxilio indiget ad duo. Primo quidem ad ea quae sunt vitae necessaria, sine quibus praesens vita transigi non potest: et ad hoc auxiliatur homini domestica multitudo, cuius est pars. Nam quilibet homo a parentibus habet generationem et nutrimentum et disciplinam. Et similiter singuli, qui sunt partes domesticae familiae, seinvicem iuvant ad necessaria vitae. Alio modo iuvatur homo a multitudine, cuius est pars, ad vitae sufficientiam perfectam; scilicet ut homo non solum vivat, sed et bene vivat, habens omnia quae sibi sufficiunt ad vitam: et sic homini auxiliatur multitudo civilis, cuius ipse est pars, non solum quantum ad corporalia, prout scilicet in civitate sunt multa artificia, ad quae una domus sufficere non potest; sed etiam quantum ad moralia; inquantum scilicet per publicam potestatem coercentur insolentes iuvenes metu poenae, quos paterna monitio corrigere non valet. Sciendum est autem, quod hoc totum, quod est civilis multitudo, vel domestica familia, habet solam unitatem ordinis, secundum quam non est aliquid simpliciter unum. Et ideo pars eius totius, potest habere operationem quae non est operatio totius, sicut miles in exercitu habet operationem quae non est totius exercitus. Habet

The order obtaining in voluntary actions lies within the competence of moral philosophy. Lastly, the order produced by reason in those external things invented by man lies within the province of the mechanical arts. So the task of moral philosophy, with which we are here dealing, is the study of human actions in so far as they are related to one another and have some end in view. It must be noted that we are dealing only with those human actions which proceed from human volition as by man's own creation. For there are certain human actions which are not so subject to volition or reason, but proceed spontaneously. As, for instance, the purely vegetative processes of the body. Such actions cannot strictly be called human, and do not enter in any way into the considerations of moral philosophy. So, as the object of natural philosophy is the study of movement or of things in movement, the object of moral philosophy is the action of man ordered to a certain end: or, in more precise terms, it is man in so far as he acts voluntarily with some end in view.

There is a further observation to be made. The fact that man is by nature a social animal—being compelled to live in society because of the many needs he cannot satisfy out of his own resources—has as a consequence the fact that man is destined by nature to form part of a community which makes a full and complete life possible for him. The help of such a communal life is necessary to him for two reasons. In the first place it is necessary to provide him with those things without which life itself would be impossible. For this purpose there is the domestic community of which man forms a part. We all get life and food and education from our parents, and it is thus that the various individuals of a family assist one another with what is necessary to existence. But life in a community further enables man to achieve a plenitude of life; not merely to exist, but to live fully, with all that is necessary to well-being. In this sense the political community, of which man forms a part, assists him not merely to obtain material comforts, such as are produced by the many diverse industries of a state, but also spiritual well-being, as when youthful intemperance, which paternal admonishment is unable to control, is restrained by public authority.

But it must be noted that this unity which is the political community or the unity of the family, is only a unity of order and not an unconditional unity. Consequently the parts which form it can have a sphere of action which is distinct from that of the whole; just as in an army a soldier can perform actions which are not proper to the whole army. At the same time the whole has a sphere of action

nihilominus et ipsum totum aliquam operationem, quae non est propria alicuius partium, sed totius, puta conflictus totius exercitus. Et tractus navis est operatio multitudinis trahentium navem. Est autem aliquid totum, quod habet unitatem non solum ordine, sed compositione, aut colligatione, vel etiam continuitate, secundum quam unitatem est aliquid unum simpliciter; et ideo nulla est operatio partis, quae non sit totius. In continuis enim idem est motus totius et partis; et similiter in compositis, vel colligatis, operatio partis principaliter est totius; et ideo oportet, quod ad eamdam scientiam pertineat talis consideratio et totius et partis eius. Non autem ad eamdem scientiam pertinet considerare totum quod habet solam ordinis unitatem, et partes ipsius. Et inde est, quod moralis philosophia in tres partes dividitur. Quarum prima considerat operationes unius hominis ordinatas ad finem, quae vocatur *monastica*. Secunda autem considerat operationes multitudinis domesticae, quae vocatur *oeconomica*. Tertia autem considerat operationes multitudinis civilis, quae vocatur *politica*.

which is not proper to any of its parts; as for example the general action in battle of the entire army: or again like the movement of a ship which results from the combined action of the rowers. There is on the other hand a whole which has not only a unity of order but also of composition, of aggregation, or of physical continuity; a unity which can be called absolute. In such a case there is no action of the parts which is not also action of the whole. In continuous things the movement of the whole is in fact identical with that of the part: and similarly in a composite or aggregate the action of any part is principally that of the whole; and in consequence the study of the part should be included in that of the whole. On the other hand it is not right that the study of what is only a unity of order, and of the parts which so compose it, should be undertaken under one head. For this reason moral philosophy should be divided into three parts. The first studies men as individuals and as ordered to a certain end: this is called monastic. The second is concerned with the domestic community and is called economic; and the third studies the action of the civil community and is called political.

N

COMMENTUM IN LIBROS POLITICORUM
SEU DE REBUS CIVILIBUS

Liber Primus

Lectio I.

Sicut Philosophus docet in secundo *Physicorum*, ars imitatur naturam. Cuius ratio est, quia sicut se habent principia adinvicem, ita proportionabiliter se habent operationes et effectus. Principium autem eorum quae secundum artem fiunt est intellectus humanus, qui secundum similitudinem quamdam derivatur ab intellectu divino, qui est principium rerum naturalium. Unde necesse est, quod et operationes artis imitentur operationes naturae: et ea, quae sunt secundum artem, imitentur ea, quae sunt in natura. Si enim aliquis instructor alicuius artis opus artis efficeret, oporteret discipulum, qui ab eo artem suscepisset, ad opus illius attendere, ut ad eius similitudinem et ipse operaretur. Et ideo intellectus humanus, ad quem intelligibile lumen ab intellectu divino derivatur, necesse habet in his quae facit informari ex inspectione eorum quae sunt naturaliter facta, ut similiter operetur. Et inde est quod Philosophus dicit, quod si ars faceret ea quae sunt naturae, similiter operaretur sicut et natura: et e converso, si natura faceret ea quae sunt artis, similiter faceret sicut ars facit. Sed natura quidem non perficit ea, quae sunt artis, sed solum quaedam principia praeparat, et exemplar operandi quodam modo artificibus praebet. Ars vero inspicere quidem potest ea quae sunt naturae, et eis uti ad opus proprium perficiendum; perficere vero ea non potest. Ex quo patet quod ratio humana eorum quae sunt secundum naturam est cognoscitiva tantum: eorum vero, quae sunt secundum artem, est et cognoscitiva et factiva: unde oportet quod scientiae humanae, quae sunt de rebus naturalibus, sint speculativae; quae vero sunt de rebus ab homine factis, sint practicae, sive operativae secundum imitationem naturae. Procedit autem natura in sua operatione ex simplicibus ad composita; ita quod in eis quae per operationem naturae fiunt, quod est maxime compositum est perfectum et totum et finis aliorum; sicut apparet in omnibus totis respectu suarum partium. Unde et ratio hominis operativa ex simplicibus ad composita procedit tanquam ex

COMMENTARY ON THE POLITICS
OF ARISTOTLE

BOOK ONE

INTRODUCTION

As the Philosopher teaches in Book II of the *Physics*, art imitates nature. The reason for this is that actions and their effects stand in the same relationship to one another as do principles among themselves. Now the human intellect is the principle of all things created by art, and, at the same time, itself derives in a certain sense from the divine intellect which is the principle of natural things. So works of art necessarily imitate the works of nature, and the processes of art are modelled upon those found in nature. When the teacher of some art is creating something it is good for the pupil who is learning from him to observe with attention the way he goes about it; thus learning to act with the skill of the master. So the human intellect, which obtains the light of intelligence from the divine intellect, must go for inspiration in what it does to the architecture of nature, and imitate that as its model. So the Philosopher says that if art were to succeed in creating the things that are in nature, it would have to operate in the same way as nature itself; and conversely if nature were to create things which are proper to art, it would act according to the model of the latter. Nature, however, does not create things which are proper to art, but only sets out certain principles, and, in a way, offers a model to the artist. While as far as art is concerned, it can see the things which are to be found in nature, and make use of them to perform its own task, but cannot create such things itself. So it is clear that reason can only know the things of nature, while it can both know and make the things of art. It follows also that those human sciences which are about the things of nature are speculative, while those which are concerned with the things made by man are practical sciences, operating in imitation of nature. Now nature proceeds in its operations from the simple to the complex; and among things which result from natural agency that which is more complex is the more perfect and constitutes the integration and purpose of the others. One can at once see this in respect of any whole and its parts. The operative reason in man also proceeds from the simple to the complex, as from the imperfect to the

195

imperfectis ad perfecta. Cum autem ratio humana disponere habeat non solum de his quae in usum hominis veniunt, sed etiam de ipsis hominibus qui ratione reguntur, in utrisque procedit ex simplicibus ad compositum. In illis quidem rebus quae in usum hominis veniunt, sicut cum ex lignis constituit navem, et ex lignis et lapidibus domum. In ipsis autem hominibus, sicut cum multos homines ordinat in unam quamdam communitatem. Quarum quidem communitatum cum diversi sint gradus et ordines, ultima est communitas civitatis ordinata ad per se sufficientia vitae humanae. Unde inter omnes communitates humanas ipsa est perfectissima. Et quia ea quae in usum hominis veniunt ordinantur ad hominem sicut ad finem, qui est principalior his quae sunt ad finem, ideo necesse est quod hoc totum quod est civitas sit principalius omnibus totis, quae ratione humana cognosci et constitui possunt. Ex his igitur quae dicta sunt circa doctrinam politicam, quam Aristoteles in hoc libro tradit, quattuor accipere possumus. Primo quidem necessitatem huius scientiae. Omnium enim quae ratione cognosci possunt, necesse est aliquam doctrinam tradi ad perfectionem humanae sapientiae quae philosophia vocatur. Cum igitur hoc totum quod est civitas, sit cuidam rationis iudicio subiectum, necesse fuit ad complementum philosophiae de civitate doctrinam tradere quae politica nominatur, idest civilis, scientia. Secundum possumus accipere genus huius scientiae. Cum enim scientiae practicae a speculativis distinguantur in hoc quod speculativae ordinantur solum ad scientiam veritatis, practicae vero ad opus; necesse est hanc scientiam sub practica philosophia contineri, cum civitas sit quoddam totum, cuius humana ratio non solum est cognoscitiva, sed etiam operativa. Rursumque cum ratio quaedam operetur per modum factionis operatione in exteriorem materiam transeunte, quod proprie ad artes pertinet, quae mechanicae vocantur, utpote fabrilis et navifactiva et similes: quaedam vero operetur per modum actionis operatione manente in eo qui operatur, sicut est consiliari, eligere, velle et huiusmodi quae ad moralem scientiam pertinent: manifestum est politicam scientiam, quae de hominum considerat ordinatione, non contineri sub factivis scientiis, quae sunt artes mechanicae, sed sub activis quae sunt scientiae morales. Tertio possumus accipere dignitatem et ordinem politicae ad omnes alias scientias practicas. Est enim civitas principalissimum eorum quae humana ratione constitui possunt. Nam ad ipsam omnes communitates humanae referuntur. Rursumque

perfect. But since man's reason must be concerned not only with what is useful to man, but also with men themselves, in that it governs their actions, it proceeds in both these cases from the simple to the complex. In the case of that which serves man's needs, as when making a ship out of timbers for example, or when constructing a house from wood and stone: in the case of man himself when, for example, it brings order into a community composed of individuals. Among such communities there are different grades and orders, the highest being the political community, which is so arranged as to satisfy all the needs of human life; and which is, in consequence, the most perfect. For since all things which serve men's needs have the fulfilment of this purpose as their end, and since ends are more important than the means thereto, it follows that this unity which we call a city takes pre-eminence over all smaller unities which the human reason can know and construct. From these considerations about political theory which Aristotle makes in this book we can draw four conclusions. First, as to the necessity of such a science. If we are to perfect the science of human wisdom, or philosophy, it is necessary to give an explanation of all that can be understood by reason. But that unity which we call the city is subject to the judgement of reason. It is necessary, then, for the completeness of philosophy, to institute a discipline which will study the city: and such a discipline is called politics or the science of statecraft. Secondly, we can distinguish the generic form of this particular science. The speculative sciences are distinguished from the practical in that the speculative aim only at knowing the truth, while the practical are concerned with action. So our present science is a practical one; for reason not only knows but also creates the city. Furthermore reason can operate about things either as making something (*per modum factionis*), in which case its action passes on to some external material, as we see in the mechanical arts of the smith and the shipwright; or by doing something (*per modum actionis*) in which case the action remains intrinsic to the agent, as we see in deliberation, making choice, willing, and all that pertains to moral science. It is clear that political science, which is concerned with the ordered relationship between men, belongs, not to the realm of making or factitive science or mechanical art, but rather to that of doing or the moral sciences. In the third place we may enlarge upon the dignity and value of politics compared with all other sciences. The city is, in fact, the most important thing constituted by human reason. For it is the object and final aim of all lesser communities.

omnia tota quae per artes mechanicas constituuntur ex rebus in usum
hominum venientibus, ad homines ordinantur, sicut ad finem. Si
igitur principalior scientia est quae est de nobiliori et perfectiori,
necesse est politicam inter omnes scientias practicas esse principaliorem
et architectonicam omnium aliarum, utpote considerans ultimum et
perfectum bonum in rebus humanis. Et propter hoc Philosophus dicit
in fine decimi *Ethicorum* quod ad politica perficitur Philosophia, quae
est circa res humanas. Quarto ex praedictis accipere possumus modum
et ordinem huiusmodi scientiae. Sicut enim scientiae speculativae,
quae de aliquo toto considerant, ex consideratione partium et principiorum notitiam de toto perficiunt passiones et operationes totius
manifestando; sic et haec scientia principia et partes civitatis considerans
de ipsa notitiam tradit, partes et passiones et operationes eius
manifestans: et quia practica est, manifestat insuper quomodo singula
perfici possunt: quod est necessarium in omni practica scientia.

And again, all those completed things which are fashioned by the mechanical arts out of what is useful to man are ordered to man as to their end. If, then, the most important science is that which treats of the noblest and most perfect things, it must follow that politics is the most important of all practical sciences and the keystone of them all; for it treats of the highest and perfect good in human affairs. For this reason the Philosopher, in the tenth book of the *Ethics*, says that philosophy which regards human affairs finds its perfection in politics. Fourthly: from the considerations we have set out above, we can deduce the method and system of this science. It proceeds in similar manner, in fact, to the speculative sciences, which study some unity, completing their knowledge by observation of its parts and principles and by throwing into relief the actions and changes of the whole. So our present science by studying the principles and various parts of the city teaches us more about it by throwing light upon its elements, its movements and its changes: and, being also a practical science, it shows us also how these various elements may be perfected; for this is necessary in every practical science.